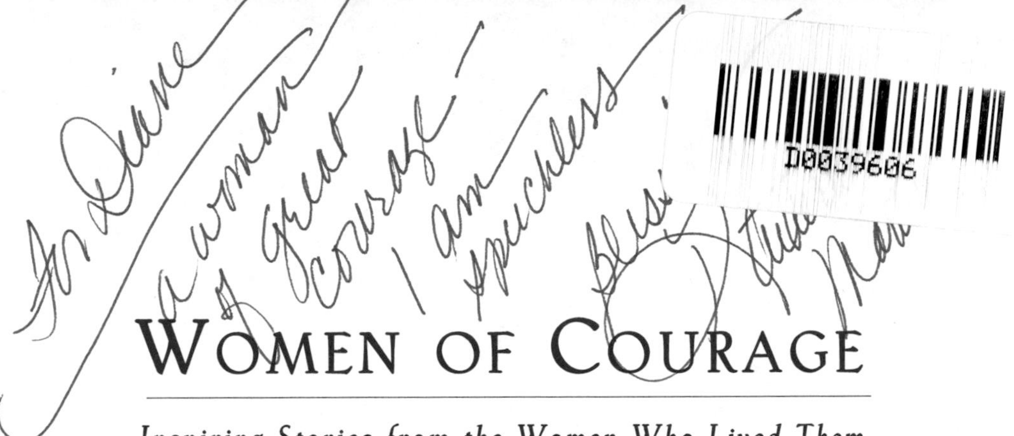

WOMEN OF COURAGE

Inspiring Stories from the Women Who Lived Them

Katherine Martin

Book I in New World Library's People Who Dare Series

New World Library
Novato, California

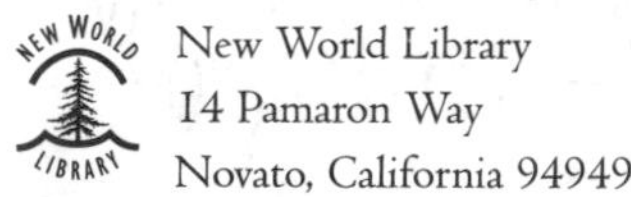
New World Library
14 Pamaron Way
Novato, California 94949

Cover design: Mary Ann Casler
Cover illustration: Roxanna Villa
Editorial: Becky Benenate
Text design and layout: Mary Ann Casler
Cover photo: Julian Goble

Library of Congress Cataloging-in-Publication Data

Women of courage: inspiring stories from the women who lived them / edited by Katherine Martin.
p. cm.
ISBN 1-57731-093-4 (alk. paper)
1. Women social reformers — United States — Biography. I. Martin, Katherine.
HQ1412.P46 1999
305.4'092'273 — DC21 97-14204
CIP

First printing, August 1999
ISBN 1-57731-093-4
Printed in Canada on acid-free, recycled paper
Distributed to the trade by Publishers Group West

10 9 8 7 6 5 4 3 2 1

To my mother
Virginia Lane

You start out with one thing, end
up with another, and nothing's
like it used to be, not even the future.

— Rita Dove, from her poem "Ö"

TABLE *of* CONTENTS

Courage has many faces: Challenging injustice, breaking barriers, reaching out, being vulnerable, being different, persevering against all odds... just for a start. Clumping these stories into manageable categories is like trying to corral courage. What would I do with Isabel Allende, who stood boldly against a patriarchal system in Chile, risked her life to help others during a military coup, and endured the long death of her beloved daughter?

Forgive the structure here. It doesn't do justice to the rich and complex landscape within. It merely hints. Read where you are drawn to read. But also read randomly. You'll find yourself in stories that surprise you. I like to hold the book, close my eyes, ask for the thing that I need to hear or ponder at that moment... and open.

Introduction
The Spirit of Courage

"Life shrinks or expands in proportion to one's courage."

— Anaïs Nin

I started this book as a courage voyeur.

Don't get me wrong, I had had my moments of chutzpah. But courage. That's a big word. Powerful. Intense. Intimidating. It's a word for heroes, for those who brave the impossible, who live bigger than life. I wanted to vicariously feel that rush of victory from challenges conquered against all odds. I wanted to know what it was like to slay the dragon.

It was a shallow perspective, as I discovered in two and a half years of talking with women, crying with them, laughing with them, thrilling with them. Courage, I discovered, can be a fragile, vulnerable thing, a quiet moment. It can be a deep look into our souls, a stillness with our divinity. It can be found in the exhalation of love. In the speaking of truth. In forgiving and the making of peace.

I learned greatly from these women — I was humbled by them. As it turns out, courage is not about climbing unscaleable mountains, crossing unfordable rivers, flying to unreasonable heights. Even in the most bold and daring acts, courage is a matter of the heart. And, for me personally, more than anything this book has brought me home to my heart and home to myself as woman. Not a woman trying to be gutsy like a man.

Just prior to starting this book, I had been writing what I believed to be not only dramatically compelling but socially important screenplays (only four were optioned and two produced). I had moved to Hollywood with my husband and son full of big dreams and naïve about what it takes to break into the movie industry. Seven years later, I felt professionally impotent. And I hated that feeling. I desperately wanted to retrieve the part of myself that made good on things, a quality that slowly had gotten sucked out of me. I wanted her back, that part of me that became one of the only nonlawyers writing legal reports for one of the major legal publishers in the country, who stepped into the shoes of Managing Editor at one of my favorite magazines and left as Senior Editor, who plunged into freelance magazine writing after Benjamin's birth and made it happen, who said she wanted to write a book and was published by Random House. I didn't want to be the woman who took on the Hollywood Dream like every other sucker and failed. I wanted to be in the company of things that worked. In the company of ballsy women with real guts, who were out there making things happen. And so I leapt at the idea of writing about women who were potent. Potent. What a feeling. Maybe some of it would rub off on me. Maybe living vicariously would be my jump start back into potency.

Right off, I discovered that courage is a loaded word, and not one that even the most courageous of women would use to describe themselves. Why is that?

The door to her large, airy studio was open, Isabel Allende inside busy with having just arrived. The courtyard was sheltered by a wide canopy of trees, lined with moss-covered brick, and made serene by the gentle waterfall in a small pond — a good place for a woman equally at home in the natural and supernatural worlds, her grandmother having been a clairvoyant of some repute who left Isabel with memories of sugar bowls moving mysteriously about the tea service, untouched. It was, I noted, January 10 and she makes a ritual of starting all her books on the eighth of a January. She turned at the sound of footsteps and flowed across the room in purple silk, a small woman with a profound presence and a rich South American voice welcoming me into her culturally vibrant studio.

Isabel was raised in Chile, a deeply patriarchal society, and as a young woman was on the vanguard of a risky feminist movement, becoming a recognized journalist and television personality. And yet, when we sank into the big white couch and I let the word "courage" pass my lips, she who had just sat down got right back up, saying "Yes, but I'm not a very courageous person," as she walked across the room and briefly busied herself at her desk. I waited for her to return, wondering how a woman who had risked her life over and over helping strangers reach safe houses and embassies following the military coup that left her father's cousin, Salvador Allende, brutally murdered and her country in the throes of unspeakable atrocities — how could it be that this woman would say, "Yes, but I'm not a very courageous person"?

Isabel's is a life of courage. Not a moment or an event, not a single strike but a series of events, an accumulation of dared moments. You see it etched in her discipline, her candor, her vulnerability, and yet her unassailable confidence. It comes from the courage to constantly stretch into places demanding an uncompromised presence. Courage is magnificent in this way. It changes us — gives us presence, makes us humble. I saw it in woman after woman. Talking with Isabel, I was struck by how emotionally available and authentic she remained in the ever more glaring light of fame. Courageous women tend to be this way, as though they have no time for pretense.

The more I spoke with women like Isabel, the more authentic became my search for daring stories. Time and again, I was surprised by what was at the heart of courage.

I met with Isabel thinking we would talk about the coup in Chile, but that wasn't where we ended up. Ann Bancroft obliged me with a thrilling story about her South Pole expedition, but that wasn't where she had to face her biggest challenge. When we first spoke, Dr. Elizabeth Newhall had just been targeted by a national antiabortion group, advised by the FBI to wear a bulletproof vest, to bulletproof her clinic's windows, and to vary her route to work. I expected her to talk about the courage it takes to carry on her work in the face of great jeopardy, but she had something else in mind.

Courage has many faces and we lose much when women summarily dismiss their brave acts because they don't measure up to a narrow definition of traditional courage. "The way our culture is defining courage is so ridiculous," says Mary Pipher, author of the bestselling *Reviving Ophelia* about adolescent girls and *The Shelter of Each Other* about families. "Courage has become *Raiders of the Lost Ark,* or riding in spaceships, killing people, taking enormous physical risks. To me, the kind of courage that's really interesting is someone whose spouse has Alzheimer's and yet manages to wake up every morning and be cheerful with that person and respectful of that person and find things to enjoy even though their day is very, very difficult. That kind of courage is really undervalued in our culture. We need to redefine our dialogue about courage."

I first met Riane Eisler at her home, a quiet, serene place on the coast of California. Shoes came off at the front door, softening the sound of movement within. A wood paneled hall led to a great room where muted rays of late day fell on Oriental rugs and tall windows framed a garden of trees. Photographs of her two grown daughters lined shelves, tables. She slipped into the room softly, gracious in her welcome of a visitor, studied in her speech as though respectful of the power of language and delighting in the sheer resonance of the words themselves. "So many of the models of courage we've had, ones that are still taught to boys and girls, are about going out to slay the dragon, to kill," she said. "It's a courage that's born out of fear, anger, and hate. But there's this other kind of courage. It's the courage to risk your life, not in war, not in battle, not out of fear...but out of love and a sense of injustice that has to be challenged. It takes far more courage to challenge unjust authority without violence than it takes to kill all the monsters in all the stories told to children about the meaning of bravery."

Riane had the audacity and the guts to challenge the gods of history and culture in her book *The Chalice and the Blade* — which anthropologist Ashley Montagu called the most important work since Darwin's *Origin of Species* — and again in her more recent *Sacred Pleasure.* Her audacity to take on "our most hallowed and sanctified norms" is borne out of her love for humanity and her unflagging will to right injustices flowing from the far and near past.

Challenging tradition can be risky, as Rita Dove learned when she became the youngest and first black Poet Laureate. "At first, I thought I hadn't done anything courageous in my life," she said. "But then, I realized that so many women do things that I view as brave without consciously setting out to be courageous. It made me rethink what I had asked of myself as Poet Laureate, the places and times when I had held my breath and jumped. Courage has nothing to do with our determination to be great. It has to do with what we decide in that moment when we are called upon to be more."

I've learned from every woman I've spoken with in the two and a half years that I've worked on this book. Each spoke to me of what I needed to hear, what I needed to ponder in my own life at just that moment. Which is no less than what I hope for you as you read in this book, put it down, come back to it, set it aside, pick it up again, ponder.

The women here have turned themselves inside out to tell their stories, given heart and soul. They're intimate with us, vulnerable. Many experienced a profound healing, a revelation, a catharsis, as though the telling brought them home to themselves. Several women cried. At first, Heather O'Brien didn't want to revisit the story she tells. "It was more arduous and painful than I expected," she says. "Traveling back, if only in my mind, was like scraping off layers from a nightmare I wasn't eager to revisit. This story is entirely true which, to me, is what makes it so scary."

Being in the company of these women is illuminating, stimulating, uplifting, invigorating. I am honored that they spoke so vulnerably and openly. It is a gift I cherish and now give to you. My life is bigger and broader for having been immersed in their stories. I haven't scaled any mountains. I haven't slain any dragons. But I honor myself more as a woman. I am more authentic. I am willing to be strong, to seek out places where I'm nervous or afraid and purposefully go there, knowing how much I gain by so doing, not only for myself but for my husband, my son, those around me. I am finding my true voice as a woman, a potent woman — there's that word, potent — less afraid to make mistakes, more eager to see what I'm made of, to seek out challenge, not to settle for mediocrity. These women dared to go where angels tread and yes, I can dare to go there too.

I have endeavored to explore the heart, the mind, the spirit of courage and to honor her many faces. To look into the eyes of the very soul of courage. To remind us of who we are. Because in remembering, we become more.

Here, then, are the women who dare....

— Katherine Martin

The Courage to PERSEVERE

Isabel Allende

"In terrible moments, in moments of revolution, of war or repression, of illness or death, people react with incredible strength."

Isabel Allende is a widely acclaimed author whose book, The House of the Spirits, *was made into an epic movie starring Meryl Streep, Glenn Close, Jeremy Irons, Winona Ryder. Yet in the ever more glaring light of fame, she remains emotionally available and authentic. She is, above all else, straightforward and modest — an author who couldn't bring herself to say she was a writer until she had published two books.*

Raised in the deeply patriarchal society of Chile, as a young woman Allende was on the vanguard of a risky feminist movement. She became a recognized journalist and television personality and repeatedly risked her life helping people she didn't even know get to safe houses and embassies following the military coup that left her father's cousin, Salvador Allende, brutally murdered and her country in the throes of unspeakable atrocities. Yet she found her greatest test of strength on a less grand stage.

I have had a very hectic life. Very often, what may have seemed like courage was really something that came about because I didn't have a choice, there really was no option. I just had to face what came.

The difficulties started very early in my life, when my father abandoned my mother and we moved from our home in Lima, Peru, to my grandfather's house in Santiago, Chile. It was the beginning of a very difficult life because Chile is strictly Catholic, a country with no divorce. So, as children, we were often rejected, and there was much aggression against my mother because she had separated from her husband instead of properly carrying on as though he would return. It took courage for her to do this. She had three children, she wasn't prepared for work, she had no money, and Chilean society told her she could not have a life outside of the one with her husband. Later, she was even more courageous when she again challenged the very society in which we lived in order to carry on a love affair that was forbidden.

During this time, I developed a very private universe where I dwelled. In a way, it protected me from the real world. We had no television at that time and children were not taken to the movies. So, I read and invented my own games, and I lived in that private world. But then, things changed. My mother married the man of the love affair. He was a diplomat, and we started traveling. The rest of my childhood was spent moving, changing places, adapting to new countries, new languages, new friends, saying good-bye to people and places. And again, I think I found in that private world of mine a safe haven where I could be myself. I was a very silent and solitary child.

All through childhood, I went to British schools where we were taught self-control. It was the utmost goal of our education. The only emotion we were allowed to express was a little surprise. I was grateful for that kind of education because I come from a family of very dramatic and tragic people, and my schooling gave me tools for self-control. The most severe school I attended was in Lebanon. Our uniform, for example, didn't have buttons. It had strings that we had to tie, because buttons were considered frivolous. It was extreme, but I loved it. I think I needed that very tight structure because I had such an unstructured life. And the discipline helped temper my character, because I tend to be exaggerated — all of that comes out now in my writing and not in my life.

When I was fifteen, I discovered love. It was a revelation. I realized that I had a body, I realized that you could touch people. In my family, nobody touches. I love my mother, we're very close to this day, but we never touch. I was a child with no physical intimacy of any kind. And, all of a sudden, I discovered that you could touch other human beings. That opened up a whole other world for me. I came out of the cocoon I'd inhabited all of my childhood. I became a person really.

I got very involved in things that were external to my family and my life . . . news, politics, the community, everything that happened in the world was interesting to me. In my twenties, I became a journalist, both print and television. It was an exciting time in Chile. It was the beginning of the sexual revolution in a country that was very conservative, the beginning of the feminist movement. Very few women had ever heard the word, let alone become feminist. I embraced it from the very beginning. I was one of few. Chile is a very patriarchal society. By this time I had married Michael, and I found myself having to stand up to him, to my mother, to society. But, I never thought I was brave for that, I thought it was just an act of intelligence and there was a sort of humorous challenge about it. The worst thing that could happen was that people would talk behind my back, but it didn't matter to me.

During this period, socialism was a growing force in a country that had been very right wing. When Salvador Allende was elected in 1970, he represented a coalition of parties of the center and the left. I got involved in so many things because they were fascinating to me. I never thought that any of it would be risky or put me in danger. I lived in a long state of innocence in that sense. I didn't really become aware that there is evil and violence in the world until 1973, after the military coup. The right reacted violently to Salvador and they used all the errors of the government to sabotage and undermine the socialist experiment in Chile. We had a very serious economic, political, and social crisis that created a state of violence and hatred.

I was thirty-one when the military coup happened. Until then, I had been convinced that evil was a sort of accident, that it happened very seldom and only because something went wrong. But I believed that we were, by nature, good and that everything *should* turn out right if we did the right things. Then, everything changed. Within twenty-four hours. Even language changed. As a journalist, I knew what was going on, but I couldn't write about it or speak about it because the truth was censored. Many people needed help, and I wasn't allowed to help them.

In the beginning, we didn't know the rules, nobody did, because the rules were changing every day. I don't think the military even knew what was going on, what the rules were. It was all very confusing. We had never had a military dictatorship in Chile. So, we didn't know what was happening. Everything was chaos. News was censored. Nothing was confirmed.

As I got involved in helping more people get to embassies or find asylum across the border, or in hiding people, I became more aware of the repression. But, I still didn't think that by helping people I was risking my life. I became aware of that much later and, by then, it was too late to get out. I was already too involved. But, I was scared all the time. As repression became more precise and more targeted, it was more difficult to get through the loopholes. I knew now that if I was caught, I would be killed or tortured or my children would be tortured in front of me. For the first time, I had to confront my ideals and ask myself, "Who am I?" and "What do I want?" But, even then, things were happening so fast, I didn't really have time to consider too deeply, to make conscious choices. I stumbled into situations and somehow confronted whatever came, more by instinct than reason. Later, I would realize that I'd been in danger or that I'd done something I shouldn't have done because it was very risky. But, I did not make a conscious decision to be courageous or brave.

If you ask me what has been the most difficult moment in my life, the moment that has required the most strength and courage to endure, I would say it was the illness and the death of my daughter, Paula. That was far and away the worst experience in my life.

Paula was living in Madrid when she got sick. I moved to a hotel there, and stayed at her bedside for six months until finally the doctors admitted that she had severe brain damage and she was never going to wake up, she was in a profound coma. I brought her to San Francisco, an incredible trip on a commercial airplane, and from there in an ambulance to a rehabilitation hospital where she stayed for a month while I prepared my home and myself to take care of her. In every step of that ordeal, there were no alternatives. It was not a question of putting Paula in an institution, as some people thought I should. It was not a question of anything, there were never any choices.

My mother thinks that I behaved very courageously, but I was scared and in pain all the time. And I did what I had to do because there was no way out. If I could have escaped, I would have. But there was no way. I'd never known what that was like. Even in the worst situations in my life, I'd always had a way to escape. From the horror of the military coup, I could escape into exile. From a rotten marriage, I could escape through divorce. But, in this situation, there was absolutely nothing I could do. I was totally trapped, as was Paula. She was trapped in her body, and I was trapped in a situation that was worse than death.

In the beginning, I prayed that she would die before I did, because if something happened to me, who was going to care for her? And then, I started praying that she would live because I couldn't bear the idea of separating from her. I thought, let her live and when I'm dying I'll kill her and kill myself. I had this fantasy that we could both go together. And then, in the end, I finally accepted that she was in pain, and then I wanted her to die for herself, not for me, but because she was trapped.

I have seen that when people confront situations like this in which there is no alternative, they are usually very brave. It's like we have hidden resources of strength that we never use; we don't even know that we have them because we don't need them. It's just sort of an immunity of the system that is never challenged, and when it is challenged, our inner resources emerge. In terrible moments, in moments of revolution, of war or repression, of illness or death, people react with incredible strength. All those women in the concentration camps in Bosnia, raped over and over, the little girls raped in front of the grandmothers . . . and they survive. We are incredibly strong. I received hundreds, thousands of letters after I wrote *Paula* from women who are terrified of the idea of losing a child. And they say, "If something like this happened to me, I would die." And I say, no you wouldn't, you go on living and you carry the child inside you. You go on . . .

> *Listen Paula, I am going to tell you a story, so that when you wake up you will not feel so lost.*

I wrote *Paula* without knowing that it would become a book. It was the journal I kept as I sat in the dark corridors of the Madrid hospital, trying to ward off the specter of death.

> *. . . You have been sleeping for a month now. I don't know how to reach you; I call and call but your name is lost in the nooks and crannies of this hospital. My soul is choking in sand. Sadness is a sterile desert. I don't know how to pray. . . . I plunge into these pages in an irrational attempt to overcome my terror. I think that perhaps if I give form to this devastation, I shall be able to help you, and myself, and that the meticulous exercise of writing can be our salvation. Eleven years ago, I wrote a letter to my grandfather to say good-bye to him in death. On this January 8, 1992, I am writing you, Paula, to bring you back to life.*

I don't know if I would have been able to survive without the writing. It gave boundaries to something that was so awful it had no boundaries, that seemed so overwhelming that it occupied every space in my life and in my soul. When I wrote, I gave words to the pain, it had limits and boundaries and shape and color and texture, and then I could describe it and when I could describe it, it no longer occupied all the space, it became something else, something with which I could deal.

This is a book I wish I had never had to write. Paula died on December 6, 1992. I start all my books on January 8. So, a month after she died, I was supposed to start another book, but I was in such pain and shock that it was impossible. And my mother said, "If you don't write, you will die. You *have* to write." I had planned a novel before Paula got sick and I thought I would try to write that novel. One day, I was with a friend who is a Buddhist monk, and we sat together in meditation for a long time. I was deep in meditation when I heard his voice say, "Tell me the first sentence of your next book." I did not speak. My voice spoke for me. I said the first sentence of the book, *Paula*. It wasn't the other book I had intended to write. *This* book was pushing to be written. I said, without even thinking, "Listen Paula, I'm going to tell you a story so that when you wake up you will not be so lost." And I knew that was the book I was going to write. I didn't have the choice of writing or not writing it. It was there.

When I was finishing *Paula*, my assistant would come into my studio and find me crying every day and she would say, "Why are you writing this book, you don't *have* to write this book, just *stop*." And I would say, "No, on the contrary, this is helping me. All these tears I will have to cry anyway, but by writing I can control them, I can control the pain." In the beginning, when Paula was very sick, I had this feeling that I was standing in the middle of a hurricane with all this wind around me and I couldn't hear anything, I couldn't think, I couldn't talk, I was totally immersed in pain. And then, when I started writing, I could step out of the center of the hurricane and I could describe it, and by describing my pain and Paula's condition, I could breathe again.

When something happens in our lives that forces us to reach deep into the storage room where we have these hidden strengths and resources, and we use them, we become incredibly confident because we know that if *this* didn't destroy me, what can? It's not that I'm looking for trouble, but I have a feeling now that I can face pain in a better way. I always had the capacity. I just didn't know it. Whatever happens now, I am strong enough to face it.

Until now, I have never shared my past; it is my innermost garden, a place not even my most intimate lover has glimpsed. Take it, Paula, perhaps it will be of some use to you, because I fear that yours no longer exists, lost somewhere during your long sleep—and no one can live without memories.

Isabel's most recent book is Aphrodite: A Memoir of the Senses.

Kelly Stone

"I know what it's like to feel you just can't cope anymore. I'd run out of money, I didn't have a place to live, I couldn't afford to insure my car and prayed that it wouldn't break down. I had zero income."

Kelly Stone, sister of actress Sharon Stone, founded Planet Hope, a foundation that runs camps and programs in the Los Angeles area to help homeless families get back on their feet.

I'm never really satisfied with where I am. I'm comfortable with myself, but I always want to do more. My sister, my brothers, and I grew up in a middle-class family in Pennsylvania. My father was a laborer in a forging die factory. My mom was the kind of mom who was always there, putting us on the bus in the morning, opening the screen door in the afternoon when we got home from school. We grew up with a lot of stability in a beautiful little town. But still, even as a girl, I wanted more.

Later, as an adult, I said to myself that I wanted three things in life: peace in my soul, to be a mother and a good partner, and to do something that would make an impact in the world. I believe our karma is decided by what we give to the world. We can't expect the world to give to us if we don't give to it. I also believe there are no accidents in life, because what happened to me in 1990 on those slippery steps in Santa Monica, California, turned into a blessing. It pushed me to do something very special and rewarding.

I had been schooled in finance and started my career in banking. I was very good with numbers, but that path in life didn't do anything for my heart. I left and went into nursing, and I volunteered for every charity I could find, looking for work that was meaningful and fulfilling. Still, I didn't feel very centered within myself and was trying to figure out what I wanted to do with my life. I was twenty-nine years old. When the accident happened, I was the director of marketing for a large medical firm. I had a good job, I was making really good money, and life in many ways was great. Then all of a sudden, in one second, it all changed, every single bit of it.

I was leaving work one day, the stairs were wet, I was wearing high heels. I slipped.

I fell down thirteen stairs. When I hit the bottom, my legs felt like they had gone through my back. I couldn't move. I thought I was paralyzed.

Both knees were badly cut and injured — muscles were ripped and my kneecap fractured. I was in a brace for the better part of a year. When I finally got back on my feet, it didn't last long, and I had to have surgery. I had one leg operated on, and there were no problems. Then, a few months later, I had the other leg operated on. This time there was a complication during surgery. I woke up without any feeling from the knee down. The whole experience became a horrible nightmare. I was supposed to be an outpatient, and I ended up in the hospital for a month.

Confined again to a wheelchair (as I would be several times for years to come), I flew back to my parents' home in Pennsylvania with a drain in my leg. Within days, I developed adhesions and a terrible infection that left me unable to move my left leg. At one point, I was at risk of losing it.

Because I was helpless, I lost every single bit of self-confidence. I had to be carried to the bathroom. I was back at home with my parents at the age of thirty. I didn't know where I was going with my life, and I was absolutely terrified. I had been independent; I had been successful; I had been attractive and dating up a storm; I had had a tremendous earning capacity; I had been working to make a difference in the world; and I had been in good shape. Now all of this had been taken from me. Now I looked horrible and felt horrible. Regularly I woke up crying. I was on several medications. And I was on a long, long road to recovery, in such despair, with this sick feeling of not knowing what I was going to do with myself.

One day, lying in bed with the curtains drawn, I wondered if I even wanted to live, when Sharon called and said, "Okay, get dressed, we're going out." I started to moan and whine that I didn't want to, I couldn't face it. "Well, you damn well better start facing it because it's your life for now and you have a healthy brain and personality. And I need your help." She was going to visit a home for teenage girls. "Stop thinking about your problems," she said, "and come with me to help some kids who have problems of their own."

I dragged myself out of bed, put on some clothes, got my crutches, and went with her. This day was the beginning for me, the real beginning. It also just happened to be my thirty-second birthday.

We spent the evening talking with girls who had been abused sexually, emotionally, and physically. A few nights later, Sharon took me to a dinner where she was being honored for her work with these girls. To my surprise, she had been doing volunteer work with homeless and abused kids for years, being as private about it as she could be. That night, she asked me to help her organize a summer camp for homeless children . . . Camp Unity.

That was February of 1993. I started volunteering, on crutches, and spent every day, with Sharon's help, working on the preparations for that summer camp — with her pushing, pushing, pushing me — on days I didn't want to get out of bed, days I didn't want to live, days I felt I'd never be able to marry, have children, walk normally. We worked for six months, going to meetings and making calls to solicit the help of doctors and volunteers and to raise donations of shoes and clothing. In August the camp opened. It was the best day of my life, my new life.

Being with those kids, seeing Sharon and my brother Michael with them, changed me, and it was the most wonderful experience. On the last day, when camp was over, I had a panic attack: "What am I going to do with my life?"

Sharon turned to look at me. "Well, what do you want to do?"

"This is what I want to do — but I can't just stay here and live in this dreamland. I have to have a career, I have to be more solid, I can't work in a camp four days a summer and wait around for the rest of the year."

"Well," she said, "what would you do if you had the opportunity to do anything you wanted?"

I thought about that for a minute. "I'd like to help women who have lost hope and are homeless. I'd like to start an organization that would help give them back their dignity, that would help homeless families find jobs and homes."

"Then, that's what you should do."

"But how?"

She just smiled at me. "You'll figure it out. I'm behind you, whatever you want to do."

And that's how Planet Hope was born. I decided I was going to help women who had hit bottom like I had, but who were homeless, especially women with children.

First, I wanted to meet women and children in shelters, and talk with them about their experiences — how they got there, what it was like for them in the shelter. Amazingly, the first woman I spoke with was a nurse who had fallen down a flight of stairs and been critically injured. She had exhausted her disability, lost her job and her home, and ended up in a shelter with her two children. Her entire life had spun out of control.

That first visit was in West Los Angeles where even a homeless shelter is beautiful, and I suspected that Jeff Schaffer, the man from the homeless organization who had sent me there, didn't think I could handle the more desperate contact of the harder neighborhoods in East L.A. I called him up and said I wanted to go where people were living on the streets, the bad neighborhoods like Watts, the ones everyone talked about. He was reluctant, but he finally gave in. "Okay, there's a woman you can meet, but she's tough; she's going to put you through the wringer, and I think you're too sensitive. I don't even know if she'll meet with you. You have to understand she's just been burned out by the riots; she comes from a whole different world."

Her name was Teryl Watkins, vice president of the Watts Labor Community Action Committee. I called and asked to meet with her. She wasn't going to meet with me, but her assistant didn't tell me that and gave me an appointment anyway. So, I drove into Watts, nervous about this woman who was going to chew me up. I walked into the office and said, "I'm here to meet with Teryl Watkins." She was too busy, said her assistant, so I met with another woman, Louise, a senior planner, who took me into a cold conference room that looked out onto a hall. I started talking away about my idea — a camp for homeless women and children — with Louise sitting across from me. Behind her, out in the hall, a woman who had the presence of royalty, a beautiful black woman, immensely powerful, began to walk back and forth. For some reason, she seemed to have a real problem with my being there and it was unsettling. Louise wasn't very receptive to what I was saying, and I could see that she was distracted by this woman walking back and forth in the hall who, I was about to discover, was Teryl Watkins.

Suddenly, the woman walked in, sat down, looked me square in the eye, and said,

"I'm gonna tell you right now, I heard about your program and I don't need your Beverly Hills bullshit coming in here, giving me a bunch of crap. This organization was started by my father for the people of Watts, it's one of the largest foundations of its kind in the country, and I don't need no dog 'n' pony shows, people coming in here and looking for their own glorification on account of their humanitarian deeds. People in this community have been used to the hilt. I'm not interested in participating in a program that doesn't have measurable goals, a beneficial outcome for people, and a long-range plan. Homeless people are used and dropped. It doesn't benefit a kid to go ride a pony in some camp when he doesn't have a home to stay in. Ask any kid what is the only thing they want and it's this: 'My own bed and a house for my mother.'"

Well, Jeff Schaffer was right: True to what he predicted, I broke down and started crying, because I wasn't sure if I could help. "I don't want to do that. I heard you were really tough. I knew you'd be really hard on me, but I'm here because I feel like I can learn from you." I was truly humbled, and I think it took Teryl aback. This was the beginning of a lifelong education (for me) and a wonderful friendship. After our rocky start, we grew to be very close friends, and I came to have a deep respect for her. She was the one person in that community who really believed in me and helped me go into the shelters to learn during the time I was putting Planet Hope together.

It was trial by fire. Most of the time, I didn't know what I was doing; I just believed in my mission. The first evening I spent alone with homeless families in a shelter, I was scared to death. There's a point when you walk in — I don't care how tough you are — and you hear the iron gate clank shut outside, and then you hear the bullet-proof door with a one-sided latch on the inside closing, and it's scary. Inside, all the furniture was torn apart, babies were crying in their mothers' arms, all these women were watching me, and I thought, "Oh, my God, what am I doing? How can I even begin to relate to them?" And they were looking at me wondering what I was doing there, what I wanted from them. I was so out of my element and so scared, but I knew I had to know this side of homelessness if I was ever going to be any good at helping and making a difference. Many of the women were educated and had lost everything. They didn't have cars, they had lost all family contact, and they had no financial resources. They had to start over — completely over. The challenge was huge.

In the summer of 1994, we held our first Planet Hope camp in the coastal town of Malibu, California. We had several programs geared to help homeless families get back on their feet, like resume writing, Alcoholics Anonymous meetings, therapy sessions, even makeovers, plus medical care, arts and crafts, sports, and "back-to-school" clothing distribution. Listening to the women at camp, I realized that if they had a drug problem or an alcohol problem, it was part of becoming homeless. Contrary to public opinion, these problems come after you've lost hope. I understood that. When I hit bottom, I was addicted to Percodan. I overdosed on Percodan and almost died. I know what it's like to feel you just can't cope anymore. I'd run out of money, I didn't have a place to live, I couldn't afford to insure my car and prayed that it wouldn't break down. I had zero income.

At one time in my life, I had a goal to make several thousand dollars a month. I hit my goal, but I've never set another one like that since. I've come to think that my goals should almost be unreachable. I should never say, "This is all I want to do."

For a few years, I couldn't imagine my future, but I have so many dreams now of what I want to do. I find myself getting up in the middle of the night and writing notes about things going through my head, plans for my future. I don't know if they'll come true, but I'm having a great time working toward them. I'm enjoying my journey on my feet.

Kelly Stone is currently extending her foundation to help homeless organizations across the United States. Planet Hope's newest program is Computer Hope, which teaches computer literacy and places homeless adults into permanent jobs. She also owns Scene Again, an entertainment marketing agency in Los Angeles.

Jako

"I felt this panic that, if I didn't inform everyone as soon as possible, that very night they could go out and make the same mistake."

Jako is twenty-six years old as of this writing. The day she found out she was HIV positive was the biggest reality check of her life. That was six and a half years ago. She never would have believed it could happen to her.

In September 1992, HIV was the last thing on my mind when I went in for a physical. I'd been traveling alone in Europe for nine months — celibate — on a soul search. I had gone looking for myself, for some sense of who I was at the root of me, because I had had a really abusive childhood and a crazy year living on my own for the first time in my life.

Traveling gave me time alone to find my spirit. For the first time, by making choices that were right for me, I began to love myself. Me. Who I am. Not ugly. Not worthless. Not all the things I'd been raised to believe about myself. After those nine months, I felt I could come home and live a new life with a new strength. I had touched that inner power in me and I could share it — I could have a real relationship.

I came home ready to start dating again, only this time with self-respect instead of some blind need. And I knew if I got into a relationship with someone, I would want to know he was healthy. What better motivation for him to get tested than for me to have a piece of paper that said I had no sexually transmitted diseases (STDs). So, I went to a clinic, had a pap smear and a physical, and, as kind of an afterthought, an HIV test. The nurse said I probably didn't need one, but she knew why I was getting all these tests to begin with and said HIV would be a good thing to add since I'd want to ask a future partner to get tested.

I despise needles so much that I almost didn't do the test. But, as we talked about risk factors, the nurse went through a checklist and asked how many partners I had had. I said seven. Her little form indicated that more than six was high risk, which now makes me laugh because so many people have far fewer than six partners and are infected. The nurse said I should definitely take a test. And that was the sum total of my pretest counseling.

I thought I was invulnerable. When I was in high school, in the early nineties, our AIDS education emphasized that gay men and IV drug users were at high risk, but the fact that drug-free heterosexual teenage girls could be at risk was never discussed. At the time, I thought I had all the protection I needed by being on the Pill. As a young woman having sexual relationships with young men who were physically beautiful, who seemed to be healthy, I never thought about protecting myself against anything other than pregnancy. No friend of mine had ever mentioned having an STD — it simply wasn't in my reality. I didn't realize how high the statistics of teens and STDs were. Not only was I putting myself at risk for HIV, but for a whole slew of other STDs that I could have contracted. I somehow managed to get the worst one possible. I was two months shy of nineteen when I discovered I was infected.

September 16, 1992. It had been two weeks since the test. I went back to the clinic to get the results, expecting everything to be fine. I sat in the doctor's office waiting for him and, when he came in, he looked routine. I had no idea what he was about to tell me. He said my pap smear was normal, but that my HIV test was positive. And then, he turned around and left. Just left. One sentence and he was gone.

I found out later that I was his first HIV positive. He sent in a counselor, a wonderful woman who spoke with me, but whatever she said, I don't remember. I was crying. Everything was a blur. My ears were ringing. She sent me home with a bag full of literature.

I don't remember leaving the doctor's office. I went to a friend's house and cried in her arms. I finally caught a bus home. Tears were still streaming down my face. *This is real, this is real, they're not lying, this is real. The doctor told me I'm positive, this is real.* I saw a little boy with brown eyes and brown curly hair, about five years old, and it hit me that I would never have children. Children. When I was traveling in Europe, I had come to realize for the first time that I would be a good mother. Working as a nanny in Monaco, I had taken care of six-year-old twins and saw that I could be a good mother. It had worried me — this thing about having children — because a counselor in high school had told me that I would treat my children as badly as my parents had treated me and that I shouldn't have any kids.

After seeing that little boy on the bus, I cried for a future I'd never have.

I finally got home. I called my previous sexual partners. I didn't know who had infected me, but they were all at risk and one of them was the source of the disease. And then, I started calling everyone I knew and told them that they needed to get tested, that I had tested positive. I felt this panic that, if I didn't inform everyone as soon as possible, that very night they could go out and make the same mistake. I'm not sure how I did that because you risk a lot of rejection from people when you disclose that you have HIV. It's one of the scariest parts about being HIV positive: being rejected, being considered dirty, being left alone. But for some reason I was driven to tell everyone, to make sure they knew it was a reality in our lives, not just my life but theirs. I knew that many of my peers had the same sense that nothing would happen to them, that as long as they were taking small risks, nothing would hurt them.

Two weeks later, I saw a friend, a guy I had been purely platonic with before we fell fatefully into bed together. He was coming out of the doctor's office with his new girlfriend. They had both tested positive for HIV. They were both under the age of twenty. I felt furious and powerless.

I had first become sexually active at eighteen and a half. It was 1991 and I was living in downtown Portland, Oregon, sharing an apartment with another girl. Until then I'd never been allowed to make any decisions for myself, so I didn't know yet what was right and what was wrong for me. I had to experience it firsthand. And I experienced it full on, going out to clubs and cafés every night, dancing and hanging out. For the first time in my life, I was popular and men were paying attention to me. My parents had not allowed me to have a boyfriend while I lived at home. My father actually told me that if I had a boyfriend, I was a whore. Neither he nor my mother ever spoke about sex, except to say that it was dirty and wrong. By the time I left home, I had a huge fear of sex.

At first, I tried having a kind of fantasy relationship, the one I'd always dreamed of: I would make love with one man and only one man in my life and he would be the person I'd marry and have kids with and it would last forever and ever and we'd live happily ever after. When the boy in this fantasy dumped me, I was broken. I had a huge hole in me. And I filled it with other people. Over the next five months, I had six partners, each time trying to convince myself that I was in love. But it was really hurtful and it wasn't right for me.

By the time I went to Europe, I was ready for a quiet inner journey. I knew traveling would help, because I'd be able to get perspective on my life by being away from what I identified with, what was familiar. I grew so much during that time. I wrote poetry. I worked and supported myself. I made my own decisions. I was the only one responsible for myself. Whenever someone asked me out to dinner or on a date, I made it clear that the date would end without any sexual intimacy. I didn't want to share my body out of some false need for affection anymore and I didn't want to be used. I had no idea what love was, but I began to see that I needed a partner who respected me for who I was, who wanted to share a life with me.

That was the Jako who returned to the States in 1992, ready and eager for a new life.

When I found out I was HIV positive, I reverted to being a little girl. I completely regressed. I felt as if I were an embryo in a womb and I needed to be taken care of, and I needed mothering, and I needed to be held. Functioning in the world was impossible. For three days, I curled up in bed like a little baby, crying and not knowing what to do and feeling as if I should have known better and wondering why, after all I had gone through in my life, I had to be infected with HIV. Why me, of all people, who had had an extremely difficult childhood and had finally just started to strengthen and love myself for the first time in my life. Why had I allowed myself to get infected? I was smarter than that; I had walked in an AIDS march and was a busy political and social activist. I knew what AIDS was. I just didn't think it had anything to do with me. Looking back, I am amazed that I could have been so involved in other things, issues, causes, and not involved enough with myself to make sure I was protected.

In the beginning, I thought I was only going to live four or five years. I tried to figure out how to plan my life, how to live everything I had wanted to live within the next four years. I really didn't know how to do that. To this day, just talking about it makes me cry. How does a nineteen-year-old plan for a life that will end at twenty-four?

I felt isolated, like I was the only person in the world going through this. I didn't know any other young, HIV-positive women, and I wanted desperately to meet one who had dealt with her disease in a powerful way. I wanted to see what she had done and how she had done it. That's who I started looking for after the first days of shock passed, but she was nowhere to be found. She didn't exist, not in my world anyway. Somehow, I started realizing that I needed to be that person, that maybe I could do the best for myself.

I wasn't going to give up. I had tried once to escape, when the abuse had gotten really horrible at home. One night, screaming inside my head to a God I had started to think didn't exist, I swallowed some pills, and I swallowed and swallowed until I cried myself to sleep. Forty-two ibuprofen went down that night. I don't know what the effects should have been, but I'm pretty sure I should have been ill. Yet, I woke up fine the next morning and went to school. I did not want to die. I did not want attention. I only wanted the hurt to stop.

My childhood taught me to fight and, having tested positive for HIV at age nineteen, that's what I knew to do — fight. I had been through horrible pain. I had faced death as a child. I had forged an incredibly strong instinct for self-preservation, an incredibly strong will to live.

I've drawn intensely on that will to live, and I've funneled it into my own crusade to help young people avoid this disease. Over the last six years, I've been doing a tremendous amount of public speaking and I hope that my coming out about being HIV positive is a reality check for other young people, that hearing a peer speak from personal experience has an impact on them. I hope my story is something a young person holds in his or her mind when they're making sexual decisions that can affect them for the rest of their lives. Our whole sexuality, in my generation, has changed. In order to survive, we desperately need to be more cautious and to incorporate the risk of contracting a sexually transmitted disease into every decision we make. There are three new HIV infections every hour, and one of those infected is a person under the age of twenty.

Every speech I've made, every interview I've given, was done because I hoped it would reach at least one other young person who wouldn't have to live through the pain of knowing they're HIV positive. Speaking publicly, I have encountered people who were afraid to be in the same room with me. I've encountered people who felt that I deserved to be HIV positive, that premarital sex warrants such a consequence. That sort of thinking infuriates me, and it saddens me because it comes from a closed mind. It shows a willingness to reject another human being. While I have a virus in my body, I have not become inhuman. I find it very difficult not to cry when I try to explain that to someone.

I was an HIV poster girl for several years, appearing on local and national radio and television ads and in the print media. I appeared on an ABC *Afterschool Special* called "Sex Unplugged" about HIV prevention and testing. I was on the talk show *Jenny Jones* in the spring of 1996 and in *Glamour* magazine when they featured HIV-positive women and their partners (HIV negative). I was in a Population Services International education video about AIDS prevention and a number of other public service announcements about AIDS. But I'm no longer a teenager, and I'm no longer willing to sacrifice my personal life for a public life of AIDS activism, which can be hard when people within the activist community tell you that you're only worth what you do, not who you are. It's difficult now when someone wants me to do a speaking engagement and I say no and they continue to ask and ask and ask. I'm expected to be a public figure, a martyr. People are disappointed — colleges, schools, the media, AIDS organizations — when I say no. There's an unspoken pressure to keep going, doing. They don't understand that I need to just be, which may take more courage than ever. I need to live my life a little less focused on my being HIV positive. I need to feel that I'm being recognized more for who I was before I was diagnosed than for the disease. I love being a positive role model for youth with HIV, but it's difficult to be recognized on the bus as "the girl with HIV," to walk down the street and have someone say, "I know you from somewhere . . . oh, yeah, you spoke at my school, you're HIV positive. Hey, Mary, this is the HIV-positive woman who spoke to us at school. She's really cool." That's very nice, but it's hard for me that my identity has become almost entirely that of the disease. I have cringed when acquaintances introduced me as "Jako, she's HIV positive." Not Jako the director or producer or interdisciplinary artist. Not Jako who speaks Spanish, Italian, French, Hungarian, and German. Not Jako who loves to travel.

I'm moving forward in life now with Christopher, my partner. We're very much in love and hope for a long life together. For me, maintaining a better balance is what's necessary. I've had to resolve for myself that what I do and what I have done is enough — that I have left my mark.

For the past three and a half years, Jako has been working on a creative film that portrays youth living with HIV disease. With her codirector Rebecca Guberman, a young HIV-positive photographer, she has traveled around the country documenting what is happening to a generation slapped in the face with its mortality. More than a hundred and twenty hours of footage is ready to be edited. The project has been endorsed by feature film director Gus Van Sant, supported by the advertising firm Wieden and Kennedy, nationally known photographers Doug Starn and Mike Starn, and by Lovett Productions in New York City. (Joe Lovett fought for and accomplished the first AIDS reporting in 1983 on ABC's 20/20.) *Hoping to provide support to HIV-positive youth, and to increase understanding and acceptance through their film, Jako and Rebecca are seeking postproduction funding for the film, which has a working title of* Blood Lines. *A twenty-minute version of the film aired on MTV on World AIDS Day, December 1, 1998, and won the prestigious 1999 Ribbon of Hope Award given by the Academy of TV Arts and Sciences. A longer, educational version won the Silver Apple Award given by the National Educational Media Network.*

Cheri Honkala

"I want to stop seeing, feeling, moving. The pain is too great, my heart is on fire."

Cheri Honkala was a college student in Minneapolis, six months pregnant, and working nights to try to meet her rent when she was evicted from her apartment. She had nowhere to go, so she lived in her car. When a drunk driver wrecked her car, she slept on the street, and she kept working and going to college until the birth of her son forced her to turn to welfare. "Being homeless is devastating. I lived in a series of abandoned houses, always scared that we would be forced to leave at any minute. We often had no water or heat, but there was nowhere else to go."

Cheri grew up in poverty in Minneapolis. "My brother and sister and I were constantly teased at school because our old clothes didn't fit us and we looked thin. Not having enough to eat at home was common. I was regularly abused — emotionally and physically — by my stepfather, who was an alcoholic. Eventually, when I was twelve years old, I ran away. I spent the rest of my teenage years in institutions for runaways and abused kids. I was never allowed to be with my family or even visit them. I felt completely alone. Writing in my journal helped me through a lot of lonely and scary times.

Finally, I was sent to an alternative 'last chance' high school, where teachers told me I was capable of doing more than I'd ever thought possible and inspired me to go to college."

She started college in Minneapolis, working nights to support herself. "I was completely alone, and I think part of what kept me going was the rebel in me. The abuse in my childhood had taught me early on that I had two choices: give up or survive. So, I had become a survivor. In college, I began to realize through a women's studies course just how much my mother, my sister, and I had been victimized by poverty and violence. Most of the women in my class, however, didn't want to talk about issues of class, about what I as a poor woman had to do simply to live day to day. It was when I started to talk to other poor women about their lives that I knew I had to do something to fight for what our families needed."

She joined the Welfare Rights Union, a national advocacy group, and when her new husband found work in Philadelphia, she ended up in Kensington, one of the city's roughest neighborhoods, where she started a branch of the Union. Frustrated with the notorious paperwork of the Department of Housing and Urban Development, she quietly moved seventeen families into twelve vacant HUD properties. The occupation was, of course, illegal, and lasted only weeks, but soon she leveraged her action into housing vouchers for all the families, cutting through red tape and providing a legal solution without the usual "interminable delay" for most Section 8 housing. It was a strategy she used again and again. "As a result, hundreds of homeless families have received vouchers for subsidized housing or have gotten permanent homes. All of the occupations involved both men and women, young and old, people of all races and backgrounds."

According to Cheri, she's been arrested, but not convicted, more than fifty times for misdemeanor trespassing violations: squatting or sit-ins. Her defense: Her actions are motivated by a "moral sense of urgency," which sits well with most juries. "There's something disgusting about women and children with no place to live," she says.

The sun is hot. I'm sweating already at 6:10 A.M. as I lie on my lawn chair that has now worn through so that I feel the metal supports on my tail bone. Another day on Fourth and Lehigh in the heart of Philadelphia's barrio. Another heat warning has been issued; with the humidity, they expect the temperature to reach a hundred and ten degrees. The heat from the sun has now forced the homeless mothers and children from their tents. They move slowly. Everything moves slowly in the oppressive heat.

The headlines announce that forty-seven have died in this heat wave. I burn inside as I read on because I know they didn't die from heat. I know they died because they couldn't afford a simple electric fan. I know that they died from poverty. And I know that the homeless women and children on this lot will die as well if we don't find housing for them. They'll die, if not from the heat of summer, then from the cold of winter.

Yet as I look around today, it is hard for me to move on. The sun is hotter now, my clothes are soaked in sweat, I have lost my appetite. A child runs by me crying with a runny nose, and I don't even want to move. Perhaps I will just lie here and, like Langston Hughes says, dry up like a raisin in the sun. "This is it, they win," I say to myself. "I give up. I can't do this anymore." I want to swim in the ocean, feel the cool of the water as it refreshes my sunburned head. I want to stop seeing, feeling, moving. The pain is too great; my heart is on fire.

In my mind, I try to run from the pain, try to find shade from the burning thoughts. There is no shade on this lot. Just thirty-seven homeless families and rocks. Rocks and more rocks and dry land. I close my eyes to escape it all. I begin to drift into sleep but am abruptly jolted back by cold water dripping on me. Two local gangster boys stand over me, holding bags of ice. As if awakening from a coma, I open my eyes without moving and stare at them. The one who is covered in tattoos says, "Here, this is for you guys. I know it ain't much, but it's the best we can do right now." Before I'm able to move my lips, they're gone, and a young woman is standing before me with a food stamp. "Here," she says, "buy something for the kids."

As my heart burns on, Flaco and Olga joke with me that it's time to go house hunting. As I manage to lift my body into the back of the pickup truck, Elba asks me if things are going to be all right. "Are the police going to take my children from me because I don't have a house, like they took Noemi's children from her?" she asks.

"Elba," I say, "you know we won't let anyone take your children away from you, and if neither the city nor the federal government gives you a house, we will take over one for you and your children." She smiles as my words burn away her fears.

We arrive at the two-story house, and I grab the scrapers and paintbrushes and make my way up the stairs. Mariluz tries to joke with me as we scrape the walls, but she sees I am much too serious today.

As I scrape, paint chips fly, covering me. The wall itself begins to come apart. Beads of sweat make the paint chips cling to my face; my eyes are covered. Now I am crying. The tears are stamping out the fire. The room is filled with bodies covered in paint and sweat, and yet their arms, my arms, are still moving. I don't know where this courage to move on comes from, but it just keeps coming. Now they sing songs in Spanish as Marls playfully paints my leg with a brush. I chase her through the house, out the door, where there is a breeze. My tears are flowing now. I feel alive. I know why I'm alive and why I love them all, all the families who have been told just to dry up in the sun, who daily have the courage to go on, to move, to move against great odds, who daily choose to live, really live.

On November 3, 1998, Cheri spoke before the United Nations as Director of the Kensington Welfare Rights Union and national spokesperson for the Economic Human Rights Campaign.

The Kensington Welfare Rights Union is a multiracial organization of poor and homeless families based in Philadelphia that works to develop leaders from among the ranks of the poor to fight for basic human needs. The Economic Human Rights Campaign is a national effort to raise the issue of poverty as a human rights violation. During the month of June 1997, Cheri led March for Our Lives, a ten-day march by the poor from Philadelphia to New York to protest human rights violations caused by welfare reform. A year later, she spearheaded a monthlong trip by the poor on the New Freedom Bus, traveling to forty urban and rural communities to gather stories to present to the UN.

Cheri was named Woman of the Year by Philadelphia Weekly, *and is in the documentary* Poverty Outlaw, *a finalist in the Documentary Competition of the 1997 Sundance Film Festival. Pulitzer Prize winning journalist David Zucchino's incisive book,* The Myth of the Welfare Queens, *chronicles the daily lives of Cheri Honkala and Odessa Williams.*

Cora Lee Johnson

"I was sixty-two years old, a poor, uneducated, disabled, black woman. I didn't have much confidence, but I decided I couldn't just sit down and do nothin'."

Cora Lee Johnson picked cotton in the fields of Georgia. She worked in a factory. She was uneducated, poor — but she had a dream.

It feels like starting a sewing center was a dream of mine since the day I first came into the world. I always wanted to sew. When I was young, I wanted to get a sewing machine but never could.

It took me a long time before I could start talking about my dream.

I worked real hard all my life, pickin' cotton, beans, tomatoes, and fruit. I started to work in the cotton field when I was tall enough to reach the cotton, and all my life I wondered how I could work so hard, going from one field to another, and still be hungry. My family married me off when I was fourteen. I worked those fields so hard my womb wouldn't hold a child, and I lost six babies. Eventually, I moved to Palm Beach, Florida, with my husband and cleaned houses. Then, one day, I came back home to Soperton, Georgia, 'cause my mamma was sick. Soperton is where my parents growed us up, raising ten children on sharecropping. I took care of my mamma until she died. That's when I had to start my life completely over. 'Cause while I was takin' care of my mamma, my husband was takin' care of another woman. I didn't have a home to go back to. I didn't have a job. I didn't have money. I didn't have anything.

I finally got me a job and worked awhile. Then I was injured in an auto accident. It happened on a Saturday. The place where I worked called first thing Monday morning and terminated my job while I was still in the hospital. I was sixty-two years old, a poor, uneducated, disabled, black woman.

I didn't have much confidence, but I decided I couldn't just sit down and do nothin'. So, I started goin' to workshops, lookin' at things uneducated folks could do for their community if they really wanted. I didn't realize I could do so much with so little until I started.

I was sewin' some at my house. When somebody would come by, I'd say to them, "I want to get some more sewin' machines so other people can come in and learn." First thing folks said to me was, "You don't have an education. How you gonna teach somebody to sew when you can't read a pattern?" I told them I wasn't plannin' to teach nobody to read a pattern — I was gonna teach 'em to sew.

Soperton is a small town southeast of Macon, Georgia, with about three thousand people. Nobody 'round here encouraged me, not even my family, 'cause they thought I was crazy. They said, "How can you do this? You know you ain't got no money."

Well, I know'd that from jump street. But the Bible says, "You have not because you ask not." And the only thing I could do was ask somebody. I thought maybe a sewin' center don't sound crazy to everybody and somebody'll help me do it. So, I started talkin' about my dream to more people outside Soperton. By still believin' in it and talkin' about it to other people, I found help. Monica Robertson, one of the ladies who used to work at Georgia Legal Services, helped me get grant money. She wrote the words for me and put the grant applications together. First grant I got was from the Sapelo Foundation. It bought sewing machines and paid rent for the first year. That's how I started my center.

My sewing center is called the Truetlen County Community Sewing Center. I have twelve machines in operation most of the time and a table for cutting. The girls come in, and I teach 'em how to cut. I don't charge nothin' in order to move by that excuse, "I'd learn how to sew, but I don't have the money to pay." I don't want to turn down nobody that come in here.

Most times at the sewing center, I don't know if I'm goin' to have money for rent from one month to another. Grant money helps, but I get just a little bit. One grant had a small stipend for me in it, but I'm on disability now, 'cause of the car accident, and that's how I makes it. Far as the center goes, I been able to keep it goin' with the help of folks who see the results of the work I do. People are working here that never had a job and never would have had a job. I keep hearing this myth that welfare mothers are lazy and won't work, but you look at the sign in front of the clothes factory and it says, "Experienced Operators Only." Somethin' wrong there. Some of the girls who been through the sewing center get experience and go get a job. Most of the people that learned to sew are still sewin'.

I teach sewin', and I teach the value of life. I talk with welfare mothers about makin' their lives better, so that they don't have to keep goin' through the same thing. And some'll say, "Well, nobody told me." So then, I try to be there to tell 'em, to love 'em whenever their parents put 'em out. I let 'em know somebody still loves 'em, 'cause I'd've never started the sewing center without some powerful women helping me grow and lovin' me.

Veda McKnight from Georgia Legal Services was the person who saw in me what I didn't see in myself. She wouldn't talk for me, she made me talk for myself. She pushed me outta the nest. I probably woulda never got out otherwise. Now that I'm out, I out for good. I can fly now.

Then, there was Lillie Allen, who started Be Present, Inc., in Atlanta. She lectures and gives seminars for women and girls, especially black women on their particular issues. If you got a problem and you don't know how to deal with it, she sees what you need to get to and help you deal with it. She tries to help women to be free. Lot of women are afraid to take the first step.

Lillie help talk me through the hurt places and the fear. When I was first talkin' about things that hurt, I'd try to avoid certain painful areas 'cause I didn't want it to hurt again. I was scared that if I said somethin' or 'n' other, it wasn't gonna come out right or somebody was gonna think I shouldn't say it. That's because whenever I'd start outta my shell, somebody'd say, "You oughta had better sense" or "You know'd better" or "You shouldn't do that." Nobody never encouraged me on nothin' that I did.

I didn't talk much with Lillie at first. I cried a lot. But, Lillie knows how to take you right back there to the hurt. And she won't let you pass it. She keeps you right there till you're able to talk about it. She lets you see that you don't have to be what people say you are.

I never felt that I belonged to my family, that I was loved. I'm the last of ten children, and other peoples said that I didn't belong to my daddy, and that hurt me. I had to do without things, and I didn't understand that maybe my daddy couldn't have got the stuff that I wanted from his sharecropping money. I saw other girls with shoes, and I had to go to school barefeeted and in old clothes. I went to school a heap of times without a sack lunch because I didn't have any food. Going to school, a big ole thirteen-year-old girl ain't got no shoes and still in the fourth grade, I just sat down and felt sorry for myself. I thought my mamma and my daddy didn't want me, and I was scared to speak up because I might get hurt. So, I had a lot of garbage that needed to be got rid of, startin' all the way back in my childhood. Because I didn't have a formal education, people would tell me I couldn't do things, and I accepted it and didn't even try.

Lillie wouldn't let me use "they" or "them," like, "They did it to me." Lillie ask, "Okay, they did that, but how about you? How did you feel when people did this to you or when people said this to you?" She want me to feel whatever it is and talk about whatever it is and, if it hurts, she want me to cry. That's the only way I could get to the next step.

We women, no matter what color we are, we go through a lot of struggles, and we think we the only one who's going through it. Once we get bare naked and talkin', when we feel safe to talk about things we can't talk about otherwise, then we can work through all the pieces to get to where we want to be. That's how it was for me. Talkin' with Lillie helped me to get confidence in myself. It was really healing.

Veda and Lillie and others learnt me how to use the power that was in me. I have grown a lot in a few years. I know that 'cause I'm able to do things I never dreamed I could have. Like testifying about housing for the poor before a Housing Committee in Washington, D.C. You supposed to have written testimony with you. Everybody got to have it. But, after I said one or two things, I realized that what needed sayin' wasn't gonna get said if I said it from the paper. I was only gonna represent a few peoples on the paper, and I needed to represent all these peoples who wasn't ever gonna have a chance to get heard. And that wasn't on the paper. So, I put the paper down. And I spoke from what I knew, for all those peoples.

I still have a lot of folks come up — black and white — who try to discourage me, and it don't even faze me anymore. I don't let nobody tell me what I can't do. Only time I say I can't do somethin' is after I try and it don't work out. Even then, I try it so many ways, usually it works out somehow. I think that's 'cause I know who I am now.

The first thing I really had to do was to work on me, find out who I was, what

I was about, what I could do. Then, when the people come up against me, I can let them know, "That's just what you sayin'." You have to realize who you are and be who you are.

I'm still trying to keep the sewin' center goin' in order to help somebody else that wants to work, 'cause I believe that there's always somethin' that somebody can do if they really want and they really try. To do anything that's your dream, you've got to have faith. In the Bible, Paul said that faith is the substance of things that are hoped for and the evidence of things not seen. I was hopin' that I could set up the sewin' center, but I had no way of knowing that I could do it. By me just up 'n' tryin' anyway, it became a reality in more ways than I could've dreamt.

I'm not doin' anything somebody else can't do. Maybe somebody don't want to do it because it calls for a lot of work. It calls for a lot of heartache. It causes a lot of criticism. It calls for a lot of negative stuff from every side. And if you can't take it, you ain't gonna make it. Once, when I was up in Detroit, a girl said, "I always wanted to do somethin' and then when I look at what you doin', I wonder why I'm not doin' it." I told her, "'cause you don't want to. If you want to do it, then you don't let other people tell you what you can do and what you can't do. You just get up and you do it."

I get letters from women all over the country tellin' me that I encouraged them to get up and do somethin'. I just love helping people, whoever need help. Someone asked me did I help the poor colored or the poor white. I told him I help the poor who need it, I didn't know poor had a color. I talk to old peoples, to young peoples, to whoever it is that's sittin' down and ain't doin' nothing. I just can't see people sittin' down, feelin' sorry for themselves, not tryin' to do anything. I guess the work I do is meddling in other folks' business and tryin' to help everybody I can. When I go places, people still get encouraged by me talkin' about my work, about settin' up the sewin' center. People come in from different areas of the country, come and look 'cause they heard about the center in the paper or on the television. They want to come in and sit down and interview me. They even wrote up the center in the social studies book they usin' in Georgia schools up to the fourth grade. I been talkin' to students in the fourth grade. That's the grade I stopped school.

I'm still a poor, disabled, old black woman from south Georgia. I turned seventy-two the twelfth of December, 1998. The first story anybody wrote about me was in *Mother Jones* magazine, "Heroes for Hard Times," 'bout how I was somebody to be reckoned with at sixty-two when I started workin' on this dream. I guess somebody comin' up, wantin' to do somethin' for somebody else, and not havin' nothin' for themselves was a hero to them. And now, twelve years later, I'm travelin' to speak to people in other countries 'bout human rights for women and 'bout how I'm doin' the work God's been callin' me to all my life.

At the UN World Summit on Social Development held in Copenhagen in March of 1995, Cora Lee spoke on the struggle to obtain better housing and health care for the poor. She served for several years as chairperson of the Macon Regional Clients Council, was a client member to the board of the National Health Law Program, sits on the board of the Georgia Citizen Coalition on Hunger, and is a Lifetime Member of the Southern Regional Council. She has lobbied and testified repeatedly before the Georgia state legislature and Congress on behalf of poor people. She also has traveled and spoken with an exhibition of photographs from the book I Dream a World: Portraits of Black Women Who Changed America, *in which she is featured.*

Lilith Quinlan helped Cora Lee write this story. Together, they're working on Cora Lee's autobiography. Lilith founded Common Ground, an organization that educates for a less racist and violent society. An annual journal, Common Ground, *is produced by poor women in the hope that their voices will become vehicles for justice.*

Mary Pipher, Ph.D.

"The heroics of doing the right thing every day even when it is dull and inconvenient are undervalued."

One of Mary Pipher's favorite quotes is a takeoff on G. K. Chesterton and goes something like this: "Courage is the power to be cheerful under circumstances we know to be desperate." The issues that burn in her heart are the lost essence of adolescent girls and the splintering of the family, issues that have sprung from her work as a psychologist practicing in America's heartland, Lincoln, Nebraska. She wrote about adolescent girls in her bestselling book Reviving Ophelia *and turned her pen to the family in* The Shelter of Each Other.

My mother and I were wired differently. She was a fearless, confident woman pursuing a medical degree in a day when few women attempted such things. I, on the other hand, am a timid person and a worrier. Temperamentally, I'm not well suited to the life I'm living right now — in the public eye and on the move. I travel all the time; I'm constantly in hotel rooms and airports. And I'm the kind of person who is fearful of flying, who worries about missing my plane. I'm the kind of person who doesn't like icy roads or hotels in unfamiliar cities, especially when I'm alone. But I keep flying around and lecturing because I think the work I'm doing — to help families cope with our modern culture — is important. I believe it is critical to educate people about the hostile forces that affect families and about the positive ways they can work to help their families and their communities. So, even though I'm fearful, I go out into the public because I see something that needs to be done.

As a child, I was very, very shy. I had a couple of experiences as a kid standing up in front of groups and literally not being able to speak, my voice just disappearing. I couldn't eat for days before giving a speech. I was terrified. My mother wrote a note to my speech teacher in high school saying that I was too nervous to be in speech class. So it is ironic that as an adult I find myself traveling from state to state lecturing several times a month throughout the year, and if I could find the time, I'd accept the invitations to do international book tours as well.

It was indirectly and not on purpose that I developed a talent for — and subsequent career in — speaking publicly. When I was in graduate school, I was poor and secured a teaching assistantship to help pay my way. The only problem was that I had to speak in front of a whole classroom full of students. I was panicked when I learned this and would have given anything to get out of it. The first day I was to get up and speak, I entered the classroom smoking. At one point during my lecture — as I was taking a drag off a cigarette — I looked down and saw that I already had two lit cigarettes burning away in the ashtray. Almost obliviously I had been lighting up and puffing away nonstop during class. Cigarettes were my crutch for the first couple of weeks. Week one, I was still a nervous wreck facing the students. The second week, I could handle it with a little less stress. And by the third week, I could speak comfortably in front of a large group. Now, some twenty years later, it is something I do in my career that I truly enjoy.

In addition to speaking, writing was another area in which I felt like a failure as a child. I have come to think that it must be quite common for people eventually to excel in areas where, as children, they felt vulnerable. With writing, my real defining experience involved a poem I wrote in high school. I had a teacher whom I just worshiped. I wrote a sonnet in her class and, when she gave it back to me, it had the grade "C-minus" on it, with the single word "Trite" written at the top. Being the straight-A student that I was, a C-minus was an F to me. I thought this grade proved that I couldn't write, so I gave it up. I was fourteen and I told myself, "You'll never be any good at writing." I didn't pick it back up again until I was thirty-six, when my daughter was in elementary school. I thought, "Well, I might not be any good at it, but I want to write anyway." That's when I started taking classes and writing and getting published. Now, years after that demoralizing grade, I really love to write and it's an important part of my life.

Eleanor Roosevelt once said, "Most of the work that's done in the world gets done by people who weren't feeling all that well at the time that they did it." I like that. It pretty much sums up my life, in that my initial reaction is to be afraid of things or not have confidence in myself, only later to realize that I can do things if I want to and if I persevere.

My mother, on the other hand, always had great confidence in herself. Other people's opinions had no bearing on her, which was both a good thing and a bad thing. She made some fairly serious mistakes in her life by ignoring external opinion. But she also had some real victories, because she knew what she wanted and she'd go after it. She went to medical school at a time when very few women were in medical school. (I remember as a child making her doctor's rounds with her.)

She got her master's degree in chemistry during the Great Depression while living with my Aunt Margaret in southern California and attending one of the state universities. She had only two dresses to her name and would wear one of them one day, wash it, and wear the other one the next day. She had a nickel a day to cover expenses. Since the streetcar ride cost a penny each way, that left her with only three cents, which was just enough for a big candy bar. She would eat half of it in the morning and put it away. Come the afternoon, she would take it out and eat the other half. Then, when she got home at night, before going to bed, she would have a plate of something saved from dinner by Aunt Margaret.

Even though my mother's family was very poor, they never let poverty define them. It was a different time, the Depression era, when people could be poor and proud, when people could be poor and respect themselves in a way that I think is much harder now.

My mother had a tough life growing up. She lived on a ranch where the work was hard. They'd be out milking cows at four in the morning. Dealing with life so close to the earth, she had lots of near-death stories and tales of heroic acts in our family, which she passed on to me. In retrospect, I've come to appreciate all the stories she told me about people in my family doing brave things. People had such tough physical lives back then, poor people like my family. Both my parents came from poverty, so there are a lot of stories about being hungry, being cold, being out in the elements, and how people handled situations. It was exciting as a child to hear these stories about relatives who behaved bravely. It's something that children these days may miss out on, hearing stories about real people in their family whom they can admire. It's something I deal with in my work because I think it's very important that children hear stories told by people who love them and who have a deep investment in their growing up to be healthy, well-behaved people. Right now, most of the stories children hear are told by corporations. Most of the stories apply to raising profits, not raising children.

One of my mother's last heroic acts was her death. She had tremendous courage during the last year of her life — while she died very slowly and was in a hospital eleven of her last twelve months. She suffered a lot, but she never complained, ever. Her bravery really struck me, because earlier, when I had my hysterectomy and was in the hospital for three days, I had been beside myself I was so miserable with pain and nausea. It made me realize how my mother was wired, that she was just someone who didn't burden other people with her private miseries and pain. She was always cheerful and pleasant and emotionally controlled. I see that as a kind of courage, even though it's not necessarily valued by our society in the 1990s. We tend to value military heroes and Schwarzenegger types who are physically courageous. The heroics of doing the right thing every day even when it is dull and inconvenient are undervalued.

Even though I am a far different creature than was my mother, I learned great value from the way she lived her life. She taught me, by example, to do the right thing even if it scares me. And, when life becomes overwhelming and stressful, I try to face it with dignity and determination, as have all the women in my family.

Mary's most recent book is Another Country: Navigating the Emotional Terrain of Our Elders.

Rhea Seddon, M.D.

"Consider risks carefully, then hold firm the courage of your own conviction."

One of the first women astronauts, Dr. Rhea Seddon became NASA's first pregnant astronaut in 1982. She logged more than seven hundred twenty-two hours in space during her three flights.

When I'm sitting on the launch pad and the door to the space shuttle is being closed, there comes a moment when I realize that I'm taking one of the larger risks of my life. I have to be at peace with myself to be able to sit there calmly during those final minutes before the shuttle launches, waiting for the rockets to ignite and the boosters to get us going.

The first time I flew on the space shuttle, I wasn't quite prepared for the amount of vibration on launch. I looked down at my hands in my lap and they were shaking so violently that I thought we were about to blow up. I remember saying to myself, "I'm about to disintegrate." I tried to prepare myself for moments like this.

I reminded myself that whatever happens with 6.5 million pounds of thrust is going to happen real fast, and that will be that. It won't be a lingering sort of thing.

On my flights, I didn't have a major part to play in the activities during the eight and half minutes it takes to get to orbit. I didn't have to be watching systems; I didn't have to do a lot of work. In a way, I was just there for the ride, holding my breath until we got past those eight and a half minutes. The launch phase was something to get through in order to do the things in orbit that I thought were important.

Another thing that caught me off guard on my first flight was looking out the window and realizing that just a couple panes of glass separated me from the vacuum of space. It's not entirely safe to be up there. In the scorching heat of reentry, if the tiles come off the bottom of the shuttle or if there's any other significant problem, we might burn up.

People assume all this must be pretty scary, but I don't know if I'd call it frightening. NASA puts us through enough rigorous simulations that we're comfortable with the physical aspects — except maybe that vibration at blast off. I'd call it risky, but I do it because the benefits outweigh the risks. To tell the truth, my first flight was nine months before the 1986 Challenger explosion. We had never lost anyone on a space flight. People had flown on the ship before and we hadn't had any problems. So, it wasn't hard to talk myself into believing that this was a safe thing to do. I felt great confidence that the system of checks and balances and redundant systems made it a very safe vehicle. In a heartbeat, all that changed. The Challenger tragedy made profoundly clear to us that things can happen that have nothing to do with our performance or our capabilities. If equipment breaks, it breaks.

Flying after Challenger took true courage. We had watched our friends die. We watched their families cope with the loss. We all grieved deeply. Since then, I've flown two flights and, each time, I knew that we could blow up on the pad or have problems going up hill. If that happened, for me it would all be over quickly — but for my family, the tragedy would just begin. They would be the ones left behind to cope. Actually, being the one left behind, losing my husband, is a scarier thought to me than dying. He's an astronaut, too, and it's always been harder for me to watch him fly than to go up myself. He was on the second flight after Challenger, and that was frightening for me.

I guess you could look at space flight and say there's danger all the way around. And I guess you have to have some guts to be willing to do that for a living. But, other things in my career with NASA have required a different kind of gutsiness. When I came to NASA in 1978, I was in the first group of women astronauts. There were six of us, and we didn't quite know how we were going to fit in or how well we would be accepted. In the beginning, there were a lot of questions about how we women would expect to be treated, whether we would make extra demands of the system, whether we would want numerous things changed. I'm sure the men also wondered how serious we would be about our jobs. I have heard that the language at the weekly All Astronaut meetings had to be cleaned up. But, overall, we were quite well accepted. As they say at NASA, it turned out to be a "nonproblem."

I met my husband, Robert Gibson (fondly known by friends as Hoot after the pre–Gene Autry cowboy movie star Hoot Gibson), when I entered NASA, and we were married three years later. Though we wanted to start a family, we didn't know how NASA would react — after all, I would be the first pregnant astronaut.

My class was just beginning to be assigned to flights and I didn't know what a pregnancy would do to my flight status. I knew that the first female astronaut to fly would soon be chosen, and I had to decide what my top priority was: Was it to have an early flight and many flights, or was it to have a later flight and in the meantime have children? Because I was thirty-four at the time, I didn't want to postpone having children for too much longer. I thought about where I wanted to be at age sixty and I knew that if I'd never had a shuttle flight but I had children, I'd be happy. If I'd had multiple shuttle flights but never had a chance to have children, well, that wasn't where I wanted to be.

Hoot and I decided to go ahead and start our family. I found myself pregnant with our first child in late 1981. As soon as we learned, through amniocentesis, that everything was okay, we spoke with some of our NASA managers. I told them that I didn't want to quit work, I didn't plan to take a long maternity leave, I wanted to stay in the rotation, I wanted to continue training in the jobs that I was doing. I realized as we talked to them that they had their own perceptions about pregnancy, perhaps based on their own lives. Most of them probably had wives who had stayed home to raise children, but I was of a different generation. I didn't plan to quit my career. None of them said, "Oh, come on now, you're going to want to stay home," but I could tell by the way they were sizing things up that they thought I might quit.

I spent much of my pregnancy trying to prove I could do a lot of things, and that I could continue with my job. Having to prove that motherhood and flying shuttles are compatible is something that, as I look back on it, I think took more courage than getting strapped into a space shuttle. It was the uncertainty of being the first one to do something, of stepping forward and saying, I'm going to do this even though it may not be an acceptable thing to do. I imagined all the worst scenarios. But, as it turned out, NASA was quite wonderful: In spite of any preconceived notions, they were willing to let me define what was right for me and, if I wanted to continue to work and was healthy enough to work, fine. Since then, several women astronauts have had children. Eileen Collins, the first woman pilot, worked at Mission Control throughout her pregnancy, had a baby in the fall of 1995, and was back at work six weeks later.

I've had three flights and three children. And the interesting thing is that taking the risk of a space flight became more difficult for me after the children. I was no longer simply risking my life — I was risking the life of my children's mother. As they get older, they have become more aware of what's going on. When I first flew, my son wasn't quite three and I don't think he realized what was happening. Before my next flight, my second son was very perceptive and when I told him, "I've got to go down to Florida now to get ready to go on the space shuttle," he looked at me in such a way that I knew he understood the risk. It grabbed my heartstrings. To accept the risk myself was one thing, but it was quite another to have my child look at me with a question in his eyes: "What if you die?" I put him on my lap and hugged him and tried to reassure him, but as I say, it shook me. It wasn't just about me now: I had to ask my children to be courageous, too.

I've made some career decisions — to be one of the first women astronauts, to be the first pregnant astronaut, to go into the field of surgery — because I felt I had something to contribute in those fields. I didn't do it to be groundbreaking, but because I knew women could do those jobs and would be valuable. I was lucky that other brave women had prepared the way for me, and I happened to come along when people were saying, "Why not women?" I'm fortunate to have been in the right place at the right time. I've spoken to many women who never had a chance to be astronauts but would have tried if they could have, or who tried and were told, "Yes, you meet all the qualifications but you're female."

Different people take risks for different reasons. My husband takes risks for fun, for the thrill of pushing an airplane to its limits. I don't take risks for fun. I take risks for some other reason, for something that simply requires that I do. I went into the space program because I wanted to see what happened to human beings when they went into space. I wanted to see if women were different, if we coped differently, if we were physiologically different. I didn't do it to prove that women could be astronauts, and yet, in doing it, I hope I achieved something for women.

In a quiet way, my grandmother, Margaret Rhea, had a profound influence on me. She came from a rather well-to-do family back in the days when women didn't work, and yet, she felt that she had a role in the working world. Even though it wasn't socially acceptable, she worked for the welfare department in my hometown of Murfreesboro, Tennessee. She went out and made sure that children were getting food and that people got their welfare checks — basically, she was a social worker. Society frowned upon nice ladies doing this sort of work, but she felt that she needed to do it. What a great role model, someone who says, "There's a purpose and a role for me out there and I'll go against convention in order to do it."

She was a very important person in my early life, and I hope that I will be that kind of person to my daughter. I hope she will be influenced by the way I've lived my life and will understand that doing what she wants to do very often will involve risk: sometimes physical, sometimes emotional, sometimes financial, sometimes social. If I can show her anything about living boldly, it will be to consider those risks carefully and then to hold firm the courage of her own conviction.

Astronaut Rhea Seddon, M.D., retired from NASA in 1997. She currently serves as the Assistant Chief Medical Officer of the Vanderbilt Medical Group at the Vanderbilt University Medical Center in Nashville, Tennessee.

Faith Popcorn

"The women in my family were cosmopolitan cowgirls, just wild. They hated being bossed around. In my family, we didn't aspire to work for large companies, we aspired to be independent, masters of our own destiny."

Called "the Nostradamus of marketing" by Fortune *magazine, premier trend guru Faith Popcorn is the founder of BrainReserve, marketing consultants to Fortune 500 companies. In 1991, she wrote the bestselling* The Popcorn Report *— her predictions about what consumers would be buying and thinking in the next decade, where we would be working, and ideas for new products, new businesses, and new markets.*

The gutsiest thing I have ever done was start my own company. At the time I made my decision, I was creative director at an ad agency and we were producing strong, beautiful work. But we weren't so much solving our clients' problems as we were solving the agency's problem: Make the commercial and get the commission. I wanted to go for something more, something that wouldn't simply *show* a product but *predict* it. And I wanted to get out on my own. I felt compartmentalized, departmentalized, stifled. This may, I admit, be genetic. The women in my family were cosmopolitan cowgirls, just wild. They hated being bossed around. In my family, we didn't aspire to work for large companies, we aspired to be independent, masters of our own destiny.

Because of my strong advertising background, the natural course when I set out on my own would have been for me to open my own small advertising agency — in 1974, the trend in advertising leaned toward boutique agencies. But because I didn't want to simply create advertising campaigns for clients, I chose not to go that route. I wanted to solve what I had determined to be the real problem for companies trying to sell products to consumers, something that involved more than just an ad campaign — the challenge and secret to success would be to meet the consumer in "future time," to predict what, how, and where they would be spending their money far into the future. I look back now and wonder, *Why did I think that?* I can't imagine what gave me that idea, but I suspect a lot of successful people start out with concepts they don't totally comprehend.

With almost no money to speak of, just a little saved up from my advertising career, I started BrainReserve, a marketing consulting company, in my studio apartment on Sixty-sixth Street in New York City. My mission was to sit down with the Fortune 500, up close and personal, and help them figure out their futures. An art director from the old agency joined me as my partner and a third person came in as a secretary. And there we sat for about three years. We couldn't get marketing assignments because we had no marketing track record and we couldn't establish a marketing track record, because we couldn't get marketing assignments — a perfect catch-22. I was nauseous. For three years. At least.

Finally, I said, "We've got to think big anyway, to act big, to project ourselves into our own future." When the senior VP from a large marketing firm called to tour our offices as part of his considering us for a project, we flew into high gear, creating a "virtual office." We rented the whole top floor of the Lotos Club next door, brought in desks, typewriters, drawing tables, and telephones connected to nowhere. Friends and freelancers came in to make it look busy, and we crossed our fingers that he wouldn't want to use the phone. We didn't get the assignment, but the value of the meeting was that it created a future vision for our company. We saw what it could be, for a moment we lived it, felt it, breathed it. It was food for our souls in a way; it kept us going and it kept us believing that what we were doing would work, we would be successful. And now, twenty years later, we're in a limestone building of our own, only two blocks from that club. Now, the phones are connected and busily ringing, and twenty-eight employees manage projects and do trend research. If the vision is there, the means will follow.

I was convinced that I could figure out a system that would replicate what I did instinctively, which was to gather information about people, their lifestyles, their thoughts, their needs and desires; interpret it in a certain way; and predict how the consumer would be living in the future and what he or she would want. This was pretty risky, because eventually my predictions would prove on the mark or off. When I started applying this system to actual products and situations, no one understood what I was doing. I'd get comments like, "Why do we need to know about the future? We can't even handle the present."

As part of my system, we started interviewing consumers — now we do four thousand a year. We read three hundred publications a month. We watch the top ten television programs and analyze what people are wearing, what language is like, what kind of family unit is being shown. The top three or four are based on alternative families and that's very interesting to us: What is being portrayed is not mom and pop and two kids. We go to night spots around the country. We look at music, movies. I put together a talent bank of forty-five hundred experts around the globe: doctors, lawyers, rocket scientists, and such, who brainstorm on a continual basis about everything in the culture worldwide. The information culled together allows clients to understand their consumers holistically. With the help of this talent bank, the consumer, and our creative people, we try to learn where the future is, to understand things like technology, virtual reality, and then to use that vision of the future to help our clients perfectly position their products and thus their companies. But, it took me about ten years to figure the whole thing out and let the world catch up with us. To my knowledge, nobody else is doing what we're doing. We're a cross between a futurist company, a classical marketing positioning company, and a unique kind of research company.

The biggest challenge during those early years was hanging on — having faith in what I was doing and not closing shop. That was much harder, actually, than opening the business, because, as a brand new company, everything lay ahead of us and I was sure we were going to be successful. But, when we weren't, I thought, Uh-oh.

In 1981, with the seventies just barely behind us and people still into "sex, drugs, and rock 'n' roll," I predicted that this lifestyle would soon lose popularity and people would begin staying home more. I coined a word for it: cocooning. In our interviews with consumers, we had noticed a "wear out" factor, an exhaustion factor: People were tired of partying; now they were thinking of having babies. AIDS was definitely a factor, also environmental toxicity. Water became an issue, which is why all the bottled water started to do well. A little later on, Martha Stewart became the queen of cocooning, showing people how to make their homes more adaptable and wonderful. Alarm systems started to do very well, also guard dogs. Cocooning socked in and, as a result, we started to tell our clients that maybe they shouldn't operate big, glitzy restaurants, for example. Maybe they should consider delivering food to people's homes instead. Maybe they should be thinking that the microwave oven was going to be big, that people might start working at home. My colleagues and I began predicting these things very early on.

Around this time, the early eighties, Isadore Barmash, the summer replacement for the advertising columnist at the *New York Times* called to say he was intrigued by the names Popcorn and BrainReserve and wanted to set up an interview. I panicked. What should I say? How could I maximize this tremendous opportunity? If I received a favorable mention in that column, my company would be set. But I had had no major success stories, nothing concrete that I could point to and say, "Here's a product that we helped launch."

I spent the weekend before the interview with friends on the beach in East Hampton and we thought and we thought and we tried to visualize things for the future, to think of what was going to happen. I read books on alternative medicine, because I had seen how big it could become when my co-author, Lys Marigold, and I drove to Chinatown in a convertible Volkswagen Rabbit in the pouring rain to meet with the doctor of the Dalai Lama, the revered spiritual head of Tibetan Buddhism. He had come out from a tenement and sat in the front seat of the car with Lys while I scrunched up in the back and watched him study the whites of her eyes. He asked her if she had trouble breathing, diagnosing her asthma, and later sent her raw herbs from his own collection to make teas that helped her. I had never seen someone diagnose a person by looking at the whites of their eyes and that was very, very fascinating. It stimulated my understanding of how big alternative medicine could be — and herbs. I had a little herb garden in the back of my house and had just started using flowers in salads. I was a big devotee of specialty stores and roamed them all around the world looking for new kinds of herbs. I saw several indicators that they were going to be big: I saw an aging population whose palates needed more high taste kinds of foods and who would become more and more salt conscious; I saw shampoo with herbs in it; I saw older Italian people picking wild herbs along the roadside and learned that they used them to make medicinal teas. And the Dalai Lama's doctor had prescribed herbs for Lys.

By the end of the weekend, I decided that these were the kinds of things I had to talk with Isadore Barmash about, that the only way to make the most of this opportunity for exposure was to speak with him about what we talked about every day at the office — predictions, what was going to happen and why. So, when he arrived and we sat down to talk, I told him fresh herbs were going to be hot, because people were cutting back on salt for health reasons and herbs are a low-sodium alternative seasoning. With an aging population, I said it was going to be okay to be gray-haired — older would be sexy. I said glitzy convertibles would come back to replace the bland, boxy look. I said fidelity would become popular again and that there would be a renewed interest in the family. I mentioned home delivery and "cocooning."

When he left, I didn't know how he was going to write up our conversation. Ten thirty at night the day before the story was to run, I went downstairs with my dog Jimmu Tenno, named after the first Emperor of Japan. I lived on Fifty-Seventh and, with trepidation, I walked across the street to the corner newsstand. The *Times* was already out and I looked at it, so scared. I bought a copy and turned to the advertising section and there it was, a whole article about BrainReserve. Everything I had said to Isadore Barmash was there in quotes. And I thought, I'm going to make it, it's going to be easy from here on in. Well, I made it, but it wasn't easy. This was just a tiny step on a very long, long road of challenges. We did get some business from food companies, including Campbell's, off that article and we were more positioned as a trend-based company.

As each prediction "clicked" into place, people started to think, *Maybe those people at BrainReserve are on to something.* I wouldn't say thousands jumped on the bandwagon, but people became accustomed to thinking about a futurist and when they thought about one, they thought about us. It became a little more acceptable for the Fortune 500 boardroom inhabitors to work with us. BrainReserve was recognized as a marketing futurist and I was its fearless leader. After all those friendless, scary years, we had clicked — the right idea at the right time — and success was in hand.

A couple of years ago, I bought a house right around the corner from where we started out with our first tiny office. I designed it as a place where our talent bank can come to brainstorm, hoping that the house becomes a center for thinking, inventing, looking into the future. It feels a bit like living on top of the haberdashery store — which is what my Russian grandparents did when they first came to this country and bought the business. I'd say that's an American dream.

In her book Clicking, *Faith continued to identify trends that help the reader "click" into the future, into new and more rewarding careers and lifestyles. Her most recent book is* 17 Trends That Drive Your Business and Your Life.

Michele Lee

"For the first time in my career, I didn't have a job. I couldn't comprehend it. I had made two films, I had starred in Broadway shows, I had had recording contracts, I had been a guest on every conceivable variety special on television. I had moved easily from one job to another — now, nothing."

Michele Lee's distinguished performing career has spanned the Broadway stage, recording, film, and television. She is, perhaps, best known for her starring role on the history-making series Knots Landing.

When I was in my last year of high school and willful in my ambitions, I had a very long talk with my father. He warned me about the trials and tribulations of being an actor-dancer-singer. He talked about the stress of getting that first job, that first agent. He talked about "paying your dues." One day, in spite of his concerns, he brought home a paper with an ad in it for auditions for a new show at a little theater here in Hollywood. "Actors must sing. Singers must dance. Dancers must act." I decided to try.

I got the job. It was a smash hit, and it ended up on Broadway — so much for paying dues.

It was the worst thing that could have happened to me. I was on Broadway in a featured role at age seventeen — a Cinderella story. Too easy. That's why, in 1973, I was devastated when, for the first time in my career, I didn't have a job. I couldn't comprehend it. I had made two films, I had starred in Broadway shows, I had had recording contracts, I had been a guest on every conceivable variety special on television. I had moved easily from one job to another — now, nothing.

Then one day, the phone rang. It was Larry Kasha, a producer I adored and with whom I had worked before (and who would later become one of the producers of *Knots Landing*). He wanted to know if I'd be interested in flying to Detroit to see a show called *Seesaw*, an adaptation of the William Gibson play, *Two for the Seesaw*. It was on its way to Broadway soon, but the show was in trouble. "How's your voice?" he asked. "Are you in shape?" He wanted me to come out and watch the show from the back of the theater. If I took the job, I'd open on Broadway in two weeks — as the star. This was a major professional opportunity and one I could not treat lightly — you do not fool around on Broadway. I would have to have it together . . . in two weeks, as the star.

"If you want it, it's really going to be tough," he said, before hanging up. *Tough*. He was being polite, but I didn't know that yet.

They sent me the script. My part was difficult, a real character role. She was funny, she made me cry. She sang, she danced. She scared me to death.

Throughout my adult life, I've been involved in one kind of therapy or another. I haven't found any magic cure-all, but I've discovered more about myself and what I can change within me to make my life better. I think of it as "training": I'm training for happiness, training for assertiveness, training for effectiveness as a parent. This training has had a profound effect on me. One of the things I've learned is that we human beings tend to do things that feel safe and comfortable. We don't often take chances. We behave in ways that aren't threatening. We all have our reasons, usually associated with fear of failure or, yes, even fear of success. People will be watching. In my case, it's the audience.

But the quality of our lives is enhanced when we do take chances, certain chances, chances that allow us to explore a part of ourselves that is new, chances that make life richer, fuller. Taking such risks requires of us that we be free of judgments and restrictive ideas about what we can or should do or be. It requires positive thinking: Yes, I can!

That's what I was trying to think when I walked into the office of my therapist and declared, "I really need this job." Singing was my life — I loved music more than anything, and to me the Broadway stage was magical.

I found twenty-seven reasons not to go: I would have to uproot my life. It was a one-year contract. My son, David, was just a baby. I had an aunt who was ill. My mother was depressed. I would feel guilty. At the bottom of it all, though, I was just scared silly that I would fail. Everything was stacked against me.

I took a deep breath . . . and jumped.

For two weeks, I lived and breathed the show. Not only did I have to memorize lines and songs and dances, but I had to do it all with a Bronx accent. I could not do a Bronx accent. When I got to work in the morning, the composer Cy Coleman would hand me the song sheets and we'd go through all the songs. My leading man, Ken Howard, would rehearse with me and then go back on stage at night with the other actress, whom I was replacing. That's when Michael Bennett (*Chorus Line*), the director, and I would edit the script and rewrite scenes and change songs. Choreographer Tommy Tune would redo dances and teach them to me as he did. I'd go back to my room at night, order dinner, and run over my lines. I'd literally fall into bed, exhausted beyond words, and wake up and start all over in the morning. It was exhilarating.

By the time we opened on Broadway, I had memorized and unmemorized and memorized again. I had learned songs, unlearned songs, and mastered Bronxese. All in two weeks. It made me realize that the power of the mind is so much greater than I had ever dreamed. For my performance as Gittel Mosca, I received the most extraordinary reviews of my career.

I had jumped and taken a huge chance. The strength I found in doing that still helps me to this day. I gave myself a gift that I could use for the rest of my life.

Michele has garnered critical acclaim as an award-winning producer, most notably for her Lifetime movie, Color Me Perfect, *with which she became the first woman in television history to write, direct, star in, and produce an original movie for television.*

The Courage to
LISTEN TO YOUR HEART

Judith Orloff, M.D.

"I will not tolerate constriction in my life and it's a great joy to feel that freedom. I encourage people who are afraid of speaking up to be a little freer with what they're feeling, because it's utterly liberating to come into one's own voice, to feel proud of that voice despite public stereotypes that would silence it."

Judith Orloff, M.D., is a psychiatrist and intuitive. Assistant Clinical Professor of Psychiatry at UCLA, she wrote the national bestseller Second Sight. *She has been featured in* Life *magazine,* Elle, McCall's, Self, New Woman, *the* New York Post *and on CNN, PBS, Lifetime, and ABC News. She travels internationally lecturing on intuition.*

I grew up in Beverly Hills, California, the only child of prominent physicians. I have always been psychic, even as a young child. The things I saw terrified me and I had no one to turn to in order to understand what was happening, why I was having premonitions and dreams that foretold events — for example, the dinosaur who became my harbinger of earthquakes. Before a quake, I would have a repetitive dream that a big dinosaur was coming down the street (children create interesting images with psychic premonitions) and its huge tail was thwapping the street and making the earth crumble. I'd also predict death and illness and other negative things — which I know now is normal in the beginner psychic. But it felt anything but normal back then and so I kept my premonitions to myself. I was very scared.

Being extremely sensitive to people, I could "read" them instantly. When I'd meet my parents' friends, I'd know immediately if they were trustworthy and whether I liked them. I was also a psychic empath which means I would pick up energy — for example from a crowd of people in a shopping mall — that left me feeling exhausted or anxious or totally inundated and also either emotionally distraught or physically in pain. And I didn't understand why.

When I first started to tell my mother what was happening, she'd say, "Oh you're just too sensitive, you don't have a thick enough skin." Then one day, I had a premonition that would insert a deep wedge between us. My mother had a close friend, a mentor really, who was a Superior Court judge in Philadelphia and running for reelection. Not only did I have a dream about him losing the election, but I saw a vision of a woman rushing after him and viciously biting his hand. I told my mother about it because it scared me. She was exasperated with me, "Why do you say these negative things?" On election night, we sat at home in Los Angeles awaiting the outcome. Not only did he lose, but his daughter-in-law, who was manic depressive, had a psychotic break at the polls and ran after him and viciously bit his hand. When my mother heard that, she said to me, "Never mention another one of your predictions or dreams to me again." I was ten years old.

I totally shut down. I thought something was horribly wrong with me. I thought maybe I was making these things happen. I had no psychic role models, no one to say to me, "This is wonderful. You're just very sensitive and have to learn to work with it." And so I got more and more withdrawn. I became very secretive, because I didn't feel safe expressing myself. This went on well into my teen years.

Then, in the late sixties, I started to get heavily involved with drugs. Drugs numbed my sensitivities and I liked that a lot. In retrospect, it was really sad that I had no resources to deal with who I was and no one to encourage my psychic abilities. With the drugs, I didn't sense things, I didn't have visions or dreams. Finally, I felt like I belonged. I could go into malls or to parties and not pick up anybody's energy. I just shut off.

I probably would have continued on that road as long as possible had it not been for an accident that was like divine intervention. I was at a party, I had just met a guy whom I was really attracted to, it was the middle of the night. We hopped in my car, an Austin Mini Cooper, and sped up the coast to Tuna Canyon, a beautiful canyon in Malibu. We wound up, up, up the mountain, fifteen hundred feet above the ocean, looking down upon the entire Malibu coastline, talking away to one another and not paying attention to the road — and then all I remember was the smell of burnt rubber and the sound of skidding tires before we hurtled over the edge of the cliff and started to roll head over end. The sky lurched at my feet, the sounds of shrieking metal seemed oddly distant and I found myself in a beautiful tunnel, gleaming gray, long, cylindrical, and quiet. It felt like home, safe and perfectly protected. Apparently, the car somersaulted eight times as we hurled through the air but all that time I was conscious only of being in this silent, sheltered tunnel. And then abruptly, I was psychically yanked back into the car as it crashed against rock, catching just at the edge of an abyss and dangling precariously on a precipice.

We had been thrown into the backseat, miraculously unhurt. Very, very carefully, we pulled ourselves out the back window knowing that, at any moment, the car could let go of its delicate balance on the precipice and plunge into the ravine below. Safely out, we started the arduous climb back up the side of the cliff.

I didn't tell anyone about the tunnel, but I knew that something incredible had happened.

My parents, frantic that drugs and rebellion were pushing me close to a dangerous edge, forced me to see a psychiatrist. I could have been sent to a Freudian psychiatrist who would have analyzed me or a neuropharmacologist who would have put me on medications thinking I was psychotic. Serendipitously, I was sent instead to a man who understood me completely. He knew that the problems I was having were due in large part to the fact that I didn't understand my abilities. He sent me to Dr. Thelma Moss, a parapsychology researcher at the UCLA Neuropsychiatric Institute. She tested me for the first time and said, "This is a wonderful thing. I'll help you understand it." She put me to work as a psychic researcher in her lab. I was still a teenager.

It was while I was working in Thelma's lab that I had a dream in which a genderless voice told me that I was going to go to medical school to become a psychiatrist in order to get the credentials to help legitimize the psychic realm. I woke up shocked, that was the last thing I wanted to do. I was raised around physicians and I didn't like them, I found them boring. I liked artists and bohemians and people on the fringe. The thought of going to medical school was dreadful. I remembered a visit with a psychologist about a year earlier: She was a career counselor who gave me multiple-choice tests to determine what type of career I should go into and, at the end, she said, "Whatever you do, don't go into the helping professions."

I knew enough from working with Thelma that this voice in the dream was something I needed to listen to even though its advice sounded far-fetched. By this time, I had graduated from high school and I made a bargain with the dream that I would enroll in one junior college course just to see how it went, that was all I was going to do.

When spirit knocks on your door, you don't have to be 100 percent there — if you open the door just a crack, then spirit will flood in. You don't have to be totally enamored with spirit or totally believe in what's happening. If your heart is just a little bit open and you're just a little bit willing, spirit begins to work on you.

I didn't think I would like junior college, because I had hated high school. By the time I registered, the only course available was geography, which wasn't high on my list of interests. On the first day of class, the teacher talked about rain and how clouds are formed, and about stars and the earth and the winds, the planets and the galaxies. I was utterly swept away. That class led to another and another and I kept getting As. Fourteen years later, I graduated from UCLA with my residency in psychiatry — all because of that dream.

I encourage people to listen to dreams like this even if they sound really impractical. When you're given specific information in a dream, it's an absolute blessing. I've seen the price people pay — in terms of physical health and depression and unhappiness — for not listening. Listening can be hard. I talk to so many people who get specific information about what to do in their lives and they don't pay attention, especially if it's impractical. Usually there's a window of time in which you can act on a dream like this and, if you don't, then the opportunity is gone.

Since medical school immerses you in absolute science, by the time I was doing my psychiatric residency, I was entrenched in traditional medicine, giving out antidepressants and lithium and anti-anxiety prescriptions. I loved being a doctor, having that kind of control and seeing people get better by taking medication. Over time, I strayed further and further away from the psychic. I saw too many psychotics come through the emergency room claiming to be psychic. Lots of psychotic people believe they're psychic — some are and some aren't. But it was very scary to see, night after night, people claiming to be possessed by the devil or convinced that the FBI was out to get them, miserable people, depressed and paranoid. The more I saw of that, the more cynical I became about the psychic. These weren't healthy role models, they were the epitome of the negative prototype that psychiatrists associate with the psychic.

I opened up a traditional practice in Century City, right in the pulse of Los Angeles. Almost from the beginning, I seemed to have more patients than I could handle. I did psychotherapy in my office and put patients who needed it on medication. I'm a workaholic, so I saw patients seven days a week. My practice was very successful.

Then one day, Christine walked into my office. A bank teller, she led a very isolated life and was lonely and depressed. I put her on antidepressants. Over time, she got better and started developing friends and going out. She reconciled with her family and met a young man who became a steady beau. All of these were promising signs of her recovery. One day, during our therapy session as I was listening to her, I glanced out the window. From my eighteenth floor office, I had a great view of the sky and could see all the way out to the ocean. For just a moment, I became fascinated with a particular cloud formation, thinking how beautiful it was, and I forgot about what Christine was saying to me. I began drifting with this cloud and she grew more distant . . . and I went into a trance state. I hadn't been in a trance for years and it was in this very clear, cool, silent space that I had a premonition that Christine was going to try to kill herself. It wasn't based on anything that she was saying — which was confusing because she seemed so improved. And yet, I had this clear sense that she was going to try to kill herself. At that point, because I had let myself grow so far from the psychic realm, I ignored my premonition. Within a week, she overdosed on the pills that I had prescribed and ended up in an intensive care unit.

It was heart wrenching. I thought I'd done something to harm her. That's a horrible feeling as a doctor. If I had listened, perhaps I could have made some kind of difference. She was in a coma for a number of weeks. I sat with her night after night, reevaluating my life. I knew that somehow, in some way, I had to incorporate the psychic back into my work as a doctor.

Christine finally came out of coma and recovered. I never did tell her about the premonition. I was still afraid of what my peers would think of me, because it's so easy to get stigmatized. In medicine, I had found my calling, I felt secure, that I belonged. I didn't want to jeopardize that or have people look at me funny. And yet, I had opened up enough to know that my life and psychiatric practice had to change, I just didn't know how it would change or what I was going to do. I only knew that somehow I had to let the psychic come into my life, and that little bit of openness put the right people and places and situations in front of me so that I could be directed by spirit.

The next year, I was introduced to my first spiritual teacher, Brugh Joy, a doctor who had been a successful internist in Beverly Hills before coming down with a severe, untreatable pancreatic disease. Turning to meditation and spiritual and intuitive healing, he overcame the illness even though traditional doctors had given up on him. He was in his early forties when I first met him and took one of his seminars on psychic and spiritual development at his Institute of Mental Physics. This was a man who had been trained at Johns Hopkins and the Mayo Clinic and was a member of Alpha Omega Alpha, the medical honor society. He had medical credentials and he worked with the psychic — exactly what my dream had told me to do so many years earlier: Get the credentials to help legitimize the psychic realm. I had gotten the credentials and invalidated the psychic.

Soon after meeting Brugh, I came into contact with Stephan Schwartz, who was the founder and director of the Mobius Group, an organization that conducted psychic research. With his staff of psychics, he worked with police departments, insurance companies, and private individuals to help solve crimes and unearth lost archaeological relics. Goose bumps shot up my arms when I first saw his picture on the cover of *L.A. Weekly.* I felt I knew him even though we'd never met. Immediately, I wrote him, describing my experiences. He brought me into his parapsychology group and hired me as a psychic. He became my mentor and close friend and, over the course of several years, he walked me through all my fears about being psychic and helped me interpret my dreams and various psychic experiences.

As I became more secure and comfortable with my psychic abilities, I began using them with patients and it worked beautifully. Today, I have no fear whatsoever when it comes to the psychic. That's become a great strength, because so many people are frightened and I can help them. I wrote an article that ran in the March 1997 issue of *McCall's* magazine and I received about fifteen hundred letters in response. So many of them were from women and men who had been having psychic experiences all their lives and were frightened. I hear this over and over when I tour and lecture.

As it turns out, my mother was one of those people frightened by the psychic, but I didn't understand her reasons until she was dying. The period surrounding her death became the defining moment of courage in my life. As I grew stronger and more secure with my psychic abilities, my mother, who had cancer, was getting sicker and sicker. She was slipping away as I was coming into myself, discovering my ability to heal with my hands. She allowed me to help her as she was dying and it was as if all my spiritual training and psychic development had brought me to this one point where I put it all into practice.

During this time, my mother, who had a dramatic side, said to me, "I'm handing the power over to you now." What on earth did *that* mean? For the first time, she revealed to me the truth about the female lineage of her family, which was rife with psychics. She'd never told me about them because she didn't want me to follow in their path and be thought of as strange. My grandmother had been a psychic healer in Philadelphia. My aunt was a physician and psychic. My cousin was psychic, as were so many of the women on my mother's side of the family whom I had not known because we lived in California and they were all back East. And the coup de gras was that my own mother was psychic. As a physician, she had used not only her medical training but also her psychic abilities to diagnose and treat her patients. She had never told anyone because she didn't want people to think she was weird. And she had a deep fear that if she encouraged the psychic in me, I would be ostracized from the world, particularly as a doctor.

I had all kinds of reactions to what she told me. I was angry about all that I had missed growing up, about how life might have been had I known all this instead of trying to suppress an entire part of myself and being afraid that I was somehow a freak. Luckily, I had continued to find the courage to follow my own path, albeit with detours. And in retrospect, I see how much I gained by having to fight for what I believed in and making it my own rather than having it handed to me. It made me stronger in my convictions. I also realized that, however misguided, my mother had kept this information from me as an act of love.

I had dreams about my mother as she was dying. One time when I went to visit her at the intensive care unit at Cedars-Sinai Hospital, she asked, "Did you call me last night?" I said, "No, but I had a dream about you." My mother didn't want to die. She held onto life ferociously, even after she slipped into a coma. One night, I dreamt that she and I were flying, not in an airplane but free in the sky. It was exhilarating and I had a very strong feeling the next morning that she was going to die that day. I went into the hospice, sat by her bed, and meditated to help bring in the light. I had a long talk with her about how she had to let go of her body. Even though she was in a coma, she squeezed my hand. I wanted desperately to stay, to be with her when she died, and it took everything in me to leave the room. I knew that she wouldn't go if I was sitting there.

I drove downtown to a halfway house for recovering criminals where I was doing some work. The minute I arrived, I received a call that my mother had died.

That was a very powerful experience for me. I've been in communication with my mother since then and it's a beautiful thing to see that death is not an end. We're never taught to invite the death energy in to work with it as a creative force in life, a psychic force. We look at death as something that happens when we leave our bodies, which is not so. Death is with us in life from the very moment that we come to earth.

We've strayed so far from our mystical side and it's gotten such a bad rap with all the psychic phone lines and other horrible things done with the psychic in our culture. I've had to confront that prejudice and misconception every time I go out on tour or get booked on media shows. I was really naïve about it in the beginning. I didn't expect people to attack me with, "How dare you, a doctor, talk about this. You should be kicked out of the profession." People can be very hostile and there's nothing you can say to them when they're full of a kind of . . . witch-hunt hatred.

One day in Santa Barbara, in the most friendly of cities where I thought I was going to have a great book signing, a woman sat in the front row of a crowd of about seventy people and directed an intense witch-hunter energy at me. She would not let up. I could tell she was appalled by what I was doing. I felt attacked and hurt and unprepared for that kind of energy. I think this woman was deeply threatened by what I was talking about, and I've seen it again since then, people getting locked into their concept of reality and clinging to it tenaciously because it's safe and secure.

I've also had a hard time with some Christian fundamentalists who feel that I'm challenging their beliefs in a very negative way, that what I'm doing is sacrilegious. But, we usually end up on common ground when they hear that Jesus was my first spiritual teacher, that he came through in my dreams when I was a little girl, that I continue to have a strong connection to Jesus. (Being Jewish, my mother was driven slightly crazy by this.) I've learned that when people begin to attack me, I need to redefine what I'm saying in a language that makes sense to them. A woman in San Diego once said to me, "Oh you're talking about the Holy Spirit? Is that what you're talking about?" However it fits. Some people who write or call me have very traditional religious beliefs and have been psychic all their lives and been told it's the work of the devil. And it tears them up. They believe in their church and, at the same time, they're having these psychic experiences. So it is on gentle common ground where I like to meet people.

During the writing of *Second Sight,* I struggled with whether or not to use the word "psychic" or to use more mainstream language like "intuition." It took me a long time to write that book, because I first had to find my voice. I'm at a point now, after having tried for so long to please people and being so careful, where I'm tired of being in a little box and I'm just the opposite of careful and pleasing. I will not tolerate constriction in my life and it's a great joy to feel that freedom. I encourage people who are afraid of speaking up to be a little freer with what they're feeling, because it's utterly liberating to come into one's own voice, to feel proud of that voice despite public stereotypes that would silence it.

Time and again throughout my life, it's taken courage not to drown in the fears, the doubts, the misjudgments, the criticisms, the loneliness, the separation from "normal" life. I've fumbled and bumbled along my path but, in the end, I've always reached toward the light. For me, the hardest part about being psychic has been dealing with the prejudices. I've spent hours and hours with media people befriending them so they can see who I am. And I've changed a lot of minds. But it's difficult because so many of them have strong stereotypes about the psychic. In a hundred years this will be a moot point because everyone will be using their psychic abilities — it won't be any big deal. It's just a matter of time.

Judith's next book, Intuitive Healing, *is due out in March of 2000. Mandalay Pictures has purchased it, and* Second Sight, *for television.*

Barbara Brennan

"Having been trained in physics, I was skeptical at first when I began to see the energy phenomena around people's bodies."

A former research scientist for NASA with an M.S. in Atmospheric Physics, Barbara Brennan made a bold move from traditional physics to the physics of healing and has been studying the human energy field for more than twenty years. She's the author of Light Emerging: The Journey of Personal Healing *and* Hands of Light™: A Guide to Healing through the Human Energy Field. *She is also the founder and director of the Barbara Brennan School of Healing® (BBSH™).*

I came straight from a farm in Wisconsin, the only one in my family to go to college, and I worked my tail off to put myself through because my parents couldn't afford it. The only girl in Advanced Upper Atmospheric Physics, I got the highest grade. Because I had so little money, my professor, a member of President Kennedy's Science Advisory Board, gave me an assistantship so I could go on to graduate school. When I was offered a job as a research scientist at NASA in 1963,

I had been designing weather satellite sensors, which measure the heat coming off the earth.

One of only two women in my department at NASA, I soon was flying down to South America to take measurements of earth energy in the visible and infrared spectrum. I really loved science and I loved my work, but after several years, I began to feel personally unfulfilled. Much of the research we did was based on having to write the next paper in order to receive the next government grant. I wrote papers like the one titled, "Anisotropic Bi-directional Reflectances from Natural Earth Surfaces," based on work to measure the albedo of the earth, that is, the solar reflectance or how much of the energy of the sun is reflected from different earth surfaces.

At the time, I was living in Washington, D.C. The women's movement had just begun, and women's-libbers were telling me how awful I was because I worked for this terrible government. I didn't really understand what they were saying. I saw NASA as a wonderful place and was grateful to have been given all the opportunities I had there. I entered an uncomfortable period of internal reflection and questioning, heightened by the Civil Rights and humanistic psychology movements, both of which had captured my attention and interest.

I remember standing on top of a high building one night during the race riots and watching the people below, running down the street setting fire to buildings and looting. Again, I didn't understand what was happening around me, because as I was growing up on the farm in Wisconsin, racial discrimination was never an issue in my community. Because no African American people were anywhere in the vicinity, when I was a young person, racial issues hadn't been a part of my life. Martin Luther King Jr. led a march on Washington and created what was known as Resurrection City, where people camped out on the grass around the Washington Monument. When a similar Resurrection City was created in Alabama, I went down and camped out there for a few weeks.

After returning to Washington, I joined the humanistic psychology movement.

It was the first time that I met people who were in "contact groups" — people gathered together, usually with a psychologist, to learn how to have nonthreatening and nonsexual physical contact with one another, simply learning how to hug and touch. I joined a group and one of the first things I realized was that I had spent most of my life not touching anyone. I couldn't remember the last time I had actually kissed or hugged my mother or my father.

And so, I began to explore my fear of the unknown, of change. I had grown up with a social model that went something like this: Get a good education and a steady job, get married, have a family, live in a small town, go to church every Sunday, and live out a rather boring existence. My research would be the one saving grace in this scenario if I were to live it. But then, I started to question. Was my job really the right one for me? Was I accomplishing my purpose in life? What was that purpose? What was life all about? What were the secrets of the universe? These were questions I pondered deeply and, for a time, I tried to maintain my position at NASA while also delving into these intimate issues. But even though I greatly enjoyed my research, the answers to many of the personal and spiritual questions in front of me couldn't be found in my work.

During this time, I fell in love with someone who had studied alternative lifestyles (this was the sixties) and began visiting different communes on weekends, living in them in the summers. I started to think about having a child. It was a time of great personal opening, even though I didn't completely understand its significance for a long time. I began to question how the world *inside* me worked, rather than focusing all my attention on how the world *around* me worked. I began to see that there was an inner landscape within me to explore, and NASA wasn't the place to do it. I felt strongly that there was something more important for me to do with my life, so I stepped off the edge of the safe and the familiar to find it — and believe me, it was scary.

Within a month of leaving NASA, I became pregnant and moved with my husband at the time to Yucatán, Mexico, where he had relatives. Suddenly, I was no longer a NASA physicist flying around the world in a private four-engine jet doing research. I was barefoot, pregnant, and nauseated in the sweltering Mexican heat, living in a Volkswagen bus in a country whose language I didn't speak. I went from being a NASA physicist to a late-sixties hippie. It was a difficult transition. Over the Thanksgiving holiday, some friends from the States came down to visit. They were involved with bioenergetics, the study of the connection between the physical body's energy flow and psychology, which was originated by Wilhelm Reich (a student of Freud along with Carl Jung) and then developed by his two main students, Dr. Alexander Lowan and Dr. John Pierrakos.

When we went back to the States for Christmas, I needed psychological help to deal with the intensity of the transition I was going through, and I found it in bioenergetics. It worked so well with me that, within just a few weeks, I was much better and decided to enter a two-year, full-time training program to become a bioenergetic therapist.

The theory of bioenergetic therapy is that your physical body grows in response to all of your environment, not only your genetic hereditary environment but also the physical and psychological environment. Therefore, your body will show the history of your childhood development. This has been shown in the works of Lowan and Pierrakos as well as Reich. One of the things a bioenergetic therapist learns to do is to"body read." You simply look at someone's physical body and tell what their childhood environment was like by the way the body has developed. This was an area I found very interesting, especially with the additional dimension of energy flow through the body. A block in energy is created when one separates one's emotions from one's conscious awareness of a traumatic or unpleasant past event as a way of dealing with a situation that is hard to face at the time. As a result, the emotional experience — often from childhood — is held in the body. Bioenergetics helps release the experience by working directly on the body with exercises and positions that release the blocked energy, thereby freeing the unconscious memory, which can then be cleared away.

We were shown how to perceive the energy flow of the body and how to work with it. We watched as a woman with cataracts in both eyes, unable to see, nevertheless"read" a student's body, telling him exactly how his energy was flowing and where he had energy blocks. I was surprised that I understood everything she was saying and that I, in fact, perceived everything she described.

Having been trained in physics, I was skeptical when I started seeing auras, the energy phenomenon around all living things. My first perception of an auric field happened during a bioenergetic training session. Another student, Natalie, and I were doing an exercise where each of us stood on opposite sides of a student playing the role of a patient. We held our open hands about half an inch away from the"patient's" leg, one on one side and one on the other. Starting at the ankle, we slowly moved our hands up the leg, without touching it, trying to feel the energy. At one point, Natalie and I stopped to talk about something and when we looked down, we noticed that both of us had stopped our hands at the same place, at the knee. We had stopped because we felt an energy break there. The patient said that he had a knee injury. I remember getting very excited about being able to actually feel an energy break in a knee.

Then, I began to perceive hazes around people. One time, maybe a year into my training, a woman named Karen was standing in a doorway across the room from me and, suddenly, I saw a bright purple-rose color arc about a foot over her head. It faded and disappeared, but then a larger arc appeared about two feet higher above her head. That one likewise disappeared, and the lower one arced again in a bright flash. The cycle happened about three times. It was very exciting.

The most thrilling moment came when my vision was first verified. I was visiting a spiritual retreat center in the Catskill Mountains — the Center for the Living Force, which was later renamed the Pathwork Center — and was outside with Dr.

John Pierrakos. We were simply standing on the lawn looking at auras around the trees and the orgone energy — a vital energy that pervades nature — being sucked into the auras and supplying the trees with energy. He saw what I saw, and I found that terribly exciting.

After two years of study and a year of practice, I moved to the Center for the Living Force and entered a five-year program there in "Helpership" training, which was a combination of spiritual and psychological training, as well as a part-time, four-year training in Core Energetics with Pierrakos at the Institute for Core Energetics in New York City. I graduated with the first class of that institute.

I continued seeing auric fields. As people sat across from me in bioenergetic therapy sessions, I noticed energy flows around the head and body and inside the body that corresponded to what they were talking about: Every time they talked about a particular subject, I saw these currents of energy, like colored air flowing through the body and around it.

Since the aura phenomenon persisted, even if I closed my eyes or moved around the room, I decided to observe it more closely, as any good scientist would. When I noticed something changing in the energy field of a patient, I made a note of it and then noticed when the phenomenon occurred again. One of the most important things about science is to be able to observe a phenomenon that repeats itself. That way, you can study it and discover the mechanism occurring as the phenomenon repeats itself. I also applied all that I had learned about light-sensitive devices to the viewing of auric fields and tested what I saw against a scientific standard. The instruments I had used during my days at NASA measured light in different wave length bands. I realized that, in much the same way that I observed the energy of the earth in constant fluid motion through different wave length bands, I could also view human auras.

I soon realized that when I looked at someone's aura, I could recognize disease in the body — and heal it. Some people call this ability the laying on of hands, faith healing, or spiritual healing — but I knew it wasn't something special that only I could do. I knew it could be taught.

During this time, I had many spiritual experiences like perceiving nonphysical beings, or guardian angels and guides. This phenomenon has since become accepted but, at the time, it was something about which people didn't talk, unless they were referring to guardian angels in heaven. People didn't realize that angels and guides could be in the room with them, that they could see them. I began seeing them, and it was very powerful and drew me deeper into my work. Yet, at the same time, it was disconcerting to be the only one I knew who did this. I talked to nonphysical beings; I heard them; I asked them questions and got answers to things I knew nothing about. How could I maintain a stable life while allowing these great changes to be occurring in my life?

The effect of all my spiritual experiences was to dissolve the veil that most of us hold between the spiritual and material worlds. Through all of these many experiences — being able to feel the presence of, touch, hear, see, and interact with nonphysical beings — the spiritual world became as real to me as the physical world and completely transformed my experience of life. Dissolving the veil between the spiritual and physical worlds was a greater transition than the one I went through leaving NASA and coming to understand my inner landscape. The spiritual world was being integrated with the mental world, the psychological world, and the physical world.

I began teaching workshops about the aura at the Pathwork Center. Soon, I was conducting workshops all over the country, traveling twenty-nine weeks a year. Then, following internal guidance, I stepped off familiar ground again, referred all my bioenergetic clients away, and saw only clients with whom I did my own healing work. I had moved to the Pathwork Center and it was here, on three hundred acres in the Catskills, that I wrote *Hands of Light.* I didn't know I was writing a book at first, because essentially I was answering questions that people had put to me. Years earlier, I had begun to paint and draw pictures with my four-year-old daughter, because it was one of her favorite activities and a good way for us to spend time together. Whenever I couldn't think of what to paint, I would paint auras. Those pictures of auras, coupled with my answers to people's questions, formed some of the chapters in the book.

I sent the manuscript to twelve publishers, all of whom rejected it. The lone exception was a Russian publisher that wanted to break it into five books. Their offer was tempting because I had recently become a single parent, but I couldn't bring myself to do that to the book.

I had grown up with the adage, "Put your money where your mouth is." In my divorce settlement, I had gotten a piece of property, which I sold for fifty thousand dollars; now it was all the money I had in the world. *Well,* I thought, *am I really, really, going to put everything behind what I'm saying?* I agonized over this decision. It was huge. People thought I was crazy to contemplate such a thing. In order to maintain the book's integrity, I used all of the money to publish it myself. This was a bold move, especially with a daughter to support, and by the time the book was done, I had less than a thousand dollars to my name.

But, once I had made the decision, I wasn't afraid anymore. I had connected with an inner calling, and I moved very powerfully in the direction I knew was right. I told people that I was certain the book would sell at least a half million copies, and they just looked at me and laughed. Some people called it a vanity book. I had never heard that term before but soon found out that a vanity book is something you publish yourself because no one thinks it will sell, nobody's interested, and you do it for your own ego. Once the book was printed, I wrote letters to people I knew, keeping it simple, saying, "I wrote this book. I know it's really good, and I'll sell it to you for what it cost me so I can get my money back." I had paid fifty thousand dollars for only a thousand books so I had a lot at stake, but I found people who were willing to buy my book for fifty dollars. (In some cases, bookstores bought it and sold it for ninety dollars!) People thanked me for writing about things they had experienced but could never explain. And, in three months, I earned all my money back. I used some of that to print another three thousand copies. Somewhere in the middle of that print run, a friend said, "Why don't you send the finished book to publishers?"

"Nobody wants it," I said. "Twelve publishers have already rejected it."

"Yeah, but that was when it was in manuscript form, and look what you've done to it since then."

This friend was in the publishing business, so I listened to his advice. I sent copies out and waited. Sure enough, not just one, but several publishers bid on it — and it sold. Since its publication, nearly one million copies have been sold, and the book has been translated into seventeen languages.

Taking the chance to publish the book myself was another turning point for me. The success of the book and the interest it generated around the world allowed me to start a school to teach people how to heal and how to work with energy fields. I wanted to teach them not only to perceive intangible things that most people don't perceive, but also how to handle all the psychology around what they perceive, their own personal reactions to it, and the emotional reactions of the people on whom they work.

The classes I offer constitute a very strong and challenging four-year personal growth program, followed by a two-year teacher training program, in what has become the biggest laying-on-of-hands healing school in the world. Last year, we had 730 students, 230 of them from outside the continental United States — from Australia, New Zealand, Russia, South Africa, Japan, Singapore, South America, Alaska, Europe, the Middle East, and the West Indies. Five times a year, students from all over the world fly in to participate in a weeklong course. The outcome of my initial risk has proven to be tremendously successful in that it allowed me to soar, and, soaring, I dared to open the school and I will dare again and again, who knows in what way or when.

Each turning point gets bigger in my life. Expanding the school was huge for me. When the school was small, I felt very at ease running it. But taking on the bigger role of a business person has been one of my hardest challenges. I have about 150 people who work for me now. I'm the boss. I find that onerous, being the one who holds the line, sets rules and parameters, determines salaries, and hires and fires. I'm a scientist and a healer. I'm very oriented toward research and taking care of people and helping them heal themselves, not laying down the law as a boss. Also, because the work of the school has become internationally oriented, I'm traveling the world more, which is both exciting and a bit frightening. Over the past several years, I've been invited to lecture all over the world and, now, I'm making the time for it. I see that the school is evolving into a university. We're dealing with intercultural and planetary healing. Next year, we are starting a two-year graduate program that will not only include class study, but internships with complimentary care programs and research projects with university research groups. We are also beginning to look at possible advanced degree certification with a major university.

Each of us will always have something we're afraid of, that we haven't faced in our lives. Every time I challenge such fears, I build tremendous courage and power, self-respect and honor, and I build both physical and spiritual endurance. Making the decisions I have — to leap off the solid ground of security and familiarity — having faith in what I'm doing, and allowing myself to be guided has pushed me through my deepest fears and into my deepest faith. And I know life will continue to present me with my next challenge, my next fear, my next opportunity, my next healing.

Barbara's latest book is Seed of the Spirit, *a collection of what she calls "transformative poetic channelings expressing deep spiritual truth and our connection with the divine."*

Susan Winston

"Has my daring changed the world? No, but it changed the world of our family. Have I cured a disease? No, but I finally gave more than lip service to one of the true ills of humanity."

Television producer Susan Winston founded and is president of Blanki & Bodi Productions in Los Angeles.

Twenty-four of us sat nervously on unforgiving wooden benches, the cacophonous sounds of the marketplace rising up from below on the pungent Guangzhou summer air. Time stood still as we waited, our final wait. A platter dressed with fresh lychees appeared oddly out of place as the "grandmas" looked anxiously at us from the railing of the adjacent old-age home. It was a day of mixed emotions.

We all knew that behind our own personal happiness was a deeply disturbing practice here in China, a quiet genocide that yearly claims the lives of thousands of female babies and children. This was the day my husband, Jim, and I were to adopt our daughter, Nikki Kate Winston.

Up to this moment, I would never have considered myself a courageous person, forging new paths, pushing discovery to new limits, challenging tradition, defying odds. That wasn't me. I was a television producer who first made her mark as the youngest female executive producer of a major network news show. Six years of being in a studio at three o'clock in the morning was more exhausting than brave. My proudest work, the coverage of the 1984 Olympics and the 1996 Oscars for ABC weren't particularly daring. Actor Christopher Reeve was courageous in making his appearance at the Academy Awards® — Susan Winston, his producer, was simply a facilitator. It's what I do for a job and I'm proud to do it well, but it hardly makes me a brave woman.

Television comes and goes — it's a video surf, a zap of a remote control. It's where I try to have an impact. And yet, when I think of the thousands of hours of programming I've produced, only one episode stands out beyond anything else. Following an on-air medical report on new warning signs for a very specific form of cancer, I received a letter from a viewer telling me that, had she not seen the program that morning and gone directly to her doctor, she most likely would have died. I initiated something that saved someone's life. That made me feel wonderful but still not daring.

With this trip to China, I had dared to follow my heart to a place it had never been before. To a little baby girl halfway around the world. It would prove to be my life's most rewarding journey.

China, for some, is the final answer to their desire to be parents. Children are available, and couples, singles, single-sex couples, all are welcome to apply, provided they are at least thirty-five years old. For many, China is the last stop after the frustration of infertility drugs or failed in vitro fertilization. With the difficulty and uncertainty of domestic adoptions, China has become an alternative unfettered by obstacles. Single women chasing their biological clocks have found China's adoption policies to be a haven; single men have, too, though in lesser numbers.

So where do I fit in? I'm married and have been for twenty-two years. I have two fabulous biological children: a boy, nine, and a girl, six. If I chose to have more biological children, I could. I work full time and have a definite limit to my financial resources. Like many working parents, I struggle to fit everything into the day. My life is very full. So what am I doing, sitting here on this bench in the clamor of Guangzhou? I am feeding my soul.

I got to this moment on an acrid summer day not by chasing a biological clock but by chasing a story, something I do constantly as a television producer. The story had taken me to Mimi Williams — the Reverend Mimi Williams — whose road to becoming an Episcopal priest was the stuff of which movies-of-the-week are made. When I met Mimi, she was waiting for China to reopen its doors so she could enter and adopt a child. What a great tag for a movie: Controversial woman dumps husband, changes religion, becomes a priest, gets a kid — a little Chinese kid at that!

I was hooked. I dug through Mimi's history and found a great movie. What fascinated me even more, however, was her quest for a child. Why China? I got a blistering education in the answer to that question as I did extensive research, pouring through books, attending "get togethers" of a group sponsored by several adopting agencies, meeting with more agencies that specialize in adoptions from China, and speaking with those who had actually adopted from China. What I learned affected me deeply and began to stir awake in me the audacity to do something I could have never guessed I would do.

As part of China's desperate attempt to curb its staggering population growth, the government has instituted a one-child-only policy throughout most of the country. By the hundreds of thousands every year, baby girls are aborted or, more tragically, abandoned. While Beijing officials deny that only girls are abandoned, the only males found in the orphanages are those with severe birth defects or disabilities. The primary reason the Chinese want a male baby is that children are the Chinese social security system: It is the child's responsibility to care for his parents in their old age. Girls become part of their husband's household in marriage, often living with the husband's family, so it is his parents who will receive her care.

Where are the little girls and what happens to them? Many are left to die at birth by women who have hidden their pregnancy, knowing that if they give birth to a girl, they will need to dispose of it. And that's against the law. No one knows how many babies are left to die. Thousands are found abandoned by the roadside, in stores, on hospital or police station doorsteps. Their fate is uncertain. Makeshift orphanages can hardly absorb the numbers. Children sleep three and four to a small crib. Infections spread rapidly; one baby's slight cold can become the death rattle of a cribmate. Very ill children are isolated, often left to die. Many orphanages even have a dying room.

The healthy children quite literally live in their cribs. They don't go for walks or even see the outdoors. No one gives them toys or visual stimuli. No one cuddles or soothes them. They have a crib and a schedule. Bottles are placed in the crib and the child's head turned towards it to latch on. It is the baby's success rate with this simple act that determines her life: hold the bottle; do it yourself; take sustenance; you live.

It's not that the Chinese don't love these children, there are just too many of them for adequate care — thus, the foreign adoptions. China is, however, a proud, isolationist country concerned with saving face and "opens" and "closes" its door on foreign adoption at will, depending upon its attitude toward a given country at a given moment. As of this writing, that door is virtually shut, and many children will remain homeless and die as a result. Even in a good year, the adoption of several thousand children hardly makes a dent in this ongoing catastrophe.

Mimi Williams had to wait for that door to reopen. When it finally did, I had become involved in her story, monitoring the difficult journey. Yet, at the time, it was still just a television movie to me.

Mimi and Baby Grace came home to a hero's welcome. This little girl not only had a mom, but an entire parish as her family. Our first private photo captured Grace sound asleep clutching her mother's jacket with a grip that said she was not going to let go, ever. When Grace awoke, she wouldn't take her eyes off her mom, not even when Mimi had to use the bathroom. Grace, Mimi, and I all walked to the bathroom together, Grace still attached to the jacket, eyes riveted on her mother. It was a memorable pee.

This scene reached deep inside me and touched the bottom of my soul. Something about little Grace's face burned right through me. Like finding religion. Like a calling. And it scared me. While I can be impetuous, I'm fairly selfish about my life and my family. I don't like disruptions and I hate new circumstances. To all but the most intimate of intimates, I appear to be impervious to pure emotion, and here I was, barely able to breathe. It was a moment of awakening. Time to take a stand. Time to make my presence felt. Time to do something.

Some months later, after I had thoroughly researched the adoption process, I approached my husband in a conversation that went like this:

"I've been thinking . . . I'd like to adopt a child." Dead silence. " . . . from China." Stunned dead silence.

Long before I shared this shattering revelation, Jim Winston had won my award for the world's most wonderful husband and father of the century. Our decision to have children had been a thirteen-year discussion while we each built careers and followed selfish pursuits before taking action. Having our two children was, by far, our best decision in life. The reality, though, is that children are also time suckers and money suckers. Since we regularly run out of both of these commodities, this adoption made no sense.

While Jim did not give me an unqualified "no," he truly thought I had lost my mind. Then he began his own education, reading and talking to adoptive parents, parents-to-be, and adoption agencies. When Jim suggested we take up the subject with our children, I knew he was with me. For our five-year-old daughter, Dani, the idea of a little sister was delicious, and for that ever-compassionate, incredible son of mine, James, beyond his concerns of finding baby drool all over his stuff, he felt it was time to "shake it up" at home.

The subsequent nine months of paperwork and social worker's home study were uneventful, and actually served as an appropriate gestation period for our family. Now it was our family and friends who thought we were crazy. While our peers were sending kids off to college, we were thinking about cribs and diapers.

This was much more than a decision to add to the family. We were altering its dynamics. We had worked hard to teach our children to understand racial differences; now we were to become a transracial family. We would live it. We had taught our children about haves and have-nots. Now we were going to make it possible for someone who had nothing to have a family. We had taught that love multiples, it does not divide, and that love knows no boundaries, not even geographic ones. We had hit the tender age of "Where do babies come from?" and answered honestly when prodded by "Tell me, really," amused by the "Oh, gross!" reactions. Now we talked about what defines a mother and a father when biology steps aside.

The night before Jim and I left for China, I was struck by my one and only moment of doubt. Looking around the dining room table at the family we had created, two beautiful children who at that moment were not fighting with each other, I tried to imagine the same scene two weeks later. I couldn't.

As parents of biological children, we had had to agree to accept a child with a "correctable handicap." The Chinese believe that, since we should all have only one child, those in violation should take care of hard-to-place children. We had signed up, fully willing to take the child given to us, just as we did when I physically gave birth. Leaving our children at home with my still-disbelieving mother, we left to give birth again.

We flew to Hong Kong, where we met the others making this journey. Twenty-four of us, who were to be linked for life by this shared momentous experience, boarded a train for mainland China. We were strangers caught up in our private dreams and desires. On the faces of our companions, travel fatigue aside, I saw long tales of need, marked by anticipation or outright fear. One day you're just you, and the next day someone's calling you "Mom" or "Dad."

It didn't take long to realize that Jim and I were the anomaly: We weren't childless or desperate, we hadn't suffered, and we weren't new to the idea of parenting. Our companions were quiet, perhaps introspective, wanting to come and go as quickly as possible. To them, China was a means to an end. China was, to me, the beginning of a brave new journey, a beginning I wanted to absorb in great detail. I soaked up the culture, the history, the sights and sounds of this foreign world, struggling to understand a culture and a social situation I would one day have to explain to my daughter.

Thankfully, our interpreter was a kindred spirit, highly educated and the son of two physicians banished to the countryside during the Cultural Revolution. Out of earshot of our ever-constant government companion from Beijing, he talked about his country and his people. He proudly talked about his seven-year-old daughter. He talked of his sadness at not being permitted to have another child. The laws are severe. He would lose his job, his housing, his government subsidy.

Most memorably, he described his conflicting feelings about the adoption process. He shared in the joy of those of us becoming parents and was grateful that these few children would receive good care. But, at the same time, he was profoundly embarrassed for his country, ashamed of the genocide that led to these adoptions. He sang to us a traditional Chinese lullaby: The essence of a child to a nation is like that of a flower to a plant. We were taking away a bouquet.

He made me love China. He made me forgive China.

The day before we were to meet our children, we all had to be personally interviewed and our papers validated. We were waiting in a bus outside Chinese government offices when something remarkable happened. One couple had made the decision to adopt a nine-year-old child who had spent her life in an orphanage. Her name was ShaoSha. As an older, female child in China, she was considered especially unadoptable, even though the orphanage, recognizing her as an extremely quick and clever child, had managed to raise funds to send her to school. Since the doors had opened on adoptions, she had watched the ongoing exodus as babies left to go to new homes. Like any child, she desperately wanted and needed parents.

When Carol and Leland, third-generation Chinese Americans, had found out about ShaoSha, they'd begun writing and trading pictures. And the rare was about to happen, an older child was going to be adopted. By now, we had all been shown the photos of this beautiful girl, and, when I looked out the window of the bus and saw a child approaching with a caretaker, I recognized her. I hardly knew what to do or say and blurted out, "I don't know how to put this gently, but there is your daughter."

ShaoSha walked onto the bus and looked around. She recognized Carol and Leland instantly. "Mama, Papa!" Her joy at meeting her parents for the first time was overwhelming to witness and not an eye was dry. Not wanting to wait a moment longer to have her own Mama and Papa, she had come to claim her family. The head of the orphanage came to take her home, because the formal proceedings weren't until the next day. Those of us on the bus argued and won — ShaoSha stayed at her parents' side. She was home.

The next day, sitting on the hard benches, trying unsuccessfully to enjoy the lychees, a seasonal delicacy, we waited for our baby. A hot and sweaty group with ShaoSha as our cheerleader, we each stood as our names were called out for the official presentation of a daughter, complete with passport and Chinese good luck money.

"Mr. and Mrs. Winston, we are proud to present your daughter, Fou Chow Wei."

I savor the moment often, remembering as we stepped forward, and saw her for the first time. She was a bundle of attentive energy and looked tiny to me although she weighed over ten pounds. While it might sound self-serving, I could actually feel her little body relax in my arms the moment she was placed there. She knew she was home. Remarkably, she never cried on the trip home. She wanted to see everything. Having been kept inside an orphanage for her first few months, she was extremely sensitive to sunlight but accustomed to noise, because the orphanage was next to an open market.

A week later, we sat at our dinner table enjoying our first official meal as a family of five. Afterwards, the kids asked to be excused. As though he had done this all his life, my son quietly took Nikki from my arms. I heard the baseball game coming from the television in the den and peeked in to see Nikki Winston propped up between her brother and sister, a baseball cap rakishly placed on her head and a baseball glove in her lap.

Has my daring changed the world? No, but it changed the world of our family. Have I cured a disease? No, but I finally gave more than lip service to one of the true ills of humanity. Have I produced an awe-inspiring, world-renowned film? No, but my home videos are surely the stuff of which standing ovations are made around our house.

Susan and Nikki and the Winston family have been an inspiration to others who have chosen to adopt even though they already have children. "It proves that love truly does transcend for all who dare," says Susan. Nikki is now a thriving four-year-old and, according to her mom, "There's no doubt who's in charge of our family. Her brother and sister still treat her like royalty and she milks that for all it's worth. A computer whiz, when not wielding a mean keyboard, she's slam-dunking and foul-shooting, wearing her well-earned nickname of little MJ (for Michael Jordan) proudly. She has an infectious laugh and a worldly-wise face that hints a bit at where she's been and just how far she'll go."

Janelle Goetcheus, M.D.

"I learned many things through the years from those who became our guests. One of those lessons was about family, and Robert was one who taught me this."

Dr. Janelle Goetcheus — founder of Christ House, a temporary medical facility for homeless men in Washington, D.C. — has been called a "physician to the forgotten" and a "servant on the streets."

As a young teenager, I dreamed of becoming a doctor. I was very hesitant to share that dream with anyone, because I was a shy, retiring young girl, who would not have been perceived by myself or by others as one who would become a doctor. Slowly, however, as I continued through school, that dream was to emerge into reality. When I graduated from Indiana University School of Medicine, I was one of eight women in a class of a hundred and fifty.

I went to medical school knowing that I wanted to provide care to those who were medically underserved. So when my husband, Al, and I started making plans to go overseas to work with the poor, I felt right on course. We lived in the small town of Upland, Indiana. Al is a United Methodist minister and, at the time, was Chair of the Speech and Drama Department at Taylor University. I was doing emergency room work and family practice. We prepared for a year for this ministry abroad and were commissioned by the church for such a mission. We went out to churches, taking our three children with us, to speak about what we were going to be doing. While we were awaiting our visas to Pakistan, we took a weekend trip to Washington, D.C., to visit with an ecumenical community, the Church of the Saviour. During that weekend, as part of our visit, we were taken into a low-income apartment building that had decayed through the years from landlord neglect. Until I walked those halls and smelled those odors, I had never known that people in this country were forced to live in such conditions. Knowing that I was a physician, several of the tenants began to tell me how difficult it was to try to get even basic health care. These encounters had a deep effect on me, and I have never been the same.

Out of that experience, Al and I made the startling decision not to go overseas, but rather to move to Washington, D.C. At that time, our children were young, and we didn't know what work we would be able to find in D.C. We had to go on faith alone, knowing only that we were drawn to the Church of the Saviour community and the work they were doing with the poor. It was a hard thing to explain to family and friends, because it looked like we were a little looney — and we felt a little looney. It was difficult to go back to the Methodist church and say, "Sorry, we're not going abroad. We're going to Washington."

"Well, what are you going to do in Washington?" people asked.

"We don't know, except we had an experience and we feel we need to go," was all we could say, which made us feel a bit unstable, especially with three young children.

Yet, we knew we were to make this journey. So, in August of 1976, we relocated from our town of three thousand to the nation's capital.

The first thing we did was to place a small health service in the very same decayed, low-income apartment building that we had first visited. Over the next year, we also began providing health care in another low-income apartment building. From there, we went to a soup kitchen where more than a thousand homeless persons came each day to stand in line awaiting breakfast and lunch.

It was probably one of the most difficult and painful times in our lives and yet one of the richest. Few of these people had ever had any regular health care. One day, as a patient was leaving my office, she said to me, rather incredulously, "How can you be my doctor?"

"Just by your wanting me to be," I said.

"You mean I can tell people I have a private doctor?"

Most of our patients had never experienced having a private doctor; the emergency room had been their doctor. Practicing medicine for the poor who were uninsured, I encountered enormous hurdles in obtaining needed services, such as X rays, specialty consults, and hospitalizations. I often found myself on the phone begging for these services for my patients. Very often, my pleas fell on deaf ears. One afternoon, while walking home after a long day of pleading, I began to cry. One of my patients, a mother who was struggling to raise her children in the inner city, saw me and said, "Please don't give up." Her words gave me courage.

While treating homeless people, I was often faced with having to send them right back out to the street. Many times, I saw minor health problems become major ones simply because there was no place for people to lie down and rest. People came to me with open ulcers on their legs and, after treating them in the office, I had to send them back out, only to watch those ulcers become larger and larger, sometimes infected and maggot-ridden, which often led to amputation. People who had been released from emergency rooms with pneumonia came to me carrying their unfilled prescriptions. Although I could provide the medications, I had to turn them back to the streets. On one snowy day, an elderly man came to the health service. I will never forget walking into the exam room and seeing this gentleman curled up on a chair. He was very ill-clothed for the weather. His overcoat was soaked from the snow. He had no undershirt. He wore a poorly fitting old pair of shoes but had no socks. He stayed with us most of the day and obtained other clothing and a warm meal, before we made arrangements for him to go back to a shelter that night. However, he never made it to the shelter. He froze to death on the streets of Washington that night.

I began to realize that we could not continue to see people and then simply turn them back out to the streets when they were so sick. I spoke with the other physicians who had come to work with us and, together, we began to dream of having a place where sick, homeless people could not only be treated but would be allowed to stay and rest and have a time of recovery. I shared that dream with a wonderful woman who was deeply moved by it and, over time, she helped us to purchase and renovate a four-story apartment building in which homeless, sick persons could be cared for and sheltered. We named it Christ House and opened on Christmas Eve of 1985.

Our first patient was a gentleman who had heart failure. He'd been hospitalized with it but released to the streets, and now came to us. Others followed: cancer patients whom we found in shelters; persons with frostbite of hands and feet; persons with tuberculosis and with AIDS; elderly, confused, demented persons found wandering the streets; and many others. Our thirty-eight beds filled all too quickly. The people who came to us were much sicker than we had ever anticipated. Because many of them had never had any regular source of health care, they had complications that never should have occurred. All too often, I saw young men with strokes from untreated hypertension and people with diabetes needing amputations.

Al and I were grateful that we had made the decision to live at Christ House, not only to provide the medical care, but also to create a home. One of the greatest gifts we ever gave our own children was to live there and know the people who came through the doors. All of our lives were enriched daily. I learned many things through the years from those who became our guests. One of those lessons was about family, and Robert was the one who taught me this lesson.

Robert and I met at the corner of Fifth and K streets. One night, when the medical outreach van from the Health Care for the Homeless — a public and private cooperative — stopped there, he and a group of men were standing around a barrel in which a fire was built. It was very cold, and they were trying to keep warm. When I took Robert's blood pressure, it was 190 over 135, which is very high. I wanted to take him to the hospital, but he told me that he was just old and waiting there to die. I asked him how old he was. We were the same age.

Robert was willing to come back to Christ House that night. When he arrived on the nursing floor and began to take off his shoes, socks, and several layers of clothing, the stench was so putrid that a number of the other patients said to me, "Please don't let him stay in my room."

Slowly, we began to know Robert. He had grown up in Alabama on a white man's farm, living in a two-room house out back with light streaming through the cracks. He and his two brothers slept in one bed and his mother, his aunt, and his mentally handicapped sister slept in the other bed. After completing second grade, he began to work the fields. By age twelve, he was allowed to drive the white man's tractor. During the years that Robert worked those fields, he and the other young men began to drink. It didn't take much in those days for a black man in the South to wind up in jail and Robert was no exception. After he was released, he decided to head north to Washington to see if he could find work. Being illiterate, with no skills and a jail record, the only job he could find was heavy day labor. After doing this type of work for many years, he developed severe degenerative changes in his lower back and began having great difficulty performing heavy labor. That is what lead to his standing around the barrel that night just trying to keep warm.

After being at Christ House with us for awhile, Robert began learning to read and write and was eventually able to move to his own apartment nearby. But, he continued to return regularly to help coordinate a support group for older, homeless men, and to offer them hope. A year later, on a routine chest X ray, Robert was found to have lung cancer. During the time he was undergoing radiation, he came back to Christ House to live. One night, he called me on the phone and said, "Come quick!" I ran down the hall to find that he was hemorrhaging from the lung. Little could be done.

The other physicians at Christ House came as well and Robert passed very quickly as I held him in my arms. Immediately after he died, we placed a small candle beside his bed and people began to come, among them our children, for whom Robert had always had special treats. The news filtered through the neighborhood and still others came. As I was standing outside Robert's room, one of the Christ House nurses said to me, "You know, Robert got it, he really got it."

Robert grasped many things that I missed, but one of the things he taught me was a sense of family. I was his sister, but then he had many sisters and many brothers, nieces, and nephews. I often wish that, in our world, we could see each other through Robert's eyes as brothers and sisters to one another. If we could, so much needless suffering would end. I was blessed to know Robert. I am blessed to know all the people who have come to our health services and to stay with us at Christ House. All those years ago, I thought I was coming to Washington, D.C., to serve but, in truth, what happened was that my own life was transformed.

Since 1985, over 3,100 people have been admitted to Christ House. Dr. Goetcheus is also medical director of the Health Care for the Homeless Project (HCHP), which operates health facilities in twelve homeless shelters and a mobile medical van that serves homeless people living in parks, on grates, and in abandoned buildings. In 1994, HCHP served more than 10,000 patients.

Among her many awards and honors, Dr. Goetcheus was inducted into the Women's Hall of Fame in 1989, named Family Doctor of the Year by the American Academy of Family Physicians in 1991, crowned Washingtonian of the Year in 1995 by Washingtonian Magazine, *and awarded the 1997 Rosenthal Foundation Award by the American College of Physicians. She has lectured extensively, including at Yale, Harvard, the Jimmy Carter Presidential Center, and at the Albert Schweitzer International Symposium on Global Health.*

Lynne Twist

"The women held their emaciated babies up to the windows. The elders, wearing rags and leaning on their staffs, demanded to speak with the group leader. Fear suddenly gripped my chest. That leader was me."

Lynne Twist is cochair of the Board of Trustees for the State of the World Forum. She was a founding executive of The Hunger Project and was responsible for raising millions of dollars to end global hunger over the past twenty-two years.

In July of 1992, I took seventeen wealthy people from the United States, Europe, and Australia to the country of Ethiopia. My companions were major donors to The Hunger Project, an organization I helped to found in 1977. I had never been to Ethiopia, but, like my companions and most of the world, I had read about the horrors of the famine of 1984 and 1985. The Hunger Project had worked hard to make the famine known to the world and to bring news of the massive starvation to the attention of governments and the media. With our behind-the-scenes efforts and the efforts of others, Live Aid was born, and Bob Geldof and his music colleagues put on the largest television event in history to raise both money and awareness to fight the famine. After that event, Ethiopia to most people meant a dry, arid, frightening wasteland of death and hunger.

My trip in 1992 was motivated in part by an upcoming event, to be hosted by the new interim president of Ethiopia, announcing the annual Africa Prize for Leadership for the Sustainable End of Hunger, a significant initiative of The Hunger Project. I wanted our major donors, each of whom had contributed or could contribute a hundred thousand dollars or more, to witness the stature of the project at this very important event held at African Hall in Addis Ababa. I also wanted them to have a firsthand experience of hunger in Africa and to show them how their money would be used.

A few years of rain in the Ethiopian highlands had made the countryside green, and a seventeen-year civil war had come to an end. The rebels had been triumphant and had elected as the new interim president Meles, a young doctor with stars in his eyes and great humanity in his heart. The transitional government had been in place for a year and was preparing Ethiopians for the first election in the history of this most ancient country. With 55 million people to reach — 80 percent of whom were illiterate — educating the public about candidates and the mechanics of voting was a real challenge. I was deeply inspired by the people of Ethiopia, their courage in overthrowing their dictator Mengistu, and their determination to build a new nation after centuries and centuries of tyranny and monolithic rule.

Our first four days were full of amazing experiences. But, nothing could have prepared us for what lay ahead as, halfway through our trip, we packed into Land Rovers with the director of Save the Children and our Ethiopian escorts and headed out to the Great Rift Valley to see a Save the Children project in the region of Ifat Tenuga, home to some of the most remote and hard-to-reach villages in the desert. No one had traveled our route for a long time, including the Save the Children workers. As we drove hour after hour with little or no road, the air and terrain became drier, dustier, and more barren. Clearly, a terrible drought still gripped this part of Ethiopia, even though only a hundred kilometers away were green mountains with beautiful, clear streams running down the hillsides. Here, the terrain was so desolate and so forgotten that it was unsettling, even frightening.

I looked out toward the bleak and barren horizon and, at first, I didn't see them through the clouds of dust from our vehicles. Slowly, they took shape. Hundreds of them, small figures moving toward us. I remember vividly the moment when I realized that they were mothers with children and babies. Some older, emaciated men struggled along beside them. As we got closer, I could see that their faces were desperate, frightened. Death walked with them, close on the heels of starvation. Limp babies tried to suckle their mother's flat, dry breasts. Children strained under swollen bellies, a sign of serious malnutrition. Others had swollen heads. All of them were covered with flies. It was horrifying. It was the sight I had dreaded most. And here it was, in my face, so close I could smell the hunger.

We had driven into the remnants of a village. Several hundred starving people crowded around our two vehicles and pressed up against us. The women held their emaciated babies up to the windows. The elders, wearing rags and leaning on their staffs, demanded to speak with the group leader. Fear suddenly gripped my chest. That leader was me.

The women in my group were crying and screaming at me to do something. Some of the men were also crying. All of them were begging me to give the villagers the food packed in our trunks. My heart raced and I could feel the pulse in my neck. My mind screamed for an answer, something to take away the pain I saw all around us.

Even the Save the Children workers didn't know what to do. They had been completely unaware of the desperate condition of the people here. Ethiopia is a large country, and budget and staff restrictions kept them from comprehensively monitoring every region. Their staff was stretched to the limit with problems in Somalia and with border difficulties between Somalia, Djibouti, and Ethiopia. And little or no assistance was available from private voluntary organizations, in part because of the remoteness of the arid desert area, in part because of the inability of NGOs (Non-Governmental Organizations) to cover more ground in such a geographically large country.

One of the Ethiopian escorts from Save the Children offered to translate for me, and we stepped down out of our Land Rover and moved into the crowd to talk with the elders, who gathered in a circle around us and asked me to speak. They wanted to know who we were and what we were doing. One of them began to tell me their story and, as it was translated, the people in my group listened and cried, wondering what I would do, what I could do. The elders said that they had not had substantial rain in seven years and the main well had gone dry. A well in a nearby village had become toxic. They said that they were burying two to three children a day and that the rest of them would be dead within two weeks if they didn't get help. They said that they had been isolated for some time, wandering the arid plains looking for livestock, food, water, any remnant of life.

My mind clarified around a single thought: I was responsible for taking action in the presence of dying and starving people — not action triggered by fear or panic. My decision needed to be clear, authentic, sustaining. I knew that this was an opportunity to express the principles of my work as never before.

The Hunger Project and the end of chronic, persistent worldwide hunger had been my life commitment for over twenty years. The Hunger Project doesn't feed people; it doesn't do development work. It's a voice for the hungry, and its goal is clear and determined: to end hunger and starvation, globally. We work to empower people, to transform conditions in which hunger and starvation persist. We galvanize and mobilize public will to form powerful partnerships with people who are trapped in these conditions. The Hunger Project is designed to break the paradigm of "haves" and "have-nots." Our vision calls for no less than complete transformation of the conditions that drive one billion people into hunger and poverty.

And now, I stood in the midst of that hunger. And I needed an answer. My years of hard work and dedication had distilled down to this moment of profound personal confrontation.

I knew that the answer wasn't to give them our food. It wouldn't even begin to feed them and would probably make them sick. It would be a quick, insufficient, questionable fix. When people are desperately hungry and approaching starvation, the first food they receive must be very mild and bland and carefully administered so that it does not weaken their systems and even further shock their bodies. We had with us just enough to feed the seventeen healthy people with whom I was traveling, and there were hundreds of villagers who were near starvation standing before us. All of them were very weak, very fragile, and in need of medical attention. No, our food was not the answer. Instead, I needed to listen to their voices, their souls, to understand the depth of their commitment to live and to pull their village, their tribe through this crisis. I needed to hear clearly so that I would know how to involve the right partners and agencies to help them. I needed to give these people love, understanding, a sense of dignity, and an opportunity to connect with us in a way that would give them enough strength to make it until we could get them the help they needed.

With our four-wheel vehicles in the background and the sun beating down mercilessly, I listened as they told their story and spoke of their plight. They talked about the children who had died. They talked about the disease rampant among them. They talked about how few days, how few hours, they had left. They held up to my face a tiny baby who would soon be dead.

As I listened, I felt not just their hunger but their strength and courage. Their bodies were ravaged, but the light was still shining in their eyes, and that light told me that, if they believed in themselves and kept going, they could be saved. I reached out to that part of them and I felt their passion and their will. I responded to that, to the very essence of who they were — their spirit, their soul.

I told them that we were from The Hunger Project, that we were not a relief organization, but that we endeavored to be the voice of the hungry. I told them we were committed to bringing their courage, their stamina, and their passion for life to the ears of the rest of the world. We would be their link to a partnership with people who could help them transform the conditions driving them into poverty and starvation.

I saw the chiefs and elders nodding as I told them that we were privileged to be with them and that, while we could not offer them immediate aid, what we could offer them was our love, our intention, and our voice. People brightened as I told them that we would return to the capital of Addis Ababa and notify the development agencies whose job it is to provide relief, dig wells, and deliver seed. We would mobilize worldwide and national resources to assist them and to work with them to reestablish their own viability and stability.

I held a dying baby. I embraced and touched the women. I kissed the children and bowed to honor the men. I invited the people in my group to come out of the vehicles and connect with these courageous and amazing people, and they did. We all honored their courage and humanity, and let them know that there were thousands of people from all across the world in The Hunger Project who thought about them daily, who worked on their behalf hourly, monthly, yearly — people who donated money, people who lobbied governments to change policies. I told them of the power of the people who stood behind them, who would make them known to the rest of the world. They would never be forgotten — although they seemed isolated, they had now connected with a worldwide network, potent and determined, that would work tirelessly to ensure that they had a chance for healthy and productive lives.

They were moved by my words. I saw them straighten and stand taller and, for the briefest of moments, I thought about all the years that I had been working on hunger, about all the devastation and destruction brought about by charity and aid. What had been a concept to me all those years was standing right in front of me now, and that concept is this: What is most important about hungry people, about people who are in resource-poor and starving conditions, is to rebuild their own sense of self and their dignity as they pull themselves out of a physically desperate situation. That can only be done through equal partnership and respect, enabling them to author the actions needed rather than doing something "for them." We would not leave them empty-handed but with a sense of renewed commitment to their own self-reliance, a sense of powerful alliance, and an experience of not being alone. They knew and we knew that, together, we could resolve not only their immediate emergency, but their return to their natural state of self-sufficiency. It was crystal clear to me that the elders and women in particular understood this.

In retrospect, what I did sounds easy. In the moment, it took tremendous courage. I was torn by that primal pull to help, to aid, to give, to fix immediately. We all have known such moments. In this case, it was extreme and had I not had the deep conviction from my years of work with The Hunger Project, I'm quite sure I would have responded in a way that would have given short-term relief, but not essential long-term, ongoing change. That response would have relieved our suffering and not theirs.

I brought out bottled water, which we were carrying in our vehicles and gave it to them. And then, we embraced and said good-bye. I knew in my soul that they would be all right.

We drove to Addis Ababa the next day and met with officials of the World Food Program and told them about the people we had met and their condition. A nomadic tribe that moved in a circle from village site to village site according to the season, they were nevertheless located with the help of our Save the Children colleagues who knew enough about the area to give clear coordinates. The World Food Program arranged to drop-ship supplies of food and water immediately. We then met with officials at Save the Children headquarters and alerted them to the dying children. They moved at once into the region, taking water and seed and tools to dig wells and plant the meager fields.

A month later, back in the United States, we received letters from officials in

Ethiopia saying that the rains had come to that dry region and that the tribe had been saved. Doctors from the World Health Organization had arrived to immunize the babies and treat the malaria. The letters said that the villagers' passion and commitment to becoming self-reliant, to not ever again needing aid, was beyond anything they had ever seen in Ethiopia or in East Africa.

At this news, I cried with gratitude. I cried because I realized that in that moment of extreme pain in the desert, I had found within myself a deep courage to provide leadership, to act not out of fear and despair but out of a deep desire to empower. I had found in myself the courage to stand on the principles of transformation that are the very heart of my work. I had been true to my commitment to the long-term end of hunger and the self-sufficiency of all people, and to my pledge that all people be honored for who they are rather than for the circumstances in which they find themselves. I hadn't just helped to save the lives of the several hundred people who surrounded our Land Rovers in that abandoned village, but I had helped to give them a future for generations and generations to come. With that one action, my entire life was worthwhile.

In her extensive travels, Lynne would meet and come to know a remote indigenous tribe in Ecuador, the Achuar, 3,500 people occupying nearly 2 million acres of pristine tropical rain forest in one of the most biologically diverse regions on the planet. Their sparse contact with the outside world had convinced them that saving their homeland would require "changing the dream of the North." Carrying their message, Lynne and her husband, Bill Twist, created the Pachamama Alliance, a partnership with the Achuar to halt the destruction of the rain forest and the inevitable loss of indigenous tribes and to find ways to blend the wisdom and knowledge of traditional cultures and of the modern world. To create a new global vision of sustainability for us all.

Rebecca Black

"Our youth haven't been lost to us. They're just waiting for us to help. We have only to risk reaching out."

As in big cities across the country, in North Portland, Oregon, kids drop through cracks every day. Gang kids, kids on parole, kids straight out of prison, abused kids, kids on the street who can't go home. They are lost to society, but not to Becky Black.

Two images from my childhood come rushing to mind when I think about the person I am today and why I do what I do: why I am drawn to help troubled kids, abused kids, gang kids, forgotten kids. One image is from the first time I visited an orphanage. I was young, maybe six years old. I gripped my father's hand as we walked up a set of long front steps carrying boxes of clothing. I remember vividly the ghostly faces of the children behind the long skirt of the woman who opened the door. It's a scene that has never faded in my mind.

The other image is from a few years later, when I accompanied my family to my sister's college graduation. The ceremony was impressive, but the moment that stood out for me was the presentation of a watch to a black man for his years of service to the school. Here was a man who could sweep the floors and scrub the toilets, but his children couldn't attend the college because of the color of their skin. I felt a deep pain seeing this, and an anger that would not go away. It was something I didn't fully understand as a ten-year-old. But I knew that something was wrong, deeply wrong, with giving this man a watch instead of allowing his children to attend the very school he served. It struck me as so fundamentally wrong that I got up and walked out of the ceremony, embarrassing my family. I got a licking for that.

These two quintessential moments in my life have helped me understand what I'm doing today, and the path that brought me here.

As an adult, I married and had two children. My husband and I also adopted an infant, Joshua, who was Native American. The marriage ended, but my mothering instincts didn't. When I adopted Jonathon, he was considered "hard to place" because he was thought to be brain damaged and was part black. In fact, he had no disability other than an allergy to milk, and he is now a handsome, hardworking twenty-two-year-old.

One day, when Jon was about three years old, I opened my front door to discover a beer box sitting on the top step. Inside was a baby. A woman whom I had met briefly knew that I had taken in foster children, and that I also had adopted children. She felt unable to care for her child, so she left her beautiful baby girl with me. I notified the Department of Health and Welfare and became the baby's foster mother.

Baby Nicole meant that I now had four children of my own, two foster children, and two jobs. And, in my spare time, I was a student at the local university. I knew that I had to give up something and it certainly wouldn't be my children. Since my two jobs kept a roof over our heads and food on the table, my part-time college education had to come to a temporary halt. (At that time, I had spent four years trying to complete my freshman year.)

By the time Nikki was three, several changes had occurred in our lives. We had moved to a housing project on the Bannock-Shoshone Indian Reservation, where I worked with Native American youth in a residential treatment facility. Unbeknownst to me, the state of Idaho decided that it was time to place Nikki up for adoption, and I was considered a bad candidate because I was poor, had four other children, and lived in a housing project on an Indian reservation. What the state failed to consider was that Nikki had grown to be a sister to the other children and was as much a member of our family as the others, that she had very involved grandparents, who loved her dearly, and was now part of a large and caring family.

The state did not notify me of the decision, so I could take no preventive steps and was totally unprepared when two social workers showed up at my door, demanding Nikki. They literally tried to pull her from my arms. If it hadn't been so tragic and traumatic, it would have been funny: two social workers tugging at my little girl and me pulling her in the opposite direction.

A young woman I worked with was visiting when all this happened. She rushed into my bedroom and called a judge. When she told him that two state workers were on tribal land and why they were there, he asked to speak to them. One of them got on the line, and the judge told him that they were trespassing and, should they succeed in taking my child from me, he would have them arrested immediately for trespassing and kidnapping. They left right away.

Days of panic and chaos followed. Eventually, the tribal Chair, a friend of mine, officially made me and Nikki honorary tribal members, making it possible for me to be represented in court by tribal attorneys. Because the tribe had protected us, my Black-Hispanic daughter became legally mine.

I remained in Idaho for several more years, but as my younger children approached their teen years, I realized the need to have exposure to diversity and multicultural surroundings. Wanting them to have lots of options, I struck out for a big city.

The week before we arrived in Portland, Oregon, in 1988, the city had its first gang killing. Fresh from the countryside and clueless about the gangs, the Crips and the Bloods, I unknowingly moved us right into the heart of gang turf. I didn't know about the attitude and hatred and posturing in gangs, but what I did see were children in pain, and I felt compelled to do something. Through a sort of "graced" innocence, I drove around rival gang territories, setting up a little card table with printed information about jobs for kids who needed work and wanted to work. The way I saw it, these children belonged to all of us and were our responsibility. Behind the gang "colors" and the guns and the "gang banging" beat the heart of a kid, an adolescent, a teenager. I had to reach out to that part of these kids.

Not really knowing any better, I did any number of things that, in retrospect, were crazy and dangerous and easily could have ended badly for me. One day I was driving three young black men to job interviews in my red (the Blood gang color) car and someone threw a rock at us. If I had had any kind of street instinct, I would have gotten out of there in a blink. Instead, I screeched to a stop and flew out of the car, stormed over to the guy and gave him hell. What right did he have to throw a rock at me, a person, a human being, someone he didn't even know? The guy backed off. I think he was shocked by this wild woman screaming at him and thought I was crazy. When I'd finished with him, I marched back to my car and saw that the three kids inside were flat on the floor anticipating a shooting. The guy who had thrown the rock was a Crip. The kids in the car were all Bloods. This is how I learned about gangs.

I also learned about gangs when I drove three young men to a Job Corps Center two hours from Portland. They wanted to play one of their rap tapes and I acquiesced — for awhile. But the language and anger in the music was difficult for me to handle, so I struck a deal with them: I would let them play their music if they would stop with me to pick wildflowers to take home. That's how I ended up prancing around a beautiful open meadow with three gang kids who had rarely been outside their 'hood. Despite the dress and the music and the attitudes and the anger, these kids had another side.

In an attempt to provide jobs, I organized a small construction crew made up of equal parts Bloods and Crips. They worked together for several months renovating a building that would house a program providing residential assistance to gang kids. I brought together the first African American wilderness fire fighting crew made up primarily of gang kids. What I came to realize was that most of these gang kids will be the lookout for drug dealers just to get money to eat. All they really want are the same things you and I want: a roof over their heads, a car, a job, food on the table . . . some respect, someone to love, someone to love them.

During the next two years, I began to see a frightening pattern. Out of the hundreds of bright, searching youth with whom I worked, few were in school. Situations early in life prevented them from being successful in the classroom, and eventually they dropped out.

In 1990, I began working with gang members returning to our community from jail. My job was to get them back in school and help them stay there. When my first official client arrived in my office, he made it clear that he was ready for a positive change in his life. He wanted to go to school, play football, go to the prom; everything that my own children wanted. He and I went to the local high school to enroll him, but because of his past problems, there was no way he could enter a public school. All the alternative schools were full, so he began to come to my office to be tutored.

Eventually, eight young men returning from juvenile incarceration began showing up at my office every day for tutoring. They had been mandated by the state to attend school, but there was no school that would accept them. Here were eight young men who expressed a sincere desire to turn their lives around, and I had no place to put them. Holding onto the belief that they would get into a school eventually, I waited for the right person to step in and remedy the situation while I provided them with sufficient activities to keep them off their neighborhood's dangerous streets. At the same time, I couldn't neglect the other dozens upon dozens of kids who were coming to my office daily looking for help finding jobs, school programs, and other alternatives.

One afternoon, I had an epiphany and suddenly realized that the "right" person wasn't going to show up and, in fact, the "right" person was none other than me. If something was going to happen for these kids, I was going to have to be the person on the inside to make it happen.

There was no income for me or my family from this work. I needed donations. I needed sponsorship. I needed an organization, either my own or one already established. Being a person who likes to see things accomplished with a minimum of red tape, I opted to begin my own organization. Gathering the application and my records, and summoning up as much courage as I could, I set out to complete the IRS application for a private, nonprofit agency. About two months later, Oregon Outreach, Inc., received its 501(c)(3) designation from the Internal Revenue Service — I was an "agency."

With Oregon Outreach placing youth in jobs, I turned to education, the other half of the equation for success. I called the Oregon Department of Education. "You must want to speak to the alternative education department," said the woman on the other end. "I'll connect you." It wasn't the call I had hoped to make, one in which I was organized and knew what I was talking about and impressed people with what I was going to do to educate at-risk youth. Instead, it was a plaintive cry for help. I requested whatever forms and paperwork were necessary to start a school.

In less than one month, my grassroots program was a state-certified school, housed in the donated basement of a church, with eight students being taught by a volunteer. Although all I could offer was a cold church basement with no textbooks, computers, or resources, the young men came, and it made me see that, while students deserve the finest technology and resources, they want to learn more than they want to wait for the right equipment.

The little school for gang youth grew to a second site for regular dropouts, which immediately filled, with a waiting list. A third site was established and it, too, quickly filled. There seemed to be no lack of students; just a lack of opportunities. The schools continued to operate at three separate sites for the next two years.

In 1993, I decided to consolidate the program and moved into our current location, changing the name to the Gladys McCoy Academy, after a black community activist in Portland who had recently died. My vision continued to evolve. Our students had peripheral issues that prevented them from succeeding in school. Why not a drug and alcohol program at school? Teen parents had no affordable child care, so they couldn't complete their education. Why not a day care center at the school? Our kids had family problems. Why not a mental health professional at the school? I contracted with a local, nationally recognized program to provide drug and alcohol counseling, intervention, and education. Drug and alcohol prevention became part of our regular curriculum. I developed an in-house day care center, and twelve teen parents suddenly began to attend school again. I employed a part-time psychologist to provide counseling to the kids and training to our staff. I held fast to the belief that "Whatever the mind can conceive, so can it achieve," and it seemed to be working.

Soon, other districts were contacting me, needing assistance with youth who were dropping out. I expanded to several sites, serving outlying suburban areas. Since that first "bargain basement" program in 1990, the education program has grown to seven sites housed in leased classroom space, churches, and storefronts. With the help of a dedicated and tireless staff, we serve more than three hundred young people whose communities have given up on them. We have provided educational services to students from fourteen different school districts, but none of this could have happened if not for the fact that our young people have a burning desire to become independent, productive adults. Youth who are out of school and involved in illegal activities are not necessarily "bad kids." If given an opportunity, they will rise to the occasion.

We can't wait for our school systems, our cities, counties, or state systems, or the federal government, to do the job of caring for and educating young people. As individuals and concerned community members, we have to take the responsibility upon ourselves. It can be done, even if we are armed only with the vision that our children need an education and the knowledge to help them obtain it. The belief and vision will take us further than thousands of dollars. Our youth have not been lost to us. They are just waiting for us to help. We have only to risk reaching out.

By 1994, all of my children except Nikki, who was still a junior, had graduated from high school. And I finally had finished what I had begun more than twenty years earlier: I graduated from college. With all of my children watching, I marched down the aisle in my cap and gown, and not only received my college diploma from Warner-Pacific College but the highest honor given to a graduating senior: The A. F. Gray Founder's Award for Achievement. As I was presented with the award, I thought of all the help I had been given along the way to earning my diploma. Our young people deserve no less. Nothing is impossible when we support those around us. It worked for me. And it will work for the youth in our communities, but the hands reaching out to help them must be ours.

In 1993, along with Hillary Clinton, Becky won the Lewis Hine Award (given by the National Child Labor Committee) for exceptional service to children. Her organization, Oregon Outreach, Inc., was made one of the Thousand Points of Light of the Bush Administration.

Barbara Trent

"We realized that in the year behind us, we had given up our trust and belief in the goodness of the universe and had lost sight of our place in it. We had been hiding from opportunity, from risk, from discomfort, and surely from the unknown."

In 1993, Barbara Trent won the Academy Award® for Best Feature Documentary. She had put her life in danger to film The Panama Deception. *But risk was no stranger to her, as she had already produced the internationally acclaimed documentaries,* Destination Nicaragua *and* COVERUP: Behind the Iran-Contra Affair. *At her side throughout was her partner, filmmaker David Kasper.*

When the U.S. invaded Panama in 1989, Trent was deeply disturbed by what she read in newspapers and saw on television: "No one questioned why Bush sent 26,000 troops and the stealth fighter to arrest one man. The media acted as cheerleaders for this invasion, never critically analyzing the reasons given by Bush and reporting only on the tactics of the invasion and the loss of American lives. No one focused on what was happening to the people and the infrastructure of Panama." She decided to find out firsthand and to document what she discovered. Organizing a film crew, she went to Panama and spoke with people in the newly U.S. installed government, in refugee camps, and in the streets to find out what really had happened and why. The end result was The Panama Deception.

In accepting the Oscar that March night in Hollywood, she dedicated the film to "all the people who have worked so hard for justice and truth and peace around the world, particularly the four people who died who were working in association with this film, and the hundreds and possibly thousands of Panamanians who died in this invasion, whose stories might never otherwise be told because of the deceptive practices and tactics of our government, with the complicity of the major media."

March, 1981. I was living in a town of 350 people in southern Illinois when my life began to unravel. Over a twenty-year period, I had developed a shining reputation as a radical activist among organizations and individuals, across the Midwest and into the South, involved in struggles for economic, political, and social justice. I had fought the FBI. I had helped to overturn corrupt village, city, and county governments, planning commissions, water districts, mental health institutions, housing authorities. I had even helped bust some of the largest landowners (landed gentry) for Fair Labor Standards Act violations with regard to their treatment of Mexican migrant farm workers. And I had helped to desegregate five towns in southern Illinois. Now, over the span of a few weeks, I lost my job, and my husband of ten years went for a ride after a dinner party and never came back.

I had been working as an EXPERT: Senior Training Specialist for the Action Agency under President Jimmy Carter. I trained VISTA volunteers — in the sister program to the more famous Peace Corps — in Region 5, which included Minnesota, Wisconsin, Illinois, Indiana, Michigan, and Ohio. My position was by appointment, and the new Reagan administration wasn't willing to wait for my appointment to expire; it really wanted to get rid of me. I had been an activist since the sixties, and I had an FBI record too long to read. This new administration didn't know the difference between dissidence and treason and continued to use its position to silence opposition to its policies. I was the opposition *ipso facto* because I had been a radical activist for twenty years.

Agents were sent out from Washington, D.C. I don't know who sent them, but they had access to FBI information on me. They demanded that my boss fire me immediately. To everyone's surprise, he refused and told them to go back to Washington and litigate if they wanted me so badly. Their response was something like "No problem; you'll regret this." Not long after, my immediate supervisor called me into his office and asked how many days were left on my contract. I told him fourteen. He said, "Use 'em up." In essence, he was saving me from a government blow that could render me unemployable and decommission me in my ability to accomplish change — I could stretch out my fourteen days and undergo a battle with the government, or I could work my fourteen days immediately and get out before any move could be made to discredit me, which is usually the objective in these kinds of government harassments within the U.S.

I used up my last days and realized there was no life left for me in Illinois. No job, a husband who lived fifteen houses down the road (the same night he walked out on me, he moved in with another woman), no future, no dream. No vision left. All of a sudden, my life was rubble again, the same rubble I had climbed out of six years earlier when I'd finally bailed off of welfare.

For the next six months, I dismantled my life, untangling myself from the past and trying to prepare for and move into a future of my own choosing. I filed for divorce at the Murphysboro courthouse, crossed the street to a travel agency, and bought two round-trip, coach tickets to Europe for my son, David, and me. Because of my experience working with at-risk people, I had been asked to speak at a conference on Humanistic Psychology in Geneva, Switzerland. Few of the Ph.D.s at the conference had similar histories or field experience working with addicts, suicidal people, youth referred from the court system, or welfare parents. I could bring to the conference a perspective otherwise missing, and I wanted to talk about how the process of emotional healing should include reaching out into the community. I thought it was important to acknowledge people's frustrations with society and to encourage them not only to change their behavior, but equally important, to change the world around them. Mine was a basic "We all need to be activists!" speech.

The speech was a hit, but I was still emotionally fragile. At times, I'd just sit down on a bench and cry, and David would put his arm around me and remind me that everything was going to be okay. I was intensely lonely, confused, and afraid of the future.

When we got back, I sent David to stay with my folks in Florida while I painted our house and settled my affairs with my ex-husband, separating out possessions, selling the rest, and splitting up the money. And then, I moved to California where I had just accepted a job as executive director of the Ocean Park Community Center in Santa Monica. David joined me several months later. By that time, it was already painfully clear that my job and I weren't seeing eye to eye. I resigned. It was a difficult decision — once again my son faced a future of complete uncertainty.

We were living in Topanga, a country town in the Santa Monica mountains. As a good little revolutionary, I always did my shopping at the organic food store there. One day as I was reading the announcements on the bulletin board, I noticed that an antinuclear war group was planning to caravan from California to New York to attend public events surrounding the Second United Nations Special Session on Disarmament, an event that would draw a million people from around the world in a united expression of commitment to peace and opposition to nuclear weapons. The group from Topanga were looking for all kinds of help, as well as volunteers to fundraise, organize, and plan the trip, which they named Pilgrimage for Peace.

Traveling *anywhere* was the last thing on my agenda at that point. But, because I had been a VISTA trainer for several years and an organizer in the Midwest for many more, I thought my contacts might be helpful to them. The people I had trained for VISTA were spread out across six states, working at the community level to help effect change and empower the poor and disenfranchised. VISTA, unlike the Peace Corps, was very activist oriented. I called and left a message that if the group from Topanga needed any contacts east of the Mississippi, to get in touch. Someone called back within minutes, thrilled to have found a compatriot who knew anyone east of the Mississippi who could help with housing, food, or publicity.

I started going to some of their planning meetings, and knew right off that I was dealing with a seriously ill-equipped group to be taking such a taxing trip. Some of them were going for no reason other than that it was a free trip to New York. Many meant well, cared fervently about the issues, but clearly had no idea what the trip would really entail. The two coordinators were wonderful maniacs in the best sense of the word, and sprinkled among the group were some seasoned activists, but all in all, the prospects seemed to favor catastrophe over success.

They were planning to conduct teach-ins en route across the country and to demonstrate outside of nuclear sites like Los Alamos Laboratory in New Mexico where research and development for the nuclear weapons industry is done; at the Pantex Plant in Amarillo, Texas, the final assembly point for all nuclear weapons made in the U.S.; at Kerr McGee (made infamous by Karen Silkwood), a corporation that mines uranium and runs the nuclear power plants that provide plutonium used in nuclear weapons; and at Rockwell International headquarters in Pittsburgh, Pennsylvania, the single largest defense contractor in the U.S. Their goal was to draw public attention to those who deal in death. The teach-ins would educate people about the impact of the nuclear industry.

So, the question for me became: how could I link these people, forty in all, to groups I had helped found and train, when some of them were likely to be incorrigible anarchists, or worse. And did I really want to hang my reputation on this ragtag group? For me, this was a seminal question. What was the value of all the incredible work I had done since the sixties? Wasn't it found in the people I had trained, the inspiration we had birthed, the leverage my reputation had earned? And what was the value of a hard-earned reputation if I had to spend the rest of my life protecting it, instead of using it to good ends? I remembered what famed futurist R. Buckminster Fuller, himself always on the cutting edge with inventions like the geodesic dome, said: that the value of your work is diminished if you're more concerned with safeguarding your reputation than with leveraging it at every reasonable opportunity.

Compelled to help, I began arranging places for them to stay, people to provide them with food, and solidarity — churches, grassroots organizations, old friends. Once I'd made the commitment and thrown myself into helping, I noticed that I was becoming more and more interested in the trip itself. I started to deeply appreciate these people. Here they were, unpolished in the ways of activism, without a common understanding of the nuclear issues to be addressed, with no grasp of the demands of a communal trip and the rigors of living with forty people you don't know, eating the same food, keeping the same schedule, sleeping on floors in church basements. But nonetheless, they were committed to submit their lives to the experience, and not for just a weekend but the better part of a month. The one thing everyone understood was that this trip was a way of taking a stand for a better world. They were average people taking on an unaverage challenge for the betterment of the planet.

My perceptions were changing and I was being drawn to join them, to risk a month of the unknown, the unexpected, but also a month of the possible. My mind told me the idea of going with them was a frightening concept, that it would be a horrible experience. I was afraid of living with so many people day in and day out. I was afraid of the conflicts. Everything about this trip scared me. But, my heart was fascinated. My son and I talked about the idea at length, but we could never come to a conclusion. I wanted to grip a decision and know it was right and kept pressing the subject, hoping that together we could figure out what we were meant to do next with our lives.

A week before the scheduled departure, David and I finally decided that we had been running scared ever since my husband had left, I had lost my job, and we had moved away from the place we had called home for all of his twelve years. We had become immobilized. We were afraid of the world and the people and places and situations outside of our small lives. We realized that in the year behind us, we had given up our trust and belief in the goodness of the universe and had lost sight of our place in it. We had been hiding from opportunity, from risk, from discomfort, and surely from the unknown.

We made a decision that we would run scared no more, that our lives were going to go on with the same gusto and sense of purpose and trust and faith that we had had before the fall. We decided to spend the little money we had to buy a computer for David, a financial decision we had agonized over for months . . . and we were both going to go on the trip.

That decision was made in a moment of blind faith. We would contradict all caution and find out once again if the universe was willing to provide, to allow us to err without destroying us — if it was a universe that appreciated and welcomed us.

I brought along my car as part of the caravan in order to make it available as an errand or scout vehicle. We all used it to run ahead of the caravan to get food for roadside meals and check on lodging locations. It also allowed me some particle of control over my experience, a small space in which to take sanctuary. It was a blue 1976 Dodge Colt, given the code name Blue Zinger for walkie-talkie purposes. It had brought me to California from Illinois, and I had no doubt that it would see us to New York and back.

Academy Award–winning filmmaker Haskell Wexler decided at the last minute to go with us and document the trip, the rallies, the marches, the demonstrations, the teach-ins along the way. He and his crew rode in a van tagged Silver Cloud. Another film team that had committed to documenting the trip came along as Haskell's second unit, riding in another van we named Yellow Thunder. (Little did

I know, Yellow Thunder transported David Kasper, the man with whom I would spend the next thirteen years of my life.) And then there was the old school bus that had been purchased for the trip and was the least likely vehicle to make it across country and might not have except for the genius of one man, Ron Rothstein, who could fix a transmission with spare bobby pins and gum.

It was one of the craziest and most intense trips of my life. It was thrilling and horrendous. As we traveled across the country, we participated in demonstrations and teach-ins organized by local community groups at fourteen sites where nuclear weapons were built and tested, where uranium was mined and enriched — a veritable Where's Where and Who's Who of the business of destruction, at the highest levels. In New Jersey, we met up with Buddhist monks from the World Peace March and walked for three days into New York City, where we joined the other 999,960 people from around the world who had made similar trips to gather for the Second U.N. Special Session on Disarmament, to stand with their bodies and their children, their petitions and origami cranes, their buttons and banners to protest and demand an end to the study, development, and deployment of weapons of destruction. People from shops and banks came out of their offices and cheered us on as we approached the international rally in Central Park. One million people joined together on June 12, 1982, and peacefully demonstrated for a unified end to nuclear annihilation. It was the largest public gathering ever held in America. There was no violence. There were no arrests. It was a moment of ultimate unity, of supreme mystical, spiritual, logistical, practical, and physical uniting of a million people who cared about saving the earth and her people. It was magic.

Barbara cofounded the Empowerment Project in 1984 with her partner, filmmaker and producer David Kasper, providing facilities, training, and other support for independent producers, artists,

activists, and organizations working in video and electronic media. The Empowerment Project works to democratize access to the media and to provide the resources necessary to put the power of the media in the hands of individuals and organizations working to further important human purposes. An active writer and lecturer, Barbara presents her films and speaks internationally at colleges and universities on subjects such as "The Economics of Censorship" and "The Search for Truth: The Responsibility of the Media, the Government, and the American Public." She was decorated with the Gasper Octavio Hernandez Award by the Journalist's Union in Panama and is a recipient of the American Humanist Association's Arts Award for her "courageous advocacy of progressive ideas."

Elizabeth Pirruccello Newhall, M.D.

"Reproductive freedom is, to those with wombs, what free speech is to those with mouths — an inalienable right."

In 1995, Dr. Elizabeth Newhall was targeted by a national anti-abortion group, the only woman put on a list called "The Deadly Dozen." The FBI advised her to wear a bulletproof vest, to install bulletproof glass at her clinic, and to alter her route to work. When interviewed about the threat, she turned from the reporter to the television camera, as though looking directly into the eyes of those tracking her. "I will not back down," she said.

People tell me I'm brave to speak the truth about abortion, things I have learned walking this path with thousands of women over the past twenty-six years. But, in this crazy time of legislative restrictions and killings over essential health care, I feel more honored than brave. It is no more than what I teach my children to do when they witness injustice.

The Advocates for Life Ministries imagine they can stop the ancient right of women to reproductive autonomy by encouraging violence against physicians and the brave women and men who work with them to provide a technically simple, ethical, yet profoundly life-changing medical option. My name on their pathetic hit list scares me much less than the prospect of living in a world where women do not have control of their reproductive destinies. The last hundred years has borne witness to women's willingness to risk death and criminal penalties to obtain this simple privilege.

It has not always been so. It has not always been a religious, moral, or social crime. I've challenged computer-equipped Bible scholars to show me where abortion is condemned — they can't. Even the Catholic Church didn't have sanctions against abortion until the new god of science arrived in the mid-1800s. Prior to the discovery that tiny embryos (many smaller than the naked eye can see) existed in early pregnancy, only the woman's testimony that she felt movement verified her pregnancy. Up until that time, about halfway through the pregnancy, what she did was her business and her business alone. Midwives and herbalists gave tinctures and remedies to interrupt pregnancies early on, and no one thought to interfere. Hippocrates was not opposed to abortion as many claim — he was opposed to surgical abortion, often a riskier procedure than ingestion of medicines. In part to eliminate their competition in this arena, the men who dominated the new science-based medicine pronounced these herbal-induced abortions immoral and convinced state legislatures to make them a crime. Women, of course, were still half a century away from obtaining effective birth control or participating in the legislative process themselves.

The new laws didn't change the incidence of abortion one whit. Illegal practices thrived openly. However, the laws did increase the risks, mostly to poor women who were forced to do their own abortions. And the laws did increase the cost to middle-class women who now, also desperate to control the size of their families, were forced to break the law to protect their futures. City hospitals now needed entire wards to care for the women who hemorrhaged, became infected, or worse.

My story is about the first abortion I performed, a feat requiring the resolution of my moral fears, manifest by the discrepancy between my ethics and my practice. Although I became a physician in 1979, like most doctors, I had "good reasons" to leave the performing of abortions to others until 1987. No one likes abortion. Our ultimate ideal is a health care system so evolved and a society so enlightened that abortions are prevented. But abortion will not go away until birth control always works, sex is always consensual, and human beings never make mistakes. We will improve on the first two, but the third is a hard fact of life. I accept it. Our world will be enriched beyond imagination when all children are wanted and when women's choices about their lives can be actualized with support and respect, not guilt and violence.

I was raised in a military, Republican, Catholic family and didn't even know abortions existed until my first year in college in 1971. Like every other devoted premedical student, I sought volunteer work that would pass as experience verifying my long commitment to the care of patients and the study of medicine. The position that found me was abortion counselor in the back of a small church in Davis, California. My job was to assist women in locating the unadvertised, obscure clinics; facilitate transportation to them (they were all quite a distance away); and keep track of how many patients we sent so we could carefully dole out the free visits earned by making referrals. Cost was an issue for everyone. This was during the time when the "self-help" movement was birthed, and we all believed and hoped that free medicine for the people was imminent.

Naïve though I was, it was powerfully clear to me that abortion was handled differently and kept separate from other medical procedures. I was fascinated with why this should be so. I marveled that these women were left to a caring virgin such as me, however capable, to guide them through this significant event in their lives. We did all the counseling that they received, listened to them process their decisions, helped them with what information we had, and explained the procedure and the risks as best we could. Listening to them — most resigned, many pained, none overtly angry — I never made the connection that some day, assuming I made it to physician, I might be called upon to perform the procedure. I didn't ponder the ethics much — these women needed my help in obtaining what I considered a standard medical procedure. I needed the experience. That was all. I was learning medicine.

Unaware of the recent historical controversy, I saw my experience in the back of that small church as a kind of curious first glimpse of the magnanimous profession I hoped to join. I didn't let the job I was doing bother me. Life is messy. I was accustomed to religious dogma conflicting with what I learned in school, science always making better intuitive sense. It's probably no coincidence that, at the conclusion of that academic year, I was finally able to act on my long-held belief that any God I could believe in was not so punitive as to send human beings to hell simply for missing mass on Sunday, and I was able to quit my weekly "just in case" masses. I had done nothing but daydream there for years anyway.

I didn't encounter abortion again until 1978, when I was a pregnant (unplanned) third-year medical student at Sacramento County Hospital. On Wednesday nights, the medical students were assigned to care for the women admitted for second trimester abortions, which were inevitably the result of some painfully compelling circumstances. Many were among the most oppressed of women, abused or otherwise unempowered. Many were scared teenagers. Others were simply unaware of their options or too paralyzed by addictions to get help any earlier. Their needs demanded the utmost respect, care, and attention. Yet, the community often didn't provide the service, and locating a provider and arranging travel took time. Even then, raising money to pay for a procedure that's frequently and shamelessly disclaimed, delayed the women further, putting them at greater risk.

The rounds would start about five in the evening. First, a resident would inject saline into the woman's uterus, using no anesthesia. This initiates labor. I don't recall any pain control. I do recall plenty of pain. We medical students stayed with the woman until the fetus passed, usually sometime in the middle of the night. Then, the woman was taken to the delivery suite, where the residents did a curettage for the placenta. Again, no anesthesia. Lots of crying women. I was once again struck by how unlike any other procedure this was. Still I wasn't angry, just miserable for the women. And still, the "just in case" Catholic part of me didn't imagine doing it myself. There seemed to be plenty of people to provide the service.

When I graduated in 1979, I learned an important lesson about following my heart and not my head. I entered training in internal medicine instead of gynecology. The price was a miserable year in a field for which I had no passion and had entered, just because it was supposedly the most respected. Another child and five years later, I began my second internship in obstetrics. Experienced now, and pregnant for a third time, I finally grasped how big an issue abortion is for women and how tough an issue for an ex-Catholic like me. I envied my fellow residents who learned abortion procedures without a trace of conflict. I even envied those patients who chose it without conflict. With what knowledge I had, I helped those who were unsure make their decisions. I knew unequivocally that we deserved a world in which women made their own decisions, especially in health care and even more especially in reproduction. Moreover, it seemed to malign the sanctity of the birth process to impose it on unwilling women. It was just the idea of being on the end of that aspirator myself that posed the dilemma. I trusted women's certainty that it was a just choice for them, yet continued to delay confronting the issue personally. It wasn't something I was ready to do, or had to do yet.

Still, I puzzled over my discomfort and became increasingly bothered about why I couldn't resolve my hesitation. Was I really so bound by the Baltimore Catechism that I couldn't see my way clear to providing a service made legal to protect the public health? I read all I could find about fetal physiology. Was it possible a fetus could feel? From all I studied, I came to believe that there is no awareness, nor any possibility of awareness, even in the second trimester. In the most common of procedures, during the first trimester, this possibility is so remote as to approach impossible. I had seen plenty of abortuses via miscarriage and, while the distinction is hard to define, that a handful of bloody glop is not imbued with humanity is pretty obvious. There is no religious service for miscarriage. It is grieved, but not honored as a death. Moreover, it is Christ's birth, not his conception that is celebrated. I was comfortable with physiologic lines being ever blurry and indistinct. That's the nature of biology. Competent practitioners must be content that we cannot know all of nature's secrets and yet, despite this, take action.

Taking action is what finally settled my hesitation, the opportunity presenting itself in which intellectual procrastination, rationalization, and confusion gave way to providing medical care. It came about in my obstetrics clinic with a patient who was schizophrenic. She was an in-patient at the nearby mental hospital at a time when only the very sickest were still institutionalized. She could not care for herself, much less a baby. Two had been taken from her already. She took lithium, a drug capable of causing heart defects. She was on multiple other medications, although none which, in my honest opinion, made abortion, *ipso facto,* indicated. Her partner was also a patient at the mental hospital and also unable to care for himself. I felt it my duty to talk with her about her options. Initially, she wanted to continue the pregnancy. But, on the day of her fourteen-week appointment, she looked me square in the eye with a clarity I'd never seen before and said, "You need to do an abortion on me today, Dr. Newhall." I knew that to tell that woman to go somewhere else was inhuman and wrong. Her doctor-patient relationship was with me. She trusted me and had asked for service. To deny her was to judge her by laying my doubts on her decision, and I supported her decision. I did the procedure with no help, and no delay, and no guilt, and no bad dreams. I had finally acted on my strong belief that excellence in obstetrics and gynecology includes the respectful provision of abortion to the women who seek it. On demand and without apology.

A year later, I graduated and spent the summer working in an abortion clinic, finally learning to do the first trimester procedure that takes about one minute and is about twenty-five times safer than childbirth. Until, together, all of us physicians step up to the responsibility of providing this simple service, women remain judged, disrespected, and inadequately cared for, particularly by the widespread practice of packing them off to a separate clinic. Our actions don't reflect the message in our health care policies. We support her right to choose in word only, when it's not so much what we say as what we do that is important to her. If we have the skill to provide the service and believe that it should be provided, yet fail to do so, we are like the physicians who refuse to treat AIDS patients because they're afraid of contracting the disease. We are ethically lacking.

The appropriate response to terrorism is for providers to draw this service into the mainstream of medicine where it belongs yet has never been. It is safe and simple to learn. Our procrastination and "just in cases" have always cost women respect and made targets of the few who offer this medically sound service. I wish every physician who, like the majority of Americans, is pro-choice would wear a button that says, "I perform abortions and/or support those who do." We are safest when we all do procedures and we do them inside big institutions.

It's time for the silent majority to speak before the well-funded opposition intrudes again into the privacy of the doctor-patient relationship. The American College of Obstetrics and Gynecology's stance is uncontroverted and clear. So is the American Medical Association's. Women's health and the public health suffer when access to abortion is restricted. How can this be happening twenty-six years after *Roe vs. Wade?*

In August of 1995, my colleagues and I completed the Oregon portion of the nationwide mifepristone (RU486) trials. Instead of happily proclaiming our involvement with this exciting breakthrough in women's medicine, we conducted these trials quietly and in secret, behind bulletproof glass, with our location intentionally obscured to protect patients, providers, and science from threatened or actual violence.

The trials, themselves, were exhilarating. Women not only wanted the option of medical abortion, but they also wanted to participate in bringing this drug to

America. They were courageous. They walked past tight security and not one asked after her own safety.

Finally, an option exists in which the woman, herself, literally performs the abortion by swallowing the pills. We have long known that a uterus can empty by itself, and many women prefer bleeding to avoid instruments and surgery. The bleeding is clinically no different from a spontaneous miscarriage, except it is usually quicker and requires a curettage much less often. Every community has at least one health care professional who can deal with a miscarriage. That's all the skill it takes. Soon, every community can safely use mifepristone. Soon, no woman under eight weeks pregnant will have to drive eight hours across an entire state to receive routine health care. Soon, no woman seeking medical treatment will have to live with the fear of being traced and targeted.

In July of 1996, the new drug application for mifepristone submitted by the New York–based Population Council to the U.S. Food and Drug Administration was heard and acted upon affirmatively. Approval was recommended, pending submission of the final data from the American trials confirming results here to be commensurate with the European data. I was thrilled to testify before the FDA subcommittee, to be among the speakers for the Population Council asked to discuss an American clinician's experience with the drug. I couldn't have asked for better closure. The lengthy public testimony was calm, clear, and dominated by eloquent supporters that ranged from conventional medical groups to women's groups to nurses and patients. The group that heard the report recommended approval nearly unanimously. One of the physician members whose questions had revealed her anti-choice beliefs throughout the hearing responsibly voted with the majority that the drug was both safe and effective. I so appreciated her professional honesty. I knew then that this drug's own merit will be all that is ultimately needed to assure its revolutionary place in the history of women's medicine.

The women and men of the choice movement are among the most committed and talented individuals with whom I've had the privilege to work. I love this work. I laugh sometimes, as I know this struggle will one day seem as quaint and self-evident as the fierce debates over women's right to vote and the morality of birth control. Reproductive freedom is, to those with wombs, what free speech is to those with mouths — an inalienable right. Women can, must, and do make competent, moral medical decisions with regard to this personal matter . . . as they have since time began. They deserve as many options as medicine is capable of offering. No less. As Liz Karlin, a much-harassed provider in the Midwest who has written eloquently on abortion, said in the *New York Times*, "Women have abortions because they want to be good mothers." I would add to that those women who elect not to be mothers because they want all children to be loved, honored, and cherished. We all deserve no less.

In late 1998, Liz joined four other doctors, Planned Parenthood, and a clinic in suing anti-abortion groups responsible for fliers made to look like wanted posters, offering a $5,000 reward for information about "The Deadly Dozen" doctors branded "Guilty of Crimes Against Humanity" and for a Web site called "The Nuremberg Files" that likens doctors who provide abortions to Nazi war criminals. The Web site lists abortion providers, their addresses, license plate numbers, and the names of their children. Lines are drawn through the names of three doctors on the list who were killed. Arguing that these actions were threats, which are not protected speech, the doctors and clinics filed a multimillion-dollar federal lawsuit under federal racketeering statutes and the 1994 Freedom of Access to Clinic Entrances Act, which makes it illegal to incite violence against abortion doctors and their patients. In early February 1999, an eight-person jury ruled in their favor.

The Courage to CHALLENGE

Anita Roddick

"There's so much outrage that's tempered and squashed and watered down in business because of these strange myths that you can't be political, that you can't challenge the system."

A woman with a fiery dedication to human rights, the environment, animal welfare, and indigenous tribes, Anita Roddick is the founder of The Body Shop. In the beauty business, she is that fierce enigma who lambastes her own industry for lying about what can and cannot be done by a wrinkle cream or sacred antiaging formulas. As the keynote speaker at a Century City Chamber of Commerce luncheon in the Los Angeles area, where she received the Women of Achievement Award, she told the audience:

> *It is so ironic that the platform on which I have chosen to stand and from which I shout for social change is a stage absolutely run by men — the cosmetics industry. Now, at best, it is dull, run by men who create needs that don't exist. At worst, it pisses me off because its main job is to make women unhappy with what they have. It plays on insecurities and self-doubt by*

> *projecting impossible ideals of feminine beauty. It is racist — never celebrating women outside of a Caucasian culture — and it sells on sex and glamour.*

Roddick, in fact, advertises her products less than she does her issues and causes, using political and social messages spread across the sides of her trucks and on billboards and posters. "We see any empty space as an opportunity to create an atmosphere, deliver a message, make a point." Pretty gutsy. Her business isn't so much about stores as about delivering those messages about our world and what is happening to it.

The big dilemma about courage is that you never think anything you do is remarkable when it's instinctive. I can tell you what I've done that's been really controversial, what's put me on a brink. But one of the scariest things I've done was around the time of the Gulf War. It was a stand I took that could have cost me my company.

I was in America on business at the time, visiting my stores in Boston. I felt strongly that we, as a company, should be supporting the notion of United Nations sanctions against Iraq because I simply felt that we should be doing anything other than supporting military engagement. We were not alone in demanding development of the sanctions — the U.S. churches and labor unions supported sanctions. The idea of going to war was so obscene to me, especially to go to war in a repressive country and not for a moral issue but because of the commercial implications of oil production in Kuwait. I initiated a big sanctions campaign in England that was directed at the U.K. government and the major players: George Bush and Saddam Hussein. We had people writing letters and phoning. We gave customers the fax numbers of Margaret Thatcher, Bush, and Hussein and asked them to send a personal message. We plied our customers with the message, "Keep the Sanctions Going." At this stage, especially in Britain, there was a huge obsession, fueled by the media's gung ho approach, with going to war. Mrs. Thatcher favored going to war, and for the rest of us, there was no chance to be asked, to debate the issues.

I had billboards put up in Littlehampton, home base of The Body Shop. Quotes from Jesus Christ. From Gandhi. From some of the great warmongers, who were actually pacifists five minutes before they died. I put them up without any permission. We took a clear stand, and the town was confused. Littlehampton is a blue-collar town. Most of the grandparents have probably experienced war, but the kids have no notion of it. The English, in general, were just gung ho for the war: forty thousand kids off to the Gulf in nanoseconds. What I was doing wasn't very popular. It riled people up, and it riled up my company, split it right down the middle, male and female — I think because of the male myths surrounding war. One of the board members rang me up in America and said, "We've got to take these billboards down." And I said, "Over my dead body. They come down and I leave. This is not negotiable."

I came back to the U.K. and closed down the offices for an afternoon, and we held a huge intercompany debate. We had staff come down from our sites in London to join in the discussions at our headquarters where we had hundreds of people working. And as we debated, I thought, *What if the whole company says, "Anita, stop this. We have to follow government policy."* What would I do? If I endorse the democratic process, I have to follow democratic minds. And I just knew, absolutely knew, I would be out of the company like a bat out of hell. I would have to leave my own company. The tension for me was huge. And I remember thinking, very fleetingly, *What would it be like if I didn't have my baby?* I birthed it. I shaped it for all those years. And I hadn't yet done all that I wanted to do with it. Yet, I was willing to leave it on an issue of principle. I had my heart in my mouth thinking, *Oh, God, they know I'm antiwar, but I'm not going to be able to persuade anybody that this campaign, this stand we're taking, is right.*

And then, I don't know, something amazing happened. Some time ago, I had spent about a week with a group of our employees, a guy who drove a truck, a guy who packed the boxes, a woman who filled the bottles, and others, about twenty of them. I had them up to my house, just talking about life. (I used to do this, take twenty people and spend three, four days and just listen to them.) That particular time, we had talked about war and we had talked about violence. One man had been in the Falkland Islands and another had served in Northern Ireland during the Irish troubles. They said that, in reality, actions change your values. The experience of participating in the Falklands War and serving in Northern Ireland had changed their whole notion about war absolutely. And it was those guys who stood up during the debate and eloquently spoke. They told what war was like, the reality of it, who benefits and who doesn't, and it was as if two guardian angels had plopped down — and I didn't need to say anything.

I didn't leave the company, but the experience brought me to a scary brink. Very few people, maybe a dozen close colleagues, knew what was going on with me, what would have happened — that I would have left the company. It was such a personal, private decision. And the strange thing is that when something like that happens, you have no options. Either you don't have the time to think — and so what comes through you is instinctive, and therefore, the most honest expression of who you are — or you just know you have no alternative. I don't know if it's courage, but there's a clarity of purpose when nothing is negotiable.

I felt that same clarity during my face-off with Shell Oil. No question, that took courage. That took incredible courage.

In *Our Agenda,* a publication of political and social issues supported by The Body Shop, we speak about this campaign, about Ken Saro-Wiwa, the Ogoni people, and Shell Oil: "On 10 November 1995, the Nigerian military dictatorship shocked the world by executing innocent writer and human rights activist Ken Saro-Wiwa and eight other environmentalists for their involvement in a long and peaceful campaign about homelands polluted by the oil-drilling activities of Royal Dutch Shell and other multinational companies over thirty years."

Although I never met him, Ken Saro-Wiwa became a good friend, through his letters, his family, and colleagues. Saying his name still makes me stop in grief that he's gone. He was an environmental activist and writer, one of the most popular in Nigeria. When he visited The Body Shop offices in the U.K., he said he wanted to go back to Nigeria, and when I heard this, I just knew he was going to be arrested. In his last speech to the military court in Nigeria, he said, "Shell is here on trial. . . . The company has ducked this particular trial, but its day will surely come and the lessons learnt here may prove useful to it for there is no doubt in my mind that the ecological war the company has waged in the Delta will be called to question sooner than later and the crimes of that war be duly punished."

I tried desperately to stop that ecological war in the Ogoni. We lobbied members of Parliament. We demonstrated at the Nigerian Embassy. We protested outside the headquarters of Shell. We organized letter writing and brought the Ogoni issue to the attention of the media. When you challenge another company on a moral issue, or an issue of human sympathy or behavior, you set yourself up for assault, unlike when you challenge for a market share, in which case you can be as mean and dirty as you like. On the Shell issue, I contacted a number of companies belonging to the socially responsible business movement and basically said to them: "You've got to help us on this one. We need to have international outrage about what the Nigerian military dictatorship and Shell have done. What Shell has done in Nigeria would be banned in the Western world." Some offered support, while others said they couldn't because they never challenge another company. Others excused themselves by saying they were not perfect as a company either. Well, neither am I perfect, but that shouldn't keep your sense of outrage in a straight jacket. There's so much outrage that's tempered and squashed and watered down in business because of these strange myths that you can't be political, that you can't challenge the system.

We challenged Shell in a very honorable way. I have learned a lot from tribal peoples, and one lesson is that you change by shaming. Gordon, my husband, spent a lot of time with top officials of Shell in England. We offered to collaborate with them. We have a very strong, very bright group of academics who work with us on environmental issues. We offered to put together the assessments on pollution, social impact, environment, and so forth. We would do all the homework, all the strategizing, all the academic stuff. And we'd plop it in their laps so they'd know what to do. But no, they wouldn't touch it.

Working with the Ogoni community in Nigeria — doing ads, standing up and speaking out — was not easy. In England, activism by women is seen either as shrill or as marketing. People never support you because you care passionately about something. They cut you off and ridicule you. Standing in this huge courtyard outside the Shell building with a microphone and hundreds of people looking at me and, in a very studied and diplomatic way, talking about what was happening — it wasn't easy. I love storytelling, but standing up there against one of the biggest multinationals in the world and challenging them . . . scary. Scary in a physical sense, certainly, but what was even scarier was how Shell officials simply looked on passively at the demonstrations against them, taking no action on the plight of the Ogoni. In the end, that corporate passivity has cost them. The constant public outcry about their conduct in Nigeria has forced them to invest heavily in reputation management.

I think whatever bravery I have in me came from my mother. We were one of a handful of Italian immigrant families in the seaside town of Littlehampton on the English Channel, and Mummy begrudgingly sent us to Catholic Mass conducted by a priest whom she hated. When my father died young of a heart attack, the priest came knocking on the door and said, "Mrs. Perella, we know your husband was an atheist, and you're lucky we're going to bury him at St. Catherine's Church." Mummy took a bucket of dirty water and threw it at him. Now there was a courageous act.

The four of us Perella children attended school at the local convent. Mummy would squash garlic between our fingers to fight the incense and there we'd be, all four of us lined up and smelling down the place. When the nuns told the Perella children to put on skirts, Mum said, "No, it's cold, wear trousers." Sacred cows were shattered early, and I learned a rebel's brand of courage.

I've done things that, when I look back on them, I wonder, "Why ever did I do that — it was crazy." I travel six months out of the year to learn from indigenous tribes, and I've known at times, in the blink of an eye, we shouldn't be someplace, that we were in danger. That's the bit I don't understand, the nonnegotiable, the driven part. George Bernard Shaw said, "Life is no brief candle . . . it is a sort of splendid torch which I've got hold of for a moment, and I want to make it burn as brightly as possible before handing it on to future generations." Anyone who does a courageous act passes it on. We learn from them. I guess, in a way, that's what I'm doing with this life of mine.

The Body Shop has grown to a $900 million business with 1,600 shops in forty-seven countries over the last twenty-two years, making it the United Kingdom's leading international retailer and giving Anita a broad platform from which to speak.

Kory Johnson

"It's hard to always be the minority, not because I'm Mexican and Native American but because I'm a woman willing to stand up and speak out. It's not normal in my town. I'm not sure what I want to do when I grow up, but I know what I won't do. I won't sit down, shut up, or go with the flow."

Awarded a 1993 Environmental Youth Award by President Clinton, Kory Johnson is a college sophomore who has already spent half her life as an environmental activist.

In 1988, my sixteen-year-old sister Amy died on Valentine's Day. She had been sick her whole life with heart problems. If you ask me, it was the contaminated water my mother drank when she was pregnant that made Amy sick.

Many children in our small community died from similar birth defects, thirty-one altogether. The water supply had been contaminated with chemicals from crop dusters. The Centers for Disease Control (CDC) said we lived in a "cancer cluster."

The number of children with cancer was twice the national average. Birth defects were high; so was asthma. But, as our local paper, the *New Times,* said, "Although the Arizona Department of Health Services (DHS) was aware that children were dying with abnormal rates of leukemia on the west side, the state agency had refused to investigate and had, in fact, labored to suppress information on the cluster."

Six months before Amy died, she and I wrote to the *New Times,* because we heard that someone at the DHS had said it was just fine that they spent $128,500 to move into new offices but didn't have a penny to spend on research on the cancer cluster. "We're just a couple of kids from Maryvale, but we're scared because our town is falling apart and nobody cares. . . . We have a big problem, and people ignore it and hope it will go away. It's not going away. . . . We need help and we need honest answers, even if they're ugly answers, we need the truth." We enclosed a drawing of a field of tombstones with children's names on them and a blank one in the middle with an epitaph that read, "Who is next and why?" We didn't know it would be Amy.

After Amy died, my mother took me to a bereavement group so I could grieve. A lot of other kids who had also lost siblings attended and, every month, we would end up crying. I asked some of the kids if they would like to start a group to work together for change instead of crying every month.

We started very small. The five of us called ourselves Children for a Safe Environment. We heard our parents talk about a hazardous waste incinerator company that wanted to come to Arizona and burn toxic waste from all over the country. Since our parents were going to public hearings, we decided to go too. I'll never forget the first time I got up and spoke. A man set a clock at five minutes and said I was not to talk about anything personal, I was to speak on facts alone. I was only eleven years old, and I didn't know about parts-per-billion, emissions, 99.99 EPA standards, particulates, or scrubbers. What I did know was that one of the incinerators was to be built in a small minority community next to a grade school and in a flood zone. And I knew that this company had a very poor track record: In other states where they operated incinerators, a high percentage of people in the area were sick. To me, this issue was *only* personal.

We had a lot of work to do and, since kids always seemed to draw the press, we had to know what we were talking about. We held candlelight rallies and protests, made signs, sent out mailers, wrote our representatives and our governor. We called a press conference to bring to people's attention the fact that this company had misspelled "environmental" on its logo. We went to many public hearings to embarrass politicians who had received campaign contributions from this company. Kids can be incredibly effective when we speak, especially when what we say comes from the heart.

We finally won. The incinerator company packed up and left Arizona.

Later, we began to receive calls from children from all over the country who wanted to organize children's environmental groups. Since I had founded Children for a Safe Environment, whose membership had grown to three hundred, they wanted my help. I was interviewed often and I was on the *Geraldo Rivera Show* for being a hero. My teachers were proud of me, but a few said I shouldn't protest. One told me that if I kept protesting, there wasn't a college in the country that would take me. Some of my other teachers whispered in my ear, "You're doing a great job. Keep up the good work." I wondered why, if I was doing such a great job, they whispered.

Over the next couple of years, we prevented two toxic dumps from being built and helped people organize recycling groups and neighborhood cleanups. I also spoke at Earth Day gatherings and rallies. Unfortunately, people would buy T-shirts and recycle a little and then forget until the next year. It's hard to make people realize that recycling, reusing, reducing; hazardous waste; and toxics issues are important and, if we want to save the planet, we have to make changes. Teaching little kids about picking up trash and planting a tree is fine, but we have a long way to go. For example, when I won an award from our mayor for getting the city to stop using Styrofoam, I was really upset that they had mounted it on Styroboard. When the media at the ceremony asked me why I was so unhappy, I said, "I guess the mayor didn't take me seriously." I didn't get any more city awards.

During my years of activism, one of the tough things was losing friends. Friends whose fathers worked for polluting companies weren't allowed to play with me anymore. People would yell things at me and my family. My aunts, uncles, and grandparents got harassed. My mother was arrested several times for trying to keep dirty industry out of poor neighborhoods and for protesting nuclear testing. The first time she was arrested, I was scared, because I thought being arrested meant you had done something bad and wrong. But when I heard that Martin Sheen had been arrested too, I relaxed a little, knowing he was a movie star and definitely not a criminal. Mom made collect calls from jail to radio stations to bring attention to the issues. She was in the news often and lost her leadership of a Girl Scout Brownie troop. She was also asked to drop out of my school's PTA because she wasn't a good role model. At first, I was embarrassed. Mom said it would just give us more time to work for change so other children didn't die.

But it seemed to me that people didn't care that our water was contaminated, that thirty-one children in our neighborhood had died, that a brown cloud hung over us during a weather condition called an inversion. The fact that my mother got cancer, that my grandmother died at fifty-three of cancer, that my sixteen-year-old sister died, all while living in this area, none of that mattered. What mattered was property and reputation and money.

Sometimes, I just want to quit. But then, the phone rings or a letter arrives, and a kid somewhere wants to know what they can do to help. And before you know it, I'm making copies and mailing out information.

Once you're in this, you're in it for life. You look at things differently. You question authority. You get in a few arguments with teachers and friends and family. But you speak up for what you believe in, even if it costs you a friend or good grades or makes you the conversation of the town. I don't mind.

I don't mind what it has cost me to do this work because my sister died and I don't have her near me to laugh with, to stay up late with, to watch scary movies with, to boy talk with, to dance with, or to do volunteer work with. I know she's watching over me. I know she's proud. But I'd rather have her here with me.

I'm a sophomore in college now. In spite of what my sixth-grade teacher told me, a couple of summers ago, I attended the University of California at Berkeley on a science and math program scholarship and spent an August working in the Raul Julia Mountain Rainforest in Puerto Rico. Like I said, once you're in it, you're in it for life.

In 1998, Kory won a prestigious Goldman Environmental Award, which is called by some the Nobel prize of the environmental movement and is given annually to six people around the world. That took her to the White House, and led to a whirlwind of interviews and speaking invitations from around the country.

Kory also received the first John Denver Windstar Youth Award for being the most environmentally active young person in the country. In addition to working for the environment, she does volunteer work with sick children, hurricane victims, and the homeless, as well as with AIDS groups. In September of 1996, she took part in a protest, along with Greenpeace and other environmental justice groups, at a railroad spur in Mobile, Arizona, to stop the arrival of forty-five train-car loads (about 80,000 tons) of DDT-contaminated dirt from a California Superfund site. It was Kory's first arrest.

Heather O'Brien

"Staring up the barrels of AK-47s into the bloodshot eyes of my Khmer Rouge captors made every muscle in my body rock tense."

Heather O'Brien has lived most of her twenty-nine years abroad, fifteen of those in Asia. She recently served with the United Nations peacekeeping operation in Eastern Slavonia, Croatia (UNTAES). As a Civil Affairs Officer in Vukovar, she assisted in negotiations between Croatian government officials and local Serb authorities, worked with the UN's multinational police and military, and organized humanitarian and economic projects. Currently, she works in Sarajevo for the UN's peacekeeping operation in Bosnia and Herzegovina (UNMIBH). She helped to conduct elections, provides political advice for the International Police Task Force, and contributes to policy on the return of refugees and displaced persons.

The effects of being a nineteen-year-old prisoner of the Khmer Rouge will, no doubt, be with me forever. And yet, what happened to me was but a small glimpse of what was forced upon an entire nation during two decades of war and poverty. It is an experience I rarely discuss, even when prodded by friends. It is very personal; it nearly killed me.

My experience in Cambodia made human rights deadly real for me. Not a concept, not a UN declaration. But flesh and blood. It put me at the cold end of an AK-47, where human rights do not exist. It gave me a new appreciation for those rights and a deeper determination to fight for them. And, it taught me about myself. I knew intellectually that within every person is a deep well of strength, always available to be tapped. But, in Cambodia, I discovered mine and found it to be far deeper than I could have imagined. Some people call this source courage.

If I learned anything from Cambodia, it is that true courage comes from within and to deepen one's sense of courage, one must not just wait for, but actively pursue, deep challenges. This is what I did every step of the way that summer and I stretched myself way beyond all preconceived limits. . . .

Southern Thai-Cambodia border, August 1989

Bouncing peacefully along in the back of a pickup truck, with the tropical evening air blowing through my hair and exotic aromas from the street hawkers randomly hitting my senses, I reflected nostalgically about the adventures of a summer that had fundamentally changed me and the course of my life. It was the end of three months traveling alone on the Thai-Cambodian "hidden border."

It had all started earlier that year in Los Angeles when I was a sophomore at Occidental College studying international relations. My favorite professor and good friend, Dr. Jane Jaquette, and I had just seen *Situation Zero*, a documentary about Site 2, a Cambodian displaced-persons camp on the border. The conditions in the camp were appalling, and the film had a considerable impact on me. As we walked out of the theater, I said with quiet conviction, "I'm going to find a way to get into that camp and report on what's really going on so the international community can do something to help." I didn't say another word to Jane about it until, after several weeks of intensive research, I had found a film crew headed for the Thai-Cambodian border who agreed to let me tag along with them to the camps.

Everyone was astonished that I'd found a way into the camps, because it was reputed to be nearly impossible. Jane and Professor Larry Caldwell got the political science department at Occidental hopping to find funding for the trip.

A few unexpected trip wires arose during my preparations and gave me the opportunity to reconsider my motivations. Why was I willing to risk my life diving into the middle of someone else's civil war and a Cold War conflict, possibly to be shelled, blown up by the mines that riddled the border, hijacked by gunrunners, or accosted by guerrillas? Trying to find a way into closed camps to bring out the stories of displaced people who had slipped from the awareness of the international community due to "compassion fatigue" — was this worth risking my life when I was only a teenager?

The Southeast Asian refugee crisis had been an integral and tangible part of my life for years. Hong Kong has been my family's home base since 1985. The Vietnamese boat people literally washed ashore right below my family's house, to be swooped down upon by the local marine police and whisked off to refugee camps. I had worked in a closed camp where outsiders were banned. It was terrible to see these desperate people within meters of freedom after traveling the South China Sea, only to be held captive in inhuman conditions for years.

Going to Cambodia was natural to me. I needed to find out the truth. Reporters seemed satisfied with dry political analyses of the shifting pawns on the Cold War chessboard. How could the international community be expected to respond to the third Indochina war without a complete picture of the human tragedy? I had to find a way to bring the personal stories back out of the camps. My heart and my mind were set.

I left Occidental after finals and flew home. That same day, the U.S. embassy in Bangkok reported border shelling in the area I planned to visit. I didn't say anything about it to Jane and Larry, hoping to save them unnecessary worry.

For the next few days, I ran around Hong Kong collecting all of the gear I'd need to be a reporter in the jungle, most of which came from the British naval headquarters. At the historically famous HMS Tamar, a generous major made sure I was "kitted up" with everything I'd need for a safe expedition, from fatigues and tropical boots, to a first aid kit and mosquito repellent that literally melted plastic on contact.

My last morning at home, the newspaper ran a huge article on the shelling of the camps I planned to visit. I tore it out before my parents could read it. At the airport, my little brother, Sean, hugged me and whispered in my ear, "Heather, I love you. Please don't get shot." Those sweet words echoed in my heart throughout the summer.

On the turbulent airwaves of the biggest typhoon of the season, I blasted off for Bangkok to begin the adventure of my life.

The only way to get into a camp was to obtain a pass from the Thai Supreme Military Command. For political and security reasons, they refused to give passes to almost everyone at that time, with the exception of relief workers. Over the course of several days, I worked my way up the ranks of the Thai military, until I managed to persuade a general to issue me passes not only to Site 2, the largest camp on the border, but also to camps run by every guerrilla faction: Site 2 (KPNLF), Site 8 (Khmer Rouge), Site B (FUNCINPEC), and Sokh Sann (KPNLF). Getting four camp passes was a major coup. Being granted entrance to a Khmer Rouge camp on Thai soil was unheard of because the international community was being told to look the other way about Thailand's harboring of communist insurgents.

I was on an adrenaline high for hours.

While the United Nations Border Relief Operation (UNBRO) provided humanitarian aid to the Cambodian displaced-persons camps (they weren't officially refugees), the camps were effectively run by each guerrilla faction and the Thai military. Being administered by different factions gave each camp a very different atmosphere, particularly the Khmer Rouge camps.

During the entire summer, I traveled the "hidden border," which was over 600 kilometers long, interviewing officials of UNBRO and non-governmental organizations, as well as the Cambodians in the camps to which I had passes and in the satellite bases around them. Every person had a story and every story was compelling. I listened to the pain of a KPNLF guerrilla who had been crucified over a fire by the Khmer Rouge. I interviewed children in Mao army uniforms who had been conscripted as soldiers at age ten for the Khmer Rouge. I spoke with smooth diplomats in Bangkok who viewed the increase in shelling only in terms of statistical battle reports and political points earned for the Paris conference that was about to start. I even followed the first UN fact-finding mission to negotiate with the Khmer Rouge deep in the steaming jungle one dawn. The summer was supersaturated with exciting intellectual and physical challenges.

I prepared for the last camp on my list, Sokh Sann, a new one and very unstable. Arriving in the southern Thai town of Chantaburi, I immediately called UNBRO to ask for a ride to the Republican KPNLF camp. The pass to this camp had been the most difficult to get. The UNBRO relief worker said that the camp had just been shelled and told me not to go, as they were expecting more shelling. I said I'd find a way there whether he took me or not, and that if he were really concerned about my safety, he'd take me. But, he wanted no responsibility for me.

Determined to get there, I got up at five the next morning, bought some steaming BBQ'd yams from the wet market, and started my search for a pickup truck driver who would take me out to Sokh Sann. An hour of negotiating with a huge group of local drivers led nowhere. No amount of money could get them to take me anywhere near Sokh Sann, because it was controlled by the Khmer Rouge. A shopkeeper who had been listening to the conversations told me that I was crazy to try. "Even the Thais don't go there," he warned.

The chief negotiator pushed his way through the crowd and announced that he had found someone crazy enough to take me. A tiny, nearly bald, decrepit old man with a few wiry hairs stringing from his face shuffled toward me. Shirtless, he wore only baggy black shorts held up by a string, and flip-flops. His skeletal frame, drooping eyes, and languid demeanor were signs of a lifelong opium addiction, and he drove a small Honda motorcycle complete with a skull-and-crossbones license plate cover. Was I really going to put my life in the hands of this guy? It was my only option.

I dislike motorcycles, and speeding along the highway, weaving through huge logging trucks that spewed smoke and were piled high with massive tree trunks was terrifying. I was sure we'd be knocked off the bike by one of the logs that stretched way beyond the end of the trucks and then be pancaked by the truck behind us.

Little by little, traffic dwindled until an hour passed with almost no other vehicles on the road. We turned off onto a smaller highway and I persuaded the driver to pull over and ask a group of women in an orchard for directions. While I waited in the sun on the bike, he descended into the orchard and squatted in the shade with the fruit pickers, all of whom had scarves wrapped high on their heads to protect them from the sun. After a long and animated discussion, he finally returned and motioned that the road to the camp was nearby. While I was worried that we had no company on the road, which was unlike routes to UNBRO camps and just what the Thais had said to beware of, the women seemed confident of their directions and so I urged us on.

We soon turned right onto a dirt road. Little did I know that by leaving the safety of the paved highway, I was leaving behind my only lifeline to civilization. But then, I didn't know what was up ahead.

The red clay road undulated with the hills through the lush green jungle. Riding the red wave was fun in the beginning — climbing up, then whizzing down the other side. The only problem was that it had recently rained and, after about a kilometer, the road turned into a leech-infested soup. The old bike had no traction to go up and no brakes to cushion going down. This meant that we kept crashing over. After landing painfully under the bike several times and after the engine finally sputtered and died from the accumulated mud, we had to walk.

My tiny driver and I carried and pushed the bike up the slippery hills and at the top, panting and exhausted, we got on, slipped down the other side with the engine off, then crashed in the soupy trough. Covered in mud, we pulled each other out of the muck, and continued to push up the next hill. At times, we had to slog through mud that was thigh deep, literally carrying the bike. I still don't know how we did it.

It wasn't just exhaustion that started to bother me. Roads leading to UNBRO camps were never this narrow and poorly kept. They were normally wide enough for two large supply trucks to pass, and the ground was always tightly packed from all of the humanitarian aid traffic streaming in and out of the camp. The state of this road was the first red flag that something was wrong. I kept repeating "UNBRO" and "Cambodian" in Thai to the driver and he kept nodding. So, I assumed he knew he was taking me to Cambodians in an UNBRO camp, and I scolded myself for not having patience. We pushed on.

At least four kilometers into the jungle, we met a group of Thai traders. By then, the road had flattened out and we were carrying the motorcycle and wading through leechy mud. The traders' pickups were so heavy with goods that they'd sunk. One vehicle had slipped off the road into the jungle. They were using bamboo poles to try to pry one of the trucks clear, but were losing out to the mud. We stopped and watched while resting. The sun was blazing and drawing out fields of freckles from my crisping skin. Not only was I burned and drenched with perspiration, I was parched so deep inside it felt like my organs had shriveled, and I was shaking from carrying the bike.

My opium friend talked to the men, while some women came over to me. "Sawadeeka," we all greeted each other. They must have noticed that I was getting sunburned, because they laughed while they took the *khrama* (long hand woven scarf) wrapped around my waist and showed me how to tip my head upside down and wrap it like theirs. We all had a good laugh at my new Thai turban fashion, which was gratefully cool. I started walking off the road a bit toward the jungle to sit in the shade, but one of the traders jumped up and caught me, vigorously motioning for me not to leave the road because of mines.

Such red flags kept signaling danger as we pressed deeper into the jungle. But each time, I kept telling myself that I hadn't come all this way to turn back just because I was a bit scared.

Farther down the road, we encountered a strange party: a family in nice, new civilian clothes and a man draped in a large, black army rain tarpaulin. From their features and dark skin, I knew they were Cambodian. Instinct told me something was amiss. The family looked acutely stressed, pulling strained smiles to cover nervous twitches. Their eyes darted constantly at the draped man who stood too closely behind them. It was sizzling hot with few clouds in the sky, so his plastic rain cover was odd. My driver tried speaking with them in Thai, but got little but nods in return. They made me feel very uneasy and were obviously under duress to be polite, so I hurried on.

When I turned to have one last look as they marched briskly away, I saw a terrible sight: the black butt of a machine gun poked out of the army tarpaulin, the other end pointed at the family. Where he was taking them and why I didn't know, but the encounter confirmed that I was in a pocket of the "hidden border" controlled by the notorious Khmer Rouge. The encounter triggered serious concern in me. This was clearly not the road to Sokh Sann. I was deep in Khmer Rouge territory, which meant one thing: I was in deep kimchee. This was a critical turning point. I had two options: turn back out of fear or challenge myself to see what I was really made of and carry on. This was a unique chance to get a scoop on the Khmer Rouge, find a hidden camp, get some exclusive photos, see a real Maoist guerrilla camp. While the danger had just ratcheted up exponentially, so had the appeal of going where few had dared to venture. More importantly, as far as I knew, no journalist had entered a real Khmer Rouge camp to carry out the stories of the families who were forced to live subhuman lives under these Maoist extremists. If the world didn't know about life under the Khmer Rouge — not just life in the showcase Site 8 Khmer Rouge camp aided by UNBRO, which was shockingly pitiful enough — how could the international community help put a stop to these human rights violations? I had to embrace the challenge and forge ahead.

From that point on, I paid even closer attention to where I walked for fear of triggering an antipersonnel mine, which the Khmer Rouge always planted in areas under their control. The sight of a small, thatched checkpoint hut as we plodded around a corner was a great relief. Finally, we had arrived. The closer we got, however, the clearer I could see the guard's distinctive uniform — the traditional Mao green army uniform and green cap with a red star over the visor. He was a Khmer Rouge guerrilla. He clutched a worn AK-47 and looked bewildered when he saw us appear out of the jungle. Hoping he would either give us directions to the UN camp — or if I was really lucky, let me slip into his camp — I took out my official documents from the plastic bag in my fatigues and walked over confidently. I asked him in English, Thai, and French if this was UNBRO's Sokh Sann camp. He stared vacantly at me, totally ignoring the documents.

Surveying the area, I was drawn to two sights. First, women with wood piled high on their *khrama*-wrapped heads were drifting in and out of the trees, fifteen meters ahead on either side of the road. Some had naked children playing at their feet. The second sight was more riveting: a vast complex of huts that snaked down and around the corner a few hundred meters beyond the checkpoint. Row after ordered row of brown-gray, dried palm thatched roofs extended into the jungle as far as the eye could see. Bingo. A real Khmer Rouge base. Now this was a story, this was big. I had to handle this right and figure out a smooth way to slip in.

Across the road was a flimsy red-and-white pole to stop traffic. Since it was linguistically useless asking permission to enter the base, I just ducked under the pole and started down the road toward the base. Big mistake. The guard yelled at me in Khmer to stop and ran down the road to catch me. He grabbed my backpack from behind and roughly dragged and pushed me back to the other side of the pole. Taken aback by his aggressiveness, yet dying to get some concrete evidence of this off-the-map place, I decided to risk taking some pictures.

The women eerily drifting along the tree line stopped as they noticed the scuffle between me and the guard. They looked picture perfect and an excellent cover for taking photos of the base. I turned my back to the guard and discreetly raised the camera to take a shot. This must have lit a fire under him, because he literally flew through the air and decked me. Stunned, I lay on the ground. Suddenly, my camera strap ripped into my neck as he tried to wrench it away from me. Luckily, it held long enough so that I could wrestle it back. No way was he getting my camera.

This time, I was lifted up off the ground by my pack and hauled on my back over to the hut. The guard was small but his strength was surprising. He didn't just drop me, he threw me on my face onto the wooden floor. Now I was scared. Now I knew I was in trouble.

Out of the corner of my eye, I watched my opiate Thai driver tactfully crawl into the jungle to lay low.

The guard stood over me, gripping his rifle tightly. He stared at me condescendingly, seeming to relish the fact that he was in command. His thin lips curled in a cold sneer over rotten teeth. He called over some comrades, who stood on all sides of the hut and pointed their guns at me. It was terrifying. Staring up the barrels of AK-47s into the bloodshot eyes of my Khmer Rouge captors made every muscle in my body rock tense. "You stay!" the guard growled, lunging his gun at me, "My Leader come!" He shouted orders at a comrade who turned and jogged off down the road toward the base, presumably to fetch "My Leader."

I sat on the wooden floor trying to figure out how to escape. Guilt crept over me as I remembered all the promises I'd made to my parents and professors: I wouldn't travel alone, I wouldn't go anywhere near a recently shelled area, I'd avoid the Khmer Rouge — the list went on. But those rules were made in safe, international, cosmopolitan cities by people (including myself) who had no idea what it took to function in an environment as challenging as the "hidden border."

While I was thinking, the women wood gatherers, children, and other men in

Mao uniforms congregated around the hut. The women wore shirts and sarongs covered in mud from the forest. Most had bare feet. The men were all in Mao uniforms with Ho Chi-Minh sandals made of rubber tires. Most of the children were naked. Soon I was surrounded by an impenetrable wall of faces. At first, I was curious, watching their expressions as they watched me. It was mutual culture shock. I had not been with real Khmer Rouge who had had no contact with the outside world, and it was clear that they had never seen a Caucasian before.

They looked me over meticulously, from my blue eyes down to my tropical jungle boots, whispering and pointing, even lying down to investigate the tread on my soles. I'm sure I was a strange sight to them — a young Caucasian woman in a T-shirt, British fatigues, and army boots, wearing a Khmer Rouge *khrama* around her head and appearing in the middle of the Thai-Cambodian border at a spot that increasingly seemed to be the doorstep of a giant hidden guerrilla base. The disconcerting part was being the focal point when their curiosity turned to suspicion and hatred. A core feature of Khmer Rouge xenophobic propaganda is that Westerners are tigers in disguise and eat children if you don't protect them. I had heard this from relief workers and refugees all summer.

After a while, the rancid stench of sweaty bodies, the unrelenting heat, and the intensity of hate became unbearable. I shot up and bolted across the hut. As soon as my feet hit the edge of the six-foot-wide platform outside, the guard caught me from behind and yanked me back down to the floor. There was no way out, I was really trapped. I felt profoundly alone, caught in an eerie otherworld. My sense of alienation from this culture of war, the mentality of these people, and the density of the jungle was overwhelming. It would have been different had someone else been with me to share the fear, to talk with, maybe to brainstorm our way out. But there was no one. And no one was going to come to my rescue. I was on my own.

By then, it was past midday. I hadn't had anything to eat or drink since five that morning and, after all of that heavy work with the motorbike, I was hungry and incredibly thirsty. Remembering that I always filled one of my pockets with candy for the kids who typically follow visitors around, I offered one to a beautiful child who had been watching me intently from the start. To my great shock and horror, as she sweetly reached out to take the candy, a soldier struck her so hard that she reeled backwards out of the crowd. As she cried into her mother's sarong, I wondered what I had done wrong. Maybe they thought I was trying to poison her. To show them my goodwill, I unwrapped and ate the very same candy. All the children were gruffly ordered out of the crowd, and I was left surrounded mostly by men who stood stroking long machetes with curved blades. A few played with handguns.

Fear was burning inside me now. Thoughts of never seeing my family, my friends and professors again, of rape and torture, seared through my mind. To try to calm myself, I hummed and whistled that inane song "Always Look on the Bright Side of Life" from the Monty Python movie, *The Life of Brian*. As ridiculous as it was, it made me feel connected to home.

A man in seventies civilian clothes pushed through the crowd. Here, I thought, is the esteemed "My Leader," but it wasn't. He was a "translator" who, in broken English, demanded to know who I was, how I had found this place, and what I was doing there. *Finally, someone with whom I can communicate,* I thought. *I'll be out of here in no time.* I dutifully presented my official documents, including my U.S. passport and my official camp passes from the Thai Supreme Military Command. I explained that we had gotten lost looking for the UNBRO camp. "I am American, I am a student," I told him, noticing with a cold grip in my gut that he was carefully pretending to study my passport — upside down.

"You lie!" he yelled.

"I am a friend of the Thais," I said, knowing that the Khmer Rouge relied heavily on the Thais for logistical support.

"You are a Soviet-Vietnamese spy!"

What? I cringed at the vehemence with which he spat at me. I tried asking him where I was, the name of the camp, but he refused to answer and yelled again, "You lie!"

I kept pointing at my U.S. passport. Until then, I had always held my passport in the highest regard and viewed it as my legitimate ticket out of any problem. But there in the jungle arguing with a Khmer Rouge interrogator over a blue book that held no meaning to him, it had lost its power as a link to the global superpower. I could rely now on nothing and no one but myself.

We kept going around and around: "I'm an American student, friend of the Thais," to which he would snap back, "You lie! You are a Soviet-Vietnamese spy!" Clueless as to where in the exosphere he had plucked such a fabricated identity for me, angry and insulted, I later learned the root cause of his suspicion.

The interrogation went on and on. He kept asking me, over and over, the details of how I had found the camp, writing copious notes as I spoke. Finally he stood up and yelled "You lie!" one last time, which was followed by an echo of "You stay. My Leader come" from the guard. *It's about time,* I thought. Half of me was looking forward to talking to the man, he had to be a more rational person — but then, the other half of me was terrified that I was now about to confront the man who could very well decide to kill me.

Fear was not an option, I decided, it simply was not. It was a weakness I couldn't afford now. No panicking, no crying, no loss of dignity by begging to be let go. I had to maintain my sense of composure, be rational, devise a strategy for escape. I had no idea how much I would need it.

The translator trotted down the road toward the base to find "My Leader," but returned alone half an hour later. "My Leader" was on his way, he informed me with a sickly sadistic grin. We sat and waited in a silence broken only by the buzzing of flies and whining of mosquitoes.

Suddenly, the guards snapped to attention. The dwindling crowd around us dispersed and was absorbed by the jungle. "My Leader" had arrived. I expected a battle-hardened, Khmer Rouge communist guerrilla commander to be an impressive figure, one who would instill chilling fear from the mere sight of him. "My Leader" was a small-framed man of dark complexion who wore Mao pants, an old white T-shirt, and Ho Chi-Minh tire sandals. He strutted over with a small entourage of advisers who lagged in the background as their commander approached the hut. The translator greeted his leader in the manner of a groveling sycophant, which made me despise him even more.

This is it, I thought, *time to stand up and persuade this man that I'm no danger to his base, to let me go.* I gathered myself for a long and detailed explanation of the situation, but was cut off. "My Leader" blatantly looked me up and down, asked me a few of the same basic questions I'd already been asked, whispered briefly with the translator, then withdrew. He curtly called over his entourage and after a few minutes' discussion, glancing and pointing at me, he turned around and walked back to the base. "Where are you going?" I wanted to shout. "You have to let me go!"

The translator returned with renewed gusto and barked at me to sit down. "My Leader" had ordered me to be taken farther into the jungle. The truck was to arrive soon. My heart started to race with panic. I'd heard the stories and read the books about what happens when one is "taken into the jungle" by guerrillas. You're murdered. That's it. "Where are you taking me?" I asked the translator. The only thing he would say, and he seemed to find great pleasure in it, was that they knew I was a Soviet-Vietnamese puppet spy. A few days earlier, a group of Soviet men had appeared at the checkpoint unexpectedly, taken photos, and left before the guard had a chance to apprehend them. Within a matter of hours, the camp was heavily shelled by the Phnom Penh–Vietnamese forces. The Khmer Rouge, therefore, concluded that the Soviets were spies disguised as cameramen who gave the enemy the coordinates to shell the guerrilla base. It was my bad luck and bad timing that I appeared right after this incident. The translator said they were going to severely punish those who had shelled the camp. I was the payback.

I could hear the roar of an enormous transport vehicle and looked up as it stopped in front of the hut. *Oh my God,* I thought, *they can't do this.* The translator shoved me toward the truck, yelling at me to get in the back with the soldiers. The truck was so huge that the tops of the deeply treaded wheels were above my head. I stood there, my mind racing, *This could be my last chance to escape.* My eyes darted around, looking for an opening. There wasn't one. If I ran, I'd surely be shot.

I felt like all the energy was draining out of my body, a cool sickening coming over me at the thought of being killed. My stomach twisted inside. My muscles tensed, my arms shook as I tried to haul myself up into the back of the truck. Suddenly, two men grabbed me from behind and threw me forward. I flew up and landed on my face in the grease and muck on the floor of the truck. The soldiers sitting inside had a good laugh. I picked myself up and sat on a crude wood bench. I was surrounded by Maoist guerrillas clutching AK-47s and leading me into the unknown.

Chugging through virgin jungle, the truck climbed over fallen trees and lurched in and out of deep ravines. The twenty-minute ride was so violent that after being thrown across the truck several times, I decided to hang from the metal frame holding up the tarpaulin cover. It was scorching hot from the sun and burned my hands, but I barely noticed. I had to find a way to detach mentally; it was the only way to deal with what was happening. I searched for a place deep inside myself, peaceful. Detachment gave me distance from the moment; it let me concentrate. While I'm not usually a very religious person, I did some heavy duty praying on that ride. But I wasn't begging God to spare my life; I wasn't angry at Him for letting me get into this nightmare. After being deeply touched all through the summer by the hundreds of children in the refugee camps and knowing that many of them would never live to be nineteen, I was grateful for the life I had lived, a colorful, fulfilling, and exciting life in a relatively short span of time. In that detached and peaceful place inside, I thanked God for my wonderful parents, professors, friends, and said that if He intended to take me now, I had only two requests: 1) Take care of my family and friends and don't let them suffer for my death, because never knowing what happened to me, they could blame themselves for letting me come to Cambodia in the first place; and 2) Please don't let them torture me — make it quick.

The brakes slammed on. We jerked to a stop a few hundred meters from a river. Before I knew what was going on, I was thrown out of the truck and barely caught by a group of soldiers waiting for us.

My senses were hyper-heightened, and I surveyed the area, absorbing every bit of information possible. Dozens of guerrillas grimly armed with AK-47s lined the perimeter of the clearing. The heat was so intense and the humidity so thick that it seemed to deaden the sounds of the jungle around us. The only noise was the incessant whining of the mosquitoes and the roaring of the river in front of us.

Someone shoved me toward the river, where "My Leader" and the translator were waiting and talking in low tones. I squinted at the river. It was a mass of brown churning water, speeding by to my right. The sheer force of it was tremendous as it roared and surged around unseen boulders below, carrying trees that had been uprooted and were now crashing and rolling downstream.

The two men stopped talking. The translator turned to me and, seemingly on edge, took a deep breath. "My Leader orders you to swim across the river to talk to the Thais. If you want to be free, you must talk to the Thais." He wouldn't look me in the eye and shifted from foot to foot. He pointed across the river.

"Where are the Thais?" I asked, seeing nothing but jungle.

"In the trees," he answered. It took a while, but eventually I could discern tree houses and, the more I looked, the more trees I could see that had been converted into military cells. I was suddenly beside myself with relief, I was that close to a U.S. ally, one who would at least be able to read my Thai Supreme Military Command camp passes, right side up. But, there was one major problem: we were separated by a raging river.

I stared at the river and, as I watched, more branches and whole trees thundered by. Suddenly, I realized what was really going on. If I tried to swim that river, I'd drown. If they wanted me in that river, they wanted me dead. It would be easier to drown me than to answer to the Thais for the bullet-ridden body of a *forang* (foreigner).

My little brother's words suddenly screamed through my mind: "Heather, I love you. Please don't get shot." I couldn't bear the thought of him, and my parents and friends, in such pain due to my stupidly getting myself killed.

"Are you crazy?" I screamed at the translator, furious at this pathetically transparent method of murder. "I'll die if I try swimming to the Thais! I refuse! You find a way to bring them here. They'll be very angry with you if you cause me to die like this!" I knew this wasn't the face-saving way to negotiate with Asians, nor with people in power, but I had to fight for my life.

The translator, still shifting, looked at his boss. I stared "My Leader" right in the eyes. If he wanted to kill me, he was going to have to do it directly, not through this wimpy puppet and not using this poorly staged murder. Minutes passed, so long that time seemed to have turned elastic. I willed myself not to be the first to break eye contact. "My Leader" surprisingly backed off.

He called over more troops while shooing the translator and me away. Shaking his head, the translator pushed me back from the river bank, where dozens of men were now talking in groups and yelling orders to one another. After tying a rope to a tree trunk, one soldier stripped down to his black underwear and was tied around the waist with the other end of the rope. Slowly, he walked into the water and started making his way across the river. The men lined up along the shore to cheer on their comrade. About ten meters out, he started to swim. The river kept sweeping him downstream, and the men on shore fought to pull him back up again. It was a long process, during which he was sucked under for long periods of time, alarming his comrades who were yelling and heaving on the rope to bring him back to the surface — and I was supposed to have blithely swum across?

Cheers went up when he climbed out onto the muddy bank on the other side and waved back at us. He disappeared into the jungle and returned half an hour later with a Thai officer. Freedom, I thought, and watched nervously as they set up the pulley system and started back across. It was equally harrowing.

"My Leader" greeted his drenched Thai counterpart at the water's edge, and, through the interpreter, briefed him on the situation. A few minutes later, the Thai officer marched over to me and asked me the obvious questions about how and why I was there, which I politely answered, producing the official Thai military documents. He took them and, thankfully, started reading them right side up. He ordered us all to sit on the ground in a circle. The soldiers stood encircling us.

The Thai and the Khmer Rouge launched an explosive round of questions. I answered as smoothly as I could under fire. They kept searching for holes in my story, kept questioning my motives: Why was I in fatigues, where did I go to school, why would any western university be so interested in sending a student to the other side of the world to research Cambodians, why would a young American care so much about Cambodian displaced people? The questions went on and on. The translator peppered the conversation with "You lie!" every few minutes. I could barely stop myself from throwing a punch at him.

The tension rose to a fever pitch. My freedom was flying in Thai, Khmer, English, and French, in debates between a dripping wet Thai officer in skimpy underwear; a military commander of a fanatic Maoist Cambodian guerrilla group that killed millions of their own people; a brainwashed, yes-man Khmer interpreter who was positive that "I lie" but couldn't read the evidence showing otherwise; and myself, a nineteen-year-old American university student who happened to have grown up in Asia and cared enough about the major political crisis there to find out how it affected the people. The scenario reached a nearly comic level. I would have laughed had I seen it on TV. But the horror of it all was that it was so vibrantly and deadly real. My life hung on a fine line, and these military fanatics were deciding how long until they would cut it. I struggled to maintain a sense of distance so I could still be rational and think.

It was late afternoon by then, and the shadows were growing long. I knew that if

I didn't make a move and force them to decide, I'd be stuck as a Khmer Rouge prisoner overnight and things were likely to disintegrate badly. My heart raced at the thought. Urgency kicked in, hot impatience with these men who refused to believe me, refused to recognize the authority of the official passes I'd worked so hard to get. I did a quick evaluation of each person in the circle — they all seemed hot and tired and disagreed with one another, weaknesses I hoped to capitalize on. Most of the soldiers were by now lying on the ground, except for a few standing behind us. My official documents and notebooks had been given to the translator, who held them loosely in his hands.

I took a deep breath.

Then, I lunged to my feet, grabbing my documents and notebooks. I yelled at the Thai officer and the Khmer leader in a loud and commanding voice that I was leaving, they had no right to keep me, and would be in serious trouble with their commanders if anything happened to an American friend of the Thais. Everyone was startled and stumbled to get to their feet. "I'm going to turn around and I'm going to walk away," I yelled. "To stop me, you'll have to shoot me!"

They looked at each other, confused, but I was sure that at least the Thai commander knew what was going on. I spun around and stormed off. I was met head on by the guerrillas who had been standing behind us. At that point, I was determined to get out and didn't care at what cost, so I barreled right through them and kept going. Thankfully, my Thai driver, who had been a ghost all day, was lying beside his motorbike a ways up the road. He saw me coming and quickly started the bike. I jumped on behind him and with one giant rev, we were off — sort of. The hill was so steep and slippery, the wheels didn't have much traction. With everything in me, I willed that bike up the hill.

I was pumped with adrenaline and gripped my camera by my side to take one last picture of the guerrillas in green Mao uniforms with AK-47s and red-and-white checked *khramas* draped across their chests, an exclusive Khmer Rouge photo. Proof that I had actually been there — as much for myself as anyone else. What I did was just plain stupid. I aimed, hoping the soldiers were in frame, and pressed the button. Suddenly, the camera whirred in auto-rewind.

From behind me, I heard the cracking of guns being loaded and a man shouting angrily, "You, stop! Stop, you!" We did not stop. I waited for the hot thud of a bullet in my back. I was positive I'd be shot, and even imagined where it would hit. A strange shift took place while I waited for that bullet. Everything warped into something marvelously surreal, like being in a different dimension. The trees ticked by in such slow motion that I swear I could have counted the bugs on their trunks. At the same time, my life flashed before me in a stunning Technicolor blaze: my family, friends from childhood, relatives, my favorite professors — I traveled to all of the places around the world where I had lived and to many I had visited, rocketed through a lifetime of experiences in a matter of minutes. The closest explanation I've been given for this surreal experience is that it was like a near-death experience. While I wasn't physically injured, I was absolutely positive that I was about to die. It gave me a glimpse into another dimension of life that I could never have imagined in my wildest dreams.

We sputtered our way back to the main highway. The sun was close to setting, and from a distance, I noticed a white UNBRO Jeep speeding toward us. I flagged it down and asked for a ride; I was so shaky, I was afraid I'd fall off the motorbike.

The young UN official rolled down his window, releasing a blast of pop music and a cool wave of air-conditioning. Ironically, it was the very same Colombian who had refused to take me to Sokh Sann. He asked if I'd found the camp and why I was so covered with mud. I told him a little about the Khmer Rouge base, but not much about how they'd treated me. I didn't want his pity, and I didn't want to sound like some damsel in distress. All I wanted was some water and a safe ride home. He was very interested in the exact location of the camp and what and how much of it I'd seen. It sounded like a big base and not one they'd heard of before. He reached in the back seat and shoved a bottle of warm water at me. A ride was out of the question, he said. Since I'd managed to get out there by myself, I could get back by myself. With that, he rolled up the window and sped off, leaving me standing on the roadside in the dust of a fading ride home to safety and taking with him much of my faith in the UN.

I forced myself to climb back onto the bike. For the first time that day, I was about to burst into tears. Soaking wet, shaky, weak, and badly sunburned, I clutched the bony frame of the driver and we slowly drove away. To stop myself from crying or falling asleep, I sang all of the happy songs I could remember from my childhood. I belted out the popular Singaporean song, "Sing your way home at the close of the day, sing your way home, drive the shadows away, smile every mile for wherever you roam, it will lighten your load, it will brighten your road. . . ." as we sped through the blackness of the Thai jungle.

That night in her hotel room, Heather got a call as she was pulling off the day's accumulation of black leeches. It was the Colombian from the UN. He and several colleagues needed to talk with her and were downstairs in the lobby waiting. She had stumbled upon a sizable new Khmer Rouge military base.

The next day, Heather got back on the motorbike with her Thai driver and went out again to successfully find Sokh Sann.

Ann Bancroft

"The things we overcome in life really become our strengths."

Ann Bancroft, who once narrowly escaped death after falling through an ice shelf into the Arctic Ocean, is the only woman to have crossed the ice to both the North and South Poles. At 31, she was the sole woman on the Will Steger expedition to the North Pole, the first recorded unsupported expedition under human and dog power alone. Four years later, she led the first all-women's expedition to the South Pole.

Often what we're publicly known for are not the things that required the greatest courage. I initially became known as the first woman to cross the ice to the North Pole. Being on that expedition was a childhood fantasy and rather than being afraid, I was exhilarated. Later, putting together my own all-women trip to the South Pole, I began to know fear because I was the leader, not simply a member of the expedition. It wasn't the South Pole itself that scared me, but the responsibility of something so big, and all the people who would be affected if we fell short of our goal. Because this dream of mine — to lead a major expedition on unknown territory and do something epic for womankind — was so big, if I failed it would hurt more deeply.

Yet, when I look back, neither Pole was my defining moment of courage. It's not that they were devoid of challenges and danger, but the hardest thing I have ever done had nothing to do with triumphs in extreme wilderness. It had to do with a very personal challenge, something I was never expected to do: finish college, get my degree, become a teacher. And I didn't realize until much later that my dream of being a teacher and my dream of being an explorer would cross one day to form a wonderful program for children and immensely satisfying work for me.

School was always pretty iffy for me, because I'm dyslexic. Reading is laborious: I'm very slow and have a hard time retaining information I've read. Academically, I've always struggled to keep up. When I was twelve, my parents had me tested for a learning disability at a time when dyslexia was fairly unknown, and we endured a barrage of tutors, starting in my elementary school years.

My parents never expected me to graduate from high school with any kind of college aspirations. I started at the University of Wyoming, but by my sophomore year, I knew it wasn't the right school for me. I decided to take off a year to look at other schools and figure out where I wanted to go. That scared the heck out of my parents, because they were sure I wouldn't go back. My older brother had just dropped out of college. My father had never finished. My mother was, she thought, a paper shy of having gotten her degree, which she found out later wasn't true. So I, the least likely academic, was our family's only hope for a college degree.

I did, in fact, go back to college the following year, because I was determined to become an elementary school teacher. I entered the teacher education program at the University of Oregon. For the next two years, I struggled with academics, like I'd always done. And I played sports, like I'd always done. But the cruncher came when my college advisor told me to give up on trying to become a teacher. Students needed to have a 3.0 grade point average in order to enter the practicum, the final phase when you actually teach, and I didn't have the minimum GPA.

"You can graduate," said my advisor, "you've done all the class work, but you can't teach."

I had never had an adult tell me to quit: Here, take the easy way out, just get your diploma. I think she saw me as one of those athletes who aren't very serious about education and, unless I was willing to devote more time to getting the grades I needed, I should just take the diploma and run.

"Well," I said, "that's not what I came here to do. The degree is worthless to me if I can't teach."

She suggested that I drop sports. At that point, I was playing field hockey. What she didn't understand was that athletics kept my spirit alive. It was something I excelled at, that gave me confidence, and it taught me more than just the game itself. By playing and by watching my coaches, I learned about teaching and coaching. I explained all this to my advisor, but she was unmoved. She still thought I should "get serious" about my course study and quit sports.

I refused. And it took everything in me to stick up for myself.

This woman was extremely strong, very intimidating, accomplished in her field, and very "old school." Standing up to her was frightening. But I knew myself, and I knew that a part of my spirit would die if I quit sports. If I hadn't had athletics in high school, I don't know if I would have finished. It was a critical part of my life, the place where I expressed myself. I had been a pretty shy kid, quiet and introverted. Athletics was where I held onto my self-confidence, where I learned my leadership skills. Kids have to feel they're good at something in order to be able to do the harder things. The harder thing for me was academics. Without sports, I'd never have made it.

It was my bad luck that my advisor sat on the committee that heard petitions from people who failed to get into the practicum and wanted to try again. I was faced with the very real possibility of not being able to do what I'd always thought I would do.

After several petitions to the committee, I finally got into the practicum, only to learn that my advisor was the person who would be grading my student teaching. I knew, however, that I'd do fine once I was in front of kids and, sure enough, from the moment I walked into the classroom as a teacher, not a student, I was in my element. The practicum flew by and even my advisor was surprised at how well I did.

So, my graduation was a pretty big deal. My entire family came to the ceremony. I was our first college graduate. And, as it turns out, my learning disability and my struggle to get through school was a marvelous training that I would use later on when I needed perseverance and courage.

Ten years later, standing in the bitter cold at the North Pole, I had the distinct thought, *This is not worse than school.* When I was having a bad day on the Arctic ice, that's what I would dredge up in my mind to keep me going: *School was harder.* The North Pole was a long endeavor — but school was longer. Most people think that my polar expeditions must have been the hardest thing I've ever done. In actuality, they were physical and that's where I excel, that's where I feel at home. They were not foreign environments to me. They felt very natural.

The North Pole expedition came about in one of those serendipitous ways that start when you bump into somebody. I was teaching at Clara Barton Open School, an elementary school in Minneapolis, Minnesota, and working at Midwest Mountaineering, an outdoor store, when I met up with Will Steger, the leader of the upcoming expedition. I had dreamt of dog sledding in the high Arctic and, in fact, had kept in my basement old articles that I'd cut out when I was younger, one of them about Will Steger and his dog sledding. We had met years earlier and when he walked into Midwest Mountaineering one day, we vaguely recognized each other. He was looking specifically for a woman to add to his North Pole team and, after checking up on me — asking people we knew in common questions like, what is she like under stress, how is she to travel with, how does she hold up elbow-to-elbow in a small tent — he called me and asked if I'd like to come up to Ely in northern

Minnesota to interview for a place on the team.

I jumped at it. I had a sense that this was the chance of a lifetime and I'd better scoop it up. I don't know where that sense came from, but somewhere deep inside, things like that register and you just react. I got in my car and headed up to Ely for three days to hang out with this guy. And it changed my life. It put me on a new track. I would never go back to a formal classroom as a full-time teacher, but this turn in the road would allow me to put two dreams together — one of being a teacher and one of being an explorer — to inspire children through a school program I would later create called Explorer in Residence.

It was 1986. I was thirty-one and about to become the first woman to cross the ice to the North Pole. There hadn't been many modern-day expeditions and we were leaving much of technology behind, so we could experience what it might have felt like to be one of those early explorers. I couldn't wait to go. I was young and eager and very naïve. I joke now that the courageous act wasn't the trip but traveling with seven men and forty-nine male dogs. It was a true adventure in that the eight of us were unknown, ordinary people following a dream, and it caught people's imagination.

But you can't do that twice — which is why there was something wonderful and yet bittersweet about that first trip. At the North Pole, I kept thinking, *I will never be here again.* At first, it was in the literal sense. I will probably never stand here again on this ice. But I've come to understand the larger essence of the phrase. It will never be the same because I will never be the same, the group will never be the same, we will have moved on. You can't go back.

We returned home heroes. We were invited to the White House. We got the red-carpet treatment from dignitaries, the international press corps, and President and Mrs. Reagan. I got marriage proposals. I was invited on a Mount Everest expedition. I was offered commentator jobs at local and national television networks. I was a hot ticket. All of it, to me, was simply the absurdity of quick fame. I didn't take any of it seriously. My dream was to lead a major expedition never before done.

And I wanted to do something educational for schoolchildren and the environment. I wanted to lead an all-women expedition to the South Pole.

I called it the American Women's Expedition (AWE). My goal didn't end at the South Pole. I wanted to make history by traversing the continent from one end to the other. The South Pole would be our halfway mark — from where we would start, it was nearly halfway to the other side of the continent.

The AWE trip was much more frightening than the North Pole, because it was my idea. Going on someone else's trip, being a team member rather than the leader was a lot easier. When it's your idea and you're leading it, you're the one fund-raising, yours is the name leading off newspaper articles, and more is at stake. The investment is greater. The potential loss is greater. The risk is greater, personally and professionally.

I was doing something I'd always wanted to do. This was truly a childhood dream, to lead a major expedition on unknown territory, as much as that is possible in this day and age. But the doubts were everywhere when it came to putting it together. I saw it in my folks, who didn't have a lot of confidence that I could pull off the trip and, in the three years that I was training and fund-raising and organizing, they barely spoke about it. Over this time, I came to realize that family and friends aren't always ready to make the journey when you are, and you just have to keep plowing along whether they have confidence in you or not. That can be very lonely. The challenge, whenever you create anything, is to persevere and push away the negative voices. And the more you accomplish, the louder they get. The key is to shut them off and trust in your heart where you're going. The tricky part is that naysayers can be useful in that they remind you to question whether you're still on the right path and they make you face your fears of failing.

As it turned out, the skiing and the pulling of the sled were the easy parts. Organizing the expedition and all of the logistics were the parts that made me go gray. The fund-raisers. Letter-writing campaigns. Grant writing. Phone calls. Talking about the vision of the expedition over and over again. Selling, or trying to sell, my project to individuals and to corporations.

I struggled badly with funding. The country had gone from the middle of the eighties, when businesses were very lucrative, to a recession and the Gulf War. Times had changed dramatically and corporate support was harder to get, especially for an all-women's athletic endeavor. I worked with a public relations firm and several fund-raisers and, three years later, I still lacked corporate support. "Get a man involved and then come talk to me," said one potential sponsor. Marlboro, Coors, and Exxon were interested, but I couldn't do it. It would have been too incompatible with my environmental and educational commitment to children. The trip was in constant jeopardy as I tried to keep volunteers and team members, as well as the public, interested and excited about an expedition that kept getting postponed. Folks who helped us out came and went, discouraged and disillusioned. Team members left because the financial pressures were so great and the struggle so hard. Every time I got a "no" from a sponsor, it got harder to keep people believing in the expedition, that it was worthy, that it was going to happen. In the end, AWE was held together by grassroots support. We sold T-shirts and posters to get to the South Pole. Kids and teachers and parents were the ones behind us.

When we finally pulled out of Minnesota at the end of October in 1992, we still didn't have all of the money to board the plane in Chile that would take us to the Antarctica continent. This was the biggest chance I'd ever taken. But I knew I couldn't postpone one more time, because we'd be forced to wait an entire calendar year, since the only time to go is during the summer months of Antarctica, November through February. If I postponed once more, I knew in my heart that the trip would never happen. It was already a four-year project and the fifth year would sink us. All the volunteers and all the folks who worked for us would be spent. So I went forward as if we had the money, convinced that, if we could just do what we were meant to do, which was pull sleds, we could make the rest happen. We just had to get to the ice.

When we left, the airport was chock full of our supporters and hundreds of kids seeing us off. I was the only one who wondered if we'd be coming back the next week. It was a bold move. Most people would think it was stupid, but I felt if I could just get us to South America, which was our jumping-off spot, to the flight company that was going to fly us to the continent, I would somehow convince them to take us. We headed out — four women, skis, and 200-pound sleds — for Punta Arenas, Chile, the southernmost tip of South America. No dogs, no men, no mechanized support vehicles, no money.

When we arrived in Punta Arenas, I finally had to tell the flight company that I didn't have all of the money. "But," I tried to assure them, "it will come. If you let us do this trip, the enthusiasm will build and the folks back home will be able to continue to fund-raise as we go across the continent and you'll get all your money."

They'd done enough expeditions to know that would be quite a gamble, and they were very angry, as they should have been. They tore up our contract. Of the two people who ran the company, I felt I could reach the woman through passion and heart and a handshake. But the guy really yelled at me for a long time. He had every right to, of course. This was an awful move on my part. I had been deceptive.

With the clock ticking in Punta Arenas, I continued to negotiate heavily for our passage. This was the only flight company that could fly us to the continent and they were charging us hundreds of thousands of dollars, the lion's share of our budget. I swore in blood that they'd get all their money, that we'd pay them $50,000 every month to stay out on the continent. Otherwise, they could come in and take us off, literally. Three days passed. We needed to be on the continent by November 1 or our window of opportunity would close. Finally, they agreed to take us.

With the contract rewritten, we readied to board the plane, only to discover that it had a mechanical difficulty. More precious days slid by. Finally, we got under way and flew out. They dropped us at the edge of the continent. And disappeared.

The first week is always the worst part of a trip for me. You'd think it would be the most exciting. Everything's before you, all the possibility. You're fresh, you're fat, you're not hungry. You've just gotten out of a shower, it's the cleanest you'll be for the next four months. But when you look out at hundreds of thousands of miles of Antarctica, and you're standing at the edge and it's white in every direction and you know you have anywhere from 100 to 120 days ahead of you to get to the other side of the continent, it's pretty daunting. I felt sick to my stomach. I wanted to go home. I wanted to quit before I'd even begun. It's a good thing I do these things in remote places so there's no backing out.

After about a week, I got my sea legs. *Oh yeah, this is what I came to do.* And then, it got exciting. I trusted that I was in shape and I'd done things right and we were where we were supposed to be. And I found the rhythm with my sled. I love pulling a sled. You almost become one with it when you're feeling good and moving along, taking care of matters, with all your belongings right there. The world seems to make sense.

You don't go very fast pulling a 200-pound sled, sometimes against 50 to 75 mile an hour winds. It's about 1,800 miles from one end of the continent to the other and you're going about a mile to a mile and a half an hour, tops. That's a lot of miles to cover in the time frame that Mother Nature gives you. You need some luck with the weather in order to get out before darkness reappears and the cold gets prohibitive.

Antarctica is the coldest, windiest place on earth and drier than the Sahara Desert. The wind would get so loud that I couldn't hear my team members behind me. In every direction were hundreds of miles of rippling white snow. The undulation of the vast exposure of ice gave me the sensation of being on an ocean, frozen, with absolutely no living thing around, anywhere. Only us, tiny dots on an endless landscape, blue above us, white below. It's a remarkable thing, beautiful.

The thermometer would drop to forty below. Living in the cold is blatantly frightening to a lot of people. I, myself, don't like being cold so it's kind of funny that I would get into these polar trips, but I'm very drawn to wide open places, and in particular, the cold, wide open places. They have a magic that's really unique, both in sound and in sight. I don't know how to articulate how quiet it was in Antarctica. Sometimes, all I could hear was the blood going through my own body, I could hear the gush as my heart pounded. Silence there had a sound so quiet that I could hear me, one of the only living organisms around.

The danger we faced on this trip wasn't so much the kind of danger we'd face if we were mountaineering, where each day our lives might be in jeopardy. It wasn't a moment-by-moment fear I felt, but an occasional fear when I was terribly cold or suddenly struck by our isolation. Our jeopardy was nestled in the remoteness of where we were and the fact that, if someone got injured or sick, we were too far from doctors or hospitals to get help. And even if the injury or sickness wasn't severe, we could afford little time to tend to it. We had food and fuel for a finite number of days. And Mother Nature was slipping through her precious summer months — we had to move every day in order to make it to the other side of the continent before winter and darkness set in.

Early in the trip, one of our team members, Sunniva, sprained her ankle and had to take painkillers to keep going each day. Much later, worn down and in the colder temperatures of high elevation, she contracted bronchitis. It slowed us down, and it created a great deal of stress, both practical and personal. We were all concerned about our timeline, and we were all concerned about her health. She kept getting sicker and sicker to the point that she collapsed on two different days after pulling only a mile. She was hypothermic, edemic, and she wouldn't eat or drink. Consequently, she got very weak very fast and was in a life-threatening situation. And it was all because of our remoteness. That's when we were at our greatest risk.

We were about a 150 miles from the South Pole, ten days away from the halfway mark of our traverse. I radioed our pilot and asked about the possibility of an evacuation. "She looks like she's turning for the worse," I said, "and I'm worried

I won't be able to bring her around. She may not be with us tomorrow." They radioed back that they couldn't get to us; the weather and ice conditions were too rough. You can have all the technology at your disposal, but it isn't always going to work in the cold, and it isn't always going to be possible to be rescued. You have to be prepared to take care of yourself, which is one of the great thrills in undertaking a remote expedition like this, but also one of the great risks. We tried to minimize those risks by being very calculated, very prepared, but they remained.

We took two days off while Sunniva slept and we force-fed her and made her drink. At this point in our trek, we were going up in altitude. We'd started our trip at about 3,200 feet at the edge of the continent and we were going up to 12,000 feet at the pole, so the air was getting thinner and the temperature was dropping.

Finally, we made it to the South Pole. It's an odd place now with spacelike structures put up to house science and research teams. I'd seen pictures, but still it was a strange sight after being out in the vast expanse of snow and ice for so long. And here were people, the first people we'd seen in our sixty-seven days of isolation. I felt a tremendous pride at the four of us having made it. I felt relief. But at the same time I was apprehensive and disappointed, because it looked like we were going to have to give up the traverse, crossing the full distance of the continent from one end to the other, which is what we had come to do. We all had a big discussion about it. I made the tough decision that two of us would go on and two would go out, the injured person and another person, who was struggling emotionally from the extreme weather, whiteouts, and sensory deprivation. This wasn't a popular decision, but our whole way of living out there was divided into pairs. We lived in tents in twos, our food system was set up for twos, so to go on with three would have been logistically difficult.

The next dilemma was our ride out at the other side of the continent. We were planning to hitch a ride on a cruise ship that sails into the waters near Antarctica. People get off, look at penguins, hop back on, and float away. They pay a lot of money to do that. The company that runs this shipping line said they'd pick us up and get us out of Antarctica for nothing. "All you have to do is talk to our folks and tell them what your experience was like." The hitch was that we had to be there by February 17. They wouldn't wait for us. "We have paying customers, you understand, so you've got to be there on time or we go." I had agreed because we didn't have enough money to fly out.

By the time we'd reached the South Pole, we were ten days late, and with this illness, we hadn't been able to make up any of the lost time. We weren't going to make that ship and to pick up two of us at the other end of the continent would cost an additional $350,000. We didn't have any companies or corporations footing the bill and saying, "Keep going, we know you can do it." We had just the average, everyday person saying, "Go for it." I had to decide whether or not to let them keep saying, "Go for it," at this price. The temptation was to continue on, use our emergency money to get out. The flight company requires you to take out an insurance policy that covers an emergency rescue flight. We could fib a little, call it an emergency when it wasn't. I wanted desperately to talk with our office and have somebody else help me with this decision. Of course, our radio was out just then. I was there, by myself, making this horrific decision.

It was the hardest decision of my life. It remains that to this day. I was sitting at the bottom of the world in the best shape of my life with food for forty-five days to take me to the other end of the continent. I knew in my bones that I could make it, every indicator said "Go." And the only thing holding me back was money. It was horrible.

But, as horrible as it was, I learned that the things we do in life leave a legacy. This trip wasn't about just me. It was everyone's trip, all the supporters, all those kids. We had 250,000 kids going with us via computer linkup through an educational program we'd set up. They were learning about Antarctica, about women's issues, about the environment. The decision I had to make was for everyone, and plummeting us into $750,000 of debt felt like an irresponsible legacy to be leaving. As reluctant as I was to learn this lesson in this way, I came to understand that there was a bigger picture beyond my own ambitions. Somebody coined the phrase, "Antarctica belongs to no one, but the journey belongs to us all." That was really what our trip was all about. It was an expedition propelled not by corporations, but by a grassroots movement. No one had ever done that, so we were writing a different kind of history and perhaps a more important history.

The most painful moment came shortly after I'd made the decision to pull out. Another expedition was on the ice at the same time. They were British, two guys, and they had started from a different point but otherwise were doing the exact same trip, pulling sleds, and trying to make a traverse. They arrived at the pole two days after us. We were still there. I had just made this decision. I was heartbroken and I had done a lot of crying and soul-searching. But I still had the option to change my mind.

When they came skiing in, we were really excited to see them. The leader of that expedition had also been to the North Pole — only about ten of us in the world have been to both poles, and two of us were sitting on our sleds in the same spot, at the same moment. We talked about our differences in philosophy and strategy: He had major sponsorship and, even though he didn't think they would make it all the way across the continent because they were in pretty rough shape physically, they were going to go as far as they could go and use their emergency money, tell that little fib. I told him I couldn't do that, we were pulling out.

The moment it hit me that I had really made the decision not to go on was when I watched them ski off in the very place I would have been skiing two days earlier. Every temptation in my body was to send my team home and just ski on. It was devastating. To this day, I wonder if it was my one chance and it's gone. The British team didn't make it across the continent, they had to pull out. So, the traverse still remains one of the few challenges of its kind in the world — and one I yearn to meet.

With modern-day explorers, it's not so much the land that's being discovered, it's more an inward journey. I learn so much about myself in those faraway places. When I was on Antarctica, I came to understand my life path after all these years. I had been so envious of people who, from the age of six, knew that they were going to be physicists or surgeons or whatever. I'd always wondered where I was meant to be. Teaching was pretty darn close, but something was a little amiss. It came to me on Antarctica.

When you're pulling a sled, there's not a whole lot to do with your mind all day long. I would write my mother letters in my head, with every intention of trying to get them on paper. One day in the middle of a letter, it struck me, *This feels so great. I love doing what I'm doing.* And I suddenly remembered a moment in my childhood. We lived in a rural area, and right out the door was an alfalfa field. We had a big winter storm one day and, loving storms, I went out into it. It was snowing buckets. I went deliberately into the alfalfa field and started mimicking pulling a sled. I chose the field because the snow was thigh deep, so it was a real struggle and I could mime how heavy this imaginary sled was. I have no idea where I got that notion. But, recalling it as I was pulling my sled toward the South Pole, I thought, *Oh, I am supposed to be doing this. I've been thinking about this since I was a little girl and here I am pulling this sled.*

I finally realized that what I was doing was what I was supposed to be doing all along. I'm a teacher, but I'm also an explorer. The way I give back to society is by raising awareness of the environment, by shrinking the globe for kids and teaching them about success, failure, and risk. My classroom is these trips, these faraway places.

Ann Bancroft designed an Explorer in Residence program, which she calls her excuse to be in schools for two or three days a week. She gives presentations of both of her trips and goes from classroom to classroom, talking about science, geography, and math; the environment; and women's issues. Her AWE Educational Foundation is focused on promoting courageous endeavors by girls and women and annually gives an Ann Bancroft Award for leadership and achievement in life and work. In 1995, Ann was inducted into the National Women's Hall of Fame. She still dreams of traversing Antarctica and is currently planning that expedition through her company Base Camp Promotions.

Senator Patty Murray

"When I ran for a seat in the United States Senate, I was considered a nobody. I didn't have a long political background. I didn't come from a family of wealth. I didn't come as an insider Democrat who had risen up through the ranks. I was a common person. I was a woman."

Patty Murray is a United States Senator from the state of Washington.

I never really intended to become involved in politics. I got a degree in recreation from Washington State University and wanted to teach young kids. When I had my own two children, I enrolled in a community college parent education course that both parent and child attended. While I was in class learning parenting skills, my children were in the preschool. One day, I went to class and the teacher announced, "We're not going to have this class anymore, they're going to take it away because of funding."

I was stunned. "Who made that decision?" I asked.

"Olympia," she said, "the state legislature."

I had never been to Olympia, had never had a reason to go to our state capitol. I did now, and I didn't think twice about what I had to do. I put my two kids in my car, drove down to Olympia, and started asking people, lobbyists, interest groups, legislators, staff, "Who's making these decisions, and how can I talk to them?" I thought that if they realized the effect of what they were doing, they'd stop. That's when I was told by a state legislator that what I had to say made no difference, "You're just a mom in tennis shoes." I remember it vividly.

I drove home very angry, because I was being told that my voice wasn't as important as the opinion of these guys in suits. I was being told that what I cared about in my community wasn't as important as some other big issues in the legislature. I said to myself, "I'm not going to let them get away with this." I began by making phone calls. I called instructors in my community college program from Yakima to Spokane to Vancouver and said, "Give me the name of a parent in one of your classes." They gave me names, and I called the parents and said, "My name is Patty Murray. You've never heard of me, but here's what the state legislature is doing to the class you're in. Will you help me?" In three months time, I had joined fifteen thousand parents together in a group we named the Organization for Parent Education, and we went after the state legislature. We wrote letters and made telephone calls. We signed petitions. We held a demonstration in the state capitol. And we ended up getting the program funded again.

That's what got me into politics in the first place. And it taught me a lesson I've used ever since: You have a choice. You can gripe about what people are doing, or you can go out and get involved and work your tail off and change what they're doing. I much prefer the second alternative. You feel better at the end, win or lose.

After that experience, I wanted to stay involved in the decision-making process of my community. I decided to run for the Board of Education because I had been at their meetings, and though the school board members were all nice people, they were all retired. These older people — one woman, four men — were deciding the fate of my children's education. I thought, "Who on this board understands little kids? Who sees the realistic perspective?"

When I'd been on the school board for a while, I was asked to lobby the state legislature on behalf of education issues. I kept returning to Olympia and watching the state senate, and I kept getting frustrated. I'd talk to senators and representatives and, then, I'd watch policies get put into place, but clearly my voice wasn't registering. This may seem a horrible thing to say, but one day sitting in the gallery, looking down on the senate, it occurred to me that I was looking down on a lot of old, bald heads. Maybe one of the reasons why I wasn't being heard was that no one on the floor could understand what I, as a mom with young kids, was concerned with in our schools. It struck me that if I wanted to be heard, I was going to have to be *on* that floor. Being on the outside wasn't enough.

So, in 1987, I announced that I was going to run for the Washington State Senate against the incumbent, Bill Kiskaddon. I had no idea what I was getting into, I was so naïve. All I knew was that I was still angry at that legislator who had put me down, who had had the gall to say who I was without knowing me. I wanted to show him that moms in tennis shoes have every right. I was so angry it didn't occur to me how difficult it was going to be, how much time it was going to take, how much courage it would take, or what I would have to face up to in the next year. I was actually told that I was too short. I was told I didn't know anything, that I couldn't run against an incumbent, that I wouldn't be able to raise money. I guess my outsider status challenged me and I guess it gave people a choice they'd been looking for, because I went out and beat an incumbent who had been there for fifteen years.

I had been a state senator for three years when the Anita Hill-Clarence Thomas hearings were held in the Senate Judiciary Committee and, like the rest of America,

I watched. Looking at that panel of fourteen mostly elderly, white men presiding over the issue of sexual harassment, I thought, "Oh, wow, what have we done? These people don't mirror what I see in my community, or what I see in stores, or what I see anywhere. How can they be writing policies for this country if they don't reflect the rest of us?" I attended a community event that night with a group of friends and everyone kept saying, "Did you see the Anita Hill hearings? Can you believe this?" And I just blurted out, "I'm going to run for the Senate." I literally felt that if I wanted to go to the ballot box and vote for somebody who looked different, I needed to run. If I wanted to make a difference, I'd have to be sitting on that panel, saying what needs to be said.

The reaction from my friends was, Oh, my God, here she goes again. When I made it official, the reaction from the political insiders was: You cannot succeed. When I ran for a seat in the United States Senate, I was considered a nobody. I didn't have a long political background. I didn't come from a family of wealth. I didn't come as an insider Democrat who had risen up through the ranks. I was a common person. I was a woman. I was told there's no way I could raise enough money to campaign. I was told I had no right to run. The next person who ran for the seat had to be somebody who had paid their dues. The insiders wanted somebody who had built up all the IOUs that one accumulates over time in a political career. Maybe they wanted somebody they felt they had more control over.

In my heart, I knew that the most important thing I could do for my kids, for my community, for my country, was to run, win or lose. Giving people a choice at the ballot box was critical to me.

Running for the United States Senate is a daunting challenge. It is overwhelming to raise money. If I had known then what I would have to go through, I'm not sure I would have gone ahead. But, at the time, I wasn't thinking about the nitty-gritty, difficult things. I was thinking about the end goal: *I've got to make a difference; somebody's got to do this.*

Winning put me on the inside where the challenges are even more intense than the ones I encountered in the state senate.

One of the first chances I had to put actions to my words was the Tailhook scandal, the Navy's tacit sanctioning of their young fighter pilots in spite of sexual misconduct claims brought against them. People who had been involved in the Tailhook scandal were being promoted, given four stars, and retiring. The Senate had never questioned anybody's retirement at four stars before, and the consensus regarding this issue was, "Let's not start now." To do so would put senators in an uncomfortable position. I went home for the weekend and decided, *I didn't come here to feel comfortable.*

I knew the risk of speaking out was huge. Would anybody respect me when I was done? Would they be willing to work with me or would they be so mad at me that they'd stonewall me? My gut said, *If I want to make a difference for the future, I've got to speak out on this now.*

Around this time, while attending a Senate Democratic retreat, I went to the other women Senators and said, "I can't keep quiet about this." I think we all had come to the same conclusion, and together we decided to make an issue out of it by opposing the four-star retirement of a former commander of the Navy's Atlantic Fleet who had been accused of failing to protect a female lieutenant from reprisals by other officers after she made accusations of sexual harassment. It was a risk for all of us, but it was the right risk to take. In the end, we didn't win, but I withdrew my amendment blocking his four-star retirement in exchange for a promise that the Senate would more closely examine military nominees. I think we changed people's viewpoint on the military and made the military wake up and recognize that they live in a different time and that they, too, have to deal with issues of sexual harassment.

Respect and camaraderie are important in the Senate. *Do unto others what you want done to yourself.* You may oppose someone's position, but how you present your opposition is very critical. You don't make people look bad. With the Tailhook issue, I frankly made people look bad. But, sometimes, you've got to do that in order to move in the right direction.

While I needed a certain measure of courage to deal with these kinds of conflicts, my entire political career has also required courage on many levels from my family. When I plunged into the heat of my first political campaign, I thought I could keep what I was going through away from my kids, shield them from the ugly side. But I learned quickly. Something would appear in the paper or they would hear about a debate from a friend, and they'd have to defend me with no knowledge of the situation. I learned very early on to sit down with them when somebody was about to print something unkind or a negative television ad was about to air. "Here's what you're going to hear," I would tell them. "Here's what I believe in, here's my side. You don't have to defend me if you don't agree with me. You're more than welcome to say to your friends that you don't agree with me."

When I was in the state senate I was working on a bill to require bicycle helmets for kids under fifteen. My son Randy was twelve. He was adamantly opposed to wearing a bike helmet, and he organized a petition drive against me at school. My husband said, "Where do you think he learned that?" I respect my son for it. I've taught my kids that you don't have to sit back and take what you don't believe in. You organize people, you fight back. And I'm proud they feel that way too.

I remember one day, when my daughter Sara was in her early teens, I came home exhausted and fed up. I can't even remember what the incident was, only that, by the time I got home, I was really tired and thinking, *God, why am I doing this? I'm working so hard. Am I getting anywhere; is this really worth it?*

Sara asked me, "What's wrong?"

I said, "I don't know, it's just one of those days. I'm wondering why I'm doing this. It seems so incredibly difficult."

She just looked me in the eye and said, "You're doing this so I can one day."

I was shocked. She had spoken the absolute truth. That is exactly why I'm doing this. I know I have to do a good job, not only for myself, but for the next generation of young women.

Among other issues that she backs, Patty is a strong advocate of efforts to fight domestic violence and to increase awareness of the economic problems faced by battered women. She hailed the February 1999 announcement by the Clinton Administration that more federal funding will be made available to states and communities to help them deal with domestic violence through increased law enforcement, more shelters and victims services. "We have worked hard to bring this issue out of the shadows," she said, "and now we need to provide the resources to law enforcement, battered women shelters, and service providers to put an end to domestic violence in America." She continues to use her position on the Senate Appropriations Committee to increase funding for efforts to end domestic violence.

Sarah Weddington

"For a lot of women, one of the hardest things about leadership is the desire to be liked by everyone. That's often inconsistent with leadership. It's certainly inconsistent with taking positions on very controversial issues."

In late 1971, Sarah Weddington argued Roe vs. Wade *in front of the U.S. Supreme Court.*

Standing before the U.S. Supreme Court at age twenty-six took a lot of courage. But it was even scarier to make the decision that I would be the one to argue *Roe vs. Wade,* because the case had such huge implications: Did the Constitution, under the right to privacy, protect a woman in the making of her decision about the appropriate response to a pregnancy? The stakes were so very high and I cared so very much about the outcome.

I had filed a motion asking the court to allow two people to argue the case and the court had said no. So, the job fell upon the shoulders of one person. And it was incumbent upon that one person to prevail, because once the court makes a decision in a big case like this, it probably won't hear another case on the same issue for a long, long time. Onerous consequences.

To have argued *Roe vs. Wade* and lost would have been horrendous. I would, of course, have agonized about what I could have done differently, or that I should have let somebody else argue it, or that I should have spent more time preparing — there would have been all sorts of self-recriminations. But bigger still would have been the effect on the whole abortion rights issue to which so many people were giving so much time and energy.

Originally, I had no idea *Roe vs. Wade* would become a U.S. Supreme Court case. I was doing research for a professor at the University of Texas Law School when a group of women approached me. They were primarily graduate students at the University of Texas in Austin, involved in consciousness-raising and counseling women about how to avoid pregnancy, at the same time trying to help those who already were and wanted to abort. The law in Texas made abortion illegal except to save the woman's life and they wanted to be sure women got good treatment, not in back alleys or places with a reputation for awful medical standards. They came to me to research whether they could be prosecuted as accomplices to abortion if they told women where to get an abortion, either legally in California or illegally in Mexico.

I found a number of cases pending around the country that challenged state abortion laws. In 1969, I filed the case that became known as *Roe vs. Wade* with the help of Linda Coffee, a law school classmate and friend. Since one of the things that makes the Supreme Court more likely to take a case is if lots of similar cases are pending nationally, I simply thought we were part of the building block process, that a decision in a lower federal court pertaining to the Texas law, which is where we started with *Roe vs. Wade,* would be helpful in getting some *other* case to the Supreme Court. I frankly didn't think it would be our *Roe.*

In a way, I'm glad I didn't know. Had I known it would occupy twenty-seven years of my life, I'm not sure I would have been as eager to run down to the courthouse. I didn't realize, really, what the costs — or the gains — would be in the long term.

If somebody had asked me at the beginning of *Roe vs. Wade*, "Would you try a Supreme Court case?" I would have said, "No, I'm not competent to do that." I was twenty-six. I hadn't been with a law firm. I had never handled a contested case. I had only done uncontested divorces, wills for people with no money, an adoption for my uncle. When it became evident that the case would go to the Supreme Court, others offered to argue it. Some pointed out my inexperience, which was inarguable — almost everyone had more experience than I. But there was a group of women lawyers involved in the issues who felt very strongly that it was a woman's case and that a woman should argue it. While a man could do just as well on some of the constitutional aspects, a woman would be much more passionate in presenting the effect of pregnancy on women, the weighty importance of a decision to have an abortion, and why women are the only appropriate ones to make it, certainly not the state.

My co-counsel Linda Coffee, who had worked with me on the case from the beginning, could have been considered to argue the case, as could other women lawyers. But I guess in the long run, I felt it was right that I do it, because nobody would work harder, nobody had been more involved in the case from the beginning, nobody had spent more time on it. And, my devotion to the issue was fueled by memories of my own illegal abortion in Mexico during my last year of law school. My husband Ron, who had gone with me, was also a lawyer dedicated to *Roe vs. Wade*. When we learned that it would be accepted by the Supreme Court, we both quit our jobs in Fort Worth — I was working as the first female Assistant City Attorney for the City of Fort Worth and Ron was in a plaintiff's litigation law firm. We came back to Austin and set up our own firm, so we'd have full time to work on it.

I would put in two years of my life getting ready.

When I finally went to Washington, even though I was nervous about doing a good job, about being able to answer all the judges' questions, not overlooking anything, it was a different kind of nervousness than I felt over that original decision to argue it.

The morning of December 13, 1971, was clear and crisp. Betty Friedan told me later that she felt her "historical Geiger counter" clicking madly that day as she made her way to the Supreme Court to witness history in the making.

I got up early to review my notes and have breakfast with a couple of people like Ruth Bowers who had been very helpful in funding the case. Ron and I walked over to the Court a good hour before oral argument was to begin in order to avoid demonstrators. I couldn't be distracted by people shouting at me or shoving through a crowd. We laughed briefly that I'd probably slide right through anyway, because no one would guess I was the person arguing the case. I was too young.

As we approached the Supreme Court building, my adrenaline was pumping. And yet, this wonderful sense of calm came over me from all the months of preparation. It was as though all the pieces had been set in motion and I was just playing out the final scene. The demonstrators weren't out yet, but a line of people snaked out the front door and around the side of the building. Some I knew and they murmured, "Go get 'em, Sarah" and "We're pulling for you."

We headed straight to the clerk's office to pick up a card authorizing me to carry materials into the court. Then to the Marshall's office, which is in charge of the seating. I had arranged to have a lot of people in the court that day. Each of the attorneys is given six seats and I had convinced the clerk to give each side an additional six. Then, I found out that the Attorney General wasn't using all of his seats, so I got a few more. I began to see all these friends who had come for the case and it was very helpful because it kept me from just sitting around and being nervous. It was like having a cheering squad. Once we were in the courtroom, they couldn't say or do anything, but I knew they were there.

Thirty minutes before the court was to start, I went into the lawyer's lounge to review my notes one last time and just calm down. I discovered there was no women's room in the lounge, only a men's. So, I went to the clerk and asked, "Where is the ladies' room?"

He said, "It's down in the basement." So I had to hurry and then I was worried about being late. Today, I'd just post somebody outside the men's room, but I didn't know to do that back then. (As years passed, each time I returned to the Supreme Court building, I checked to see if a women's room had been provided in the lawyer's lounge. First, I was told "it was under consideration." More years passed. "It would probably be approved," I was reassured. Still more years: "There are tentative plans." Then: "There are definite plans." Finally, a few years ago, the lawyer's lounge boasted a women's room as well as a men's room — and women getting ready to argue a case no longer have to run to the basement before their big moment.)

It was time. I went into the courtroom. The place inspires reverence. Heavy maroon velvet curtains hang at the back of the room to cut down noise as people come and go during deliberations. Twenty-four marble columns line the sides. Thirteen kinds of marble. A very high, ornate ceiling. Vivid colors and gold gilt. It's very formal and yet feels quite intimate, holding about three hundred and fifty people. Someone mistook me for a secretary.

When you argue, you stand at a small lectern right in front of the Chief Justice. Hanging prominently behind him is a huge clock so you can watch the minutes of your argument ticking by. I would have thirty minutes.

The opening of the court was very stately. Promptly at ten, the marshal came out in cutaway tails and striped pants and struck his gavel. "The Honorable, the chief justice and the associate justices of the Supreme Court of the United States!" A hush fell over the room. The heavy velvet curtains behind the bench parted and the judges silhouetted in their black robes started marching in as the marshal continued, "Oyez, oyez, oyez! All persons having business before the Honorable, the

Supreme Court of the United States, are admonished to draw near and give their attention, for the Court is now sitting. God save the United States and this Honorable Court." It was really an awesome moment.

After the justices were seated, the gavel fell again and everyone in the courtroom sat. Clerks placed appropriate briefs and papers in front of the justices and Chief Justice Warren E. Burger peered down at me with his placid demeanor. "Mrs. Weddington, if you're ready, you may begin." I picked up my materials and stood. And it was at that moment that I quit being nervous. Once at the podium and opening my argument, I was locked so intensely into my statement that I wasn't even conscious of my surroundings. I was conscious only of those nine judges and the clock.

The judges started asking me questions, and the exchange became very intense. I had so many legal points to make and I had to remember that a judge might actually be against me, and trying to trick me into making a concession against my interests — or another might be trying to help me and I had to really listen carefully to where he was going and what he was trying to get me to point out. It was like playing a huge chess game in which there was so much I was trying to remember and so much that I was trying to do all in a very short time and under a great deal of pressure.

When it was over, after both sides had presented and the court had accepted the case for consideration, I went outside the courtroom and pulled someone aside. "What did I say? Was it okay?" I had been so concentrated during the presentation that I had no idea. I couldn't go back through it and reconstruct what I'd said. I had to ask other people what had happened. I also didn't know that my argument had been recorded. Now those recordings are public, on the Internet.

I knew from the beginning of *Roe vs. Wade* that there were people who disagreed with me intensely. I, myself, am not pro-abortion but I am fervently pro-choice. What I did not expect was that, twenty-six years after the Court's decision, the ruling — that the Texas anti-abortion statute violated the due process clause of the

Fourteenth Amendment that protects from state action the right to privacy, including a woman's qualified right to terminate pregnancy — would still be so much in the press and that so much effort would be aimed at overturning it. I did not count on so much hatred. To this day, when I travel to lecture at colleges and universities, I may end up with security guards assigned to me, I may be booked into a hotel under a false name. I've received my share of hate letters. But, if you're going to do something significant, there are going to be minuses as well as the pluses. There are costs. People will disagree with you. But, like that old saying goes, "Do nothing, say nothing, believe nothing, be nothing."

I heard that a lot when I was young.

My father was a Methodist preacher who also believed that, "To be a leader, you must be comfortable feeling different." Preachers kids always feel different. We didn't always do what everybody else did. We moved quite often. We were always having to make new friends and were taught to stand up for our own convictions. I learned characteristics of courage as a child.

My mother was somewhat unusual for her time in that she coached high school basketball. After her kids were older, she got a masters degree and taught at a business college. She was fiercely independent and wanted her children to have all the opportunities available. She encouraged me to enter contests and, from the age of four, I was making public presentations to the student body of McMurry College in Abilene, Texas, where she was active. It was leadership training at a very young age.

For a lot of women, one of the hardest things about leadership is the desire to be liked by everyone. That's often inconsistent with leadership. It's certainly inconsistent with taking positions on very controversial issues.

A lot of women simply don't see themselves as leaders. I once said to Lady Bird Johnson, "I really admire your leadership." Her response was, "Oh I wasn't a leader, I just helped my husband." Women have been trained to hold other people up and not to hold themselves up. We think of praise or acclaim as being very special, so rather than saying "I'd like it for myself," we're always saying "Let's give it to somebody else."

While taking on the abortion issue in the sixties was courageous, I personally thought of it much more as breaking new ground for women. I grew up in West Texas at a time when people often said, "Women don't, women can't, women shouldn't." Whereas to young men they often said, "Well, try it." Many of us were conscious of those differences, although not really rebelling against them until we were a little older. So, I grew up like most young women in West Texas playing half-court basketball. After two dribbles, we were called for traveling. When I asked, "Why can't we just keep running?" the answer was, "Oh, all that jiggling and bouncing and rebounding, you just don't know what harm you might do to your innards."

When I went to college, it was to get a teaching certificate. Senior year, I was told, "Now, of course, if you get pregnant, as a public school teacher in Texas, you'll have to quit because women are not allowed to be pregnant in the classroom." That made no sense to me. I thought women could walk and talk and be pregnant all at the same time and that young people had certainly seen pregnant women, so I was again one of those saying, "Why?" Later, as a member of the Texas legislature, I was part of an effort headed by female members to change that rule. Shortly after, the national law against discriminating against pregnant women was passed.

I finished practice teaching with an honors class of eighth graders and realized that they weren't nearly as dedicated to learning as I had hoped. It clearly wasn't where I was supposed to be. I went to the dean of my college. "I think I want to go to law school," I said.

Without hesitation, he replied, "Well you can't."

"Why not? I have very good grades."

"Yes, but no woman from this school has ever gone to law school, and my son is in law school and he's having a hard time. It would just be too tough for you."

So, of course, I went to law school. When I graduated and passed the bar, I applied for a credit card and they said, "You'll need your husband's signature." I explained that I was the lawyer. My husband was back from military service, I was putting him through law school and eventually hoped he would have income, but at the moment, it was mine. They said, in essence, we don't care what you think. And so, of course, later when I was in the Texas legislature, I was the principal sponsor of the equal credit bill.

And so, although the abortion issue is the one for which I'm best known, to me it was all part of my lifelong interest in opening up new possibilities for women. When I ran for office, no woman had ever been elected to the Texas legislature from Austin, Travis County. A lot of people said, "You can't win." But I thought it was important to learn how to run campaigns for women, because it was the only way to get women in the legislature, the only way to right many of the wrongs. I was in the legislature when we passed rape reform legislation, and I worked for President Jimmy Carter to find women to fill key positions in his administration and as federal judges. That was a time when we expanded opportunities for women in the military and saw the first domestic violence shelters. I'm not an advocate for just one issue, but have an overarching interest in all issues that will break new ground for women or allow them to break ground for themselves.

And, while breaking ground requires courage, so does changing course. It's something I've come to appreciate as being vital and requiring a good amount of guts. I call it course correction and it can require the greatest courage because when you alter your course, you're fully aware of the step you're taking, as opposed to following the instinctive response that may have led you on your present path.

Someone once pointed out to me that missiles are important not because they go straight to their target but because they course correct, so that if they're fired and they enter a high wind, they crab into it. If they come to a mountain, they go over it. If there's an incoming enemy missile, they evade. I've come to think of life as a series of course corrections, and I share this philosophy with my students, who are seniors at the University of Texas where I now teach. They worry so much about what they're going to be, what they're going to do when they graduate. I say to them that what is important is to have a general direction, to be heading someplace with intense effort, but then to be open to all of the course corrections that are possible or that may be compelled. The more they think of life as course corrections, the more they remain open to opportunities and the less they feel the need to have one answer. Nobody can, not at any age, these days. Which is why the courage to forge ahead anyhow is so critical now.

Sarah Weddington's first book, A Question of Choice, *was about her life and her journey through* Roe vs. Wade. *She's currently at work on a book about civic leadership, primarily from a woman's perspective and based, in part, on her own experiences as assistant to the president of the United States, working with President Carter; as the first woman general counsel for the U.S. Department of Agriculture; as the first woman to head the Texas Office of State-Federal Relations; and as the first woman elected to the Texas Legislature from Austin/Travis County, Texas. She teaches at the University of Texas in Austin and lectures internationally.*

Fanchon Blake

"I hang up. There's no turning back now. No changing my mind. I've made the decision to sue."

In 1973, Sergeant Fanchon Blake filed an historic lawsuit in the U.S. District Court against the Los Angeles Police Department. At age fifty-two and fearing retaliation, she did what no woman had dared to do — sue a law enforcement agency for sexual discrimination. By so doing, she forced the LAPD's doors open to large numbers of women police officers.

On March 14, 1973, in the Parker Center in Los Angeles, California, I broke twenty-five years of smoldering silence. Women officers of the Los Angeles Police Department were not to be seen or heard talking about our assignments or promotions. From the first day at the police academy, male officers made sure women in the Los Angeles Police Department were subservient to the men. We were viewed as too emotional and too weak to be able to handle work in the field. From the beginning, I developed a silent rebellion when denied choice assignments. It burned in me when I was told I couldn't take the lieutenant's exam, thus being denied promotion beyond sergeant.

I served in World War II, having joined the military at twenty-one, one of the first women allowed into service and one of a handful to be accepted into Officer Candidate School. At our graduation, Eleanor Roosevelt inspected our company and shook our hands, so gracious. It was a crowning moment for me. By my twenty-second birthday, I had my first command in Fort Des Moines, Iowa. I did ten years of active duty — including a year in Japan during the Korean conflict — and six years of reserve. I left the army as a major when I became pregnant with my son.

Still in the Reserve Army when I joined the LAPD in 1948, I was recalled three years later to active duty at the Presidio in San Francisco as a criminal investigator, one of the first women investigators in the history of the service. When I returned to the LAPD, I expected an assignment to the Detective Bureau. Instead, I was made a jail matron with the admonition, "Take it or resign." I was enraged at being treated with such disdain and contempt just because I was a woman. Qualification and experience didn't mean a damn. I swallowed my rage, submitting to the code of silence. I suppose if I had been qualified or educated to do other work, I might have looked elsewhere, but back in those days, opportunities for women just weren't available like they are now. I had trained for one thing, I had put in my time. And so I watched the years continue to pass, my talents go unchallenged. I saw qualified women around me denied their right to work in positions that were unavailable to them simply by virtue of their being women.

No woman since 1910 — when the first woman was allowed on the force — had dared to confront or seek redress of grievances from the Los Angeles Police Commission. In 1973, when rumors began to circulate that women were about to be phased out of the police department, a hundred of us demanded to meet with the Chief of Police. In the meeting, he said, among other things, that none of us would ever make Chief of Police because of our "little monthlies." I was stunned and something in me snapped. I could no longer remain silent against such outrageous behavior. His odious Unisex Plan — which would have effectively put a hiring freeze on women by changing physical requirements — was to be brought before the police commission and I promised myself that, on that day, I would be heard.

This is how it is that I find myself on March 14, standing before the all-male Los Angeles Police Commission. Already, the detectives I work with are avoiding me, knowing that I'm going to challenge the Commission.

I square my shoulders to hide my turmoil as I stand rigid at the rostrum, my knees shaking, my voice cracking as I begin, "Mr. President, members of the Commission . . . " The TV camera lights glare as I call for the Chief to uphold his sworn oath and enforce the Equal Rights Act, to assure equal opportunity for all police officers. I feel stronger as I go on, calling for him to remove from his Unisex Plan his recommendation to raise the female minimum height requirement from five foot four inches to five foot eight. His plan would reclassify eighty-six female officers to civilian status, meaning they would lose their badges. It would drastically narrow the availability of female applicants to the police academy. I point out that many men who were only five foot tall have gone away to war for centuries and fought bloody battles and come home heroes.

As I speak, I hope my apprehension about the consequences that surely await me from the Chief's office doesn't show. It's taken all the nerve I can muster to appear here today, to say to their faces what no woman has dared to speak. There's no question but that I'll be branded disloyal and banished from the police family. I may lose my hard-won transfer to forgery investigation. The Chief can reassign me — worse, he can put me on the "wheel," which could mean a transfer every month. I know I'm going to catch hell, but I'm not sure how it's going to come down. What I haven't anticipated, however, is that I will be tailed, my phone bugged, that I'll fear for my life — and it takes an awful lot to frighten me. Repercussions from what I'm doing, and what as yet unbeknownst to me I'm about to do, eventually will require an order from the U.S. Attorney General to put me under federal protection.

When I finish my speech, the packed room booms with applause from the women and loud talk from the men. The Chief glares at me as Michael Kohn, president of the Los Angeles Police Commission, gavels for silence. I wait, returning the Chief's stare, refusing to be intimidated. He knows something I don't, but am about to learn. I hear Kohn's voice thanking me for speaking so eloquently but informing me that in private session, the Police Commission had already voted to send the Chief's Unisex Plan to the City Council.

I reel: With a recommendation by the Police Commission, the City Council would pass an ordinance making the Unisex Plan city law. The Chief had bragged that there'd be no more than twelve women officers remaining on the Los Angeles Police Department. He had already won.

I sit down. *Come on, Fanchon,* I tell myself, *get a grip. Don't let them see weakness.* I take a deep breath, aware of sweat wetting my hair. I grasp the edge of my chair. I'm scared, my head is light. I will myself not to pass out. Another breath or two and I should be okay. Those damned TV lights make my head buzz.

The Chief's blue eyes seem to turn to piercing green as he continues to glare at me. Neither of us break eye contact. I watch his left hand reach up, a fist brushes across his left eye. His face, the same flabby roundness, suddenly transposes . . .

. . . Into Mr. Steele, our landlord when I was six years old, as he dabbed ooze with a red hankie from his missing left eye, lost in a recent auto accident. My bare feet felt warm against the hot sidewalk as the California sun beat down on my shoulders. I watched Mr. Steele, bent over, pulling weeds from the front lawn, showing his exposed back tinged pink except for the white crisscross under his overall straps. He sat back on his haunches and pulled the hankie from his rear pocket and wiped sweat from his balding head. Then he wiped the ooze from his missing eye again and looked up at me. I froze from the horror of that gaping eyehole.

"Little girls need treats," he said, "How about a glass of cold milk with a slice of Daisy's chocolate cake? We can sneak a piece before your Ma and Daisy come back from the store."

With my eyes locked on the Chief, I blink with the memory of Mr. Steele, his hairy chest, his smelly body, his left eyehole weeping a white substance as he held me down on the floor and whispered, "I won't hurt you," his breath coming in short gasps as I pushed against him, yelling, "That hurts," helpless to get him off of me. A glob of pus oozed from his missing eye and caught on his chin. I turned my head as it dripped on my neck. He lied. A piece of cake, he'd said. "Let me up," I screamed. "Let me go!"

His big hand smothered my mouth. I choked. He leaned close. His one blue eye stared into mine. "Don't tell anyone, ya hear," he hissed.

I nodded.

"Promise?" he rasped.

I couldn't move. The room darkened. He took his hand away. "I promise," I said and gulped for air.

His bristled mustache twitched. "Quiet, tiger," he said. "You'll love it in a minute." His voice faded as his sweaty head moved down between my legs. His wet tongue probed as it pushed into me. All these new sensations made me lay still. His head snapped up, drool hung on his quivering chin. "How sweet you are," he whispered. "Baby, don't move." He fumbled with his fly, his head went down again, he dragged his face across my stomach. His whiskers pierced my bare skin. His tongue, wet and warm, sent strange feelings over my body. He moved up and over me, his fat body hung down inside his overalls. He pushed something inside me.

A searing pain made me cry, "It hurts, Mr. Steele, don't!"

. . . Vaguely, I become aware of a woman's voice. "You okay?" the sergeant asks. I blink, see the Chief rising to leave, his face eerily blended with Steele's, the jowled cheeks, balding white heads, thick necks. The Commission room swirls behind him.

My God, that really happened to me. After all these years of locking it out of my mind, why would I remember it now? I blink again and the evil apparition of Steele fades, leaving only the Chief, who raped my career. The one who is violating the rights of all the women who deserve to be on the police force and, not only on it, but equally advanced. He's won this round with the Police Commission. Neither they nor the City Council will acknowledge the discrimination.

Through the ringing in my ears I hear Kohn's gavel, his faraway voice, "Quiet please." In a flash of seconds, I swallow and suck in a breath. I'd grasped my seat until my knuckles turned white. Slowly, I open my fingers as Kohn ends the session.

I stand up and start out of the hearing room. "Why don't you broads stay home?" yells a policeman. "You skirts don't belong behind the badge."

My eyes sting. My rage boils. The sound of men slapping each other on the backs boomerangs in my ears. "Sue the bastards, Fanchon," Judge Joan Dempsey Klein, of the California Court of Appeals, had said when I sought her advice. "Women officers have been waiting over half a century for the men to bestow rank. It'll never happen. They have no intention of elevating women. One of you will have to have the guts to sue. You'll have to fight for the right to compete or accept what has always been — token positions."

I'll bring the Chief a fight he'll never forget. I'm going to the press right now. The women won't back me, but I'm going to blow this mess wide open. Right now. There has to be a sacrificial lamb and it might as well be me. I'm the one woman in the department who isn't afraid of the men. I have to do something — now!

I hurry down the main floor corridor, head around the corner to the left of the lobby, and into the police press room. My friend Ken Hanson, a reporter for the *Los Angeles Times,* is asleep on a lumpy couch. I shake his shoulders. "Wake up, Hanson. Come with me. It's my turn to pay back the coverage you gave me in February. I've got an exclusive, just for you."

He stands, yawns, cleans his glasses. "What's up?" He picks up a pad and pencil, and follows me outside the building.

"I don't want leaks until I can set up what I have to do. I don't trust the telephones in this building, Scientific Investigation on the third floor can monitor any phone whenever they want. And I don't trust ears that might hear what I have to say."

"If you talk fast," he looks at his wrist watch, "I have time to make the afternoon deadline of the paper."

"It can't break until Friday. I need your solemn promise you won't tell another soul."

"I can't keep anything from my editor, but I promise he'll honor your request. What's cooking?"

"I'm suing the Los Angeles Police Department for sex discrimination."

Hanson sort of chokes. "Do you have any idea what you're doing?"

"I'll use an outside phone to make an appointment with the Federal Equal Opportunity Commission."

"All hell is going to break loose, you're going to be in deep trouble," he says.

"I know, Hanson."

He scribbles something on a piece of paper and hands it to me. "Here's my editor's number. Don't go home tonight until you hear from his office. We'll back your action. You're going to need all the help you can get."

With that, he takes off for the Times Building.

I find a phone and call the Federal Equal Opportunity Commission. They give me a Friday morning appointment. Adrenaline courses through my system as I hurry back to work. The squad room is empty and my phone is ringing when I get there. Quickly, I pick it up.

"This is Dorothy Townsend, feature writer for the *Times,"* comes the voice on the other end. "I'm assigned to your story. Hanson has filled me in on what you're doing. Have you made contact with the Federal Commission?"

"I don't like talking on these phones," I say low into the receiver.

"I understand."

"Friday morning, ten o'clock."

"Sergeant, I'd like to meet you there with our photographer. Will that be all right with you?"

"I'd be grateful. I'm already shaking just thinking about what I'm doing."

"Let me assure you," she says, "you won't be alone. And nobody will know about this until it's published by the *Times*."

I hang up. There's no turning back now. No changing my mind. I've made the decision to sue. From now until ten o'clock Friday morning, all I have to do is keep my mouth shut. I'll be a nervous wreck, but I have to do it. This is one time I can't take anyone into my confidence. Oddly, I feel elated. I'm no longer powerless. I have a voice. I will be seen. I've broken the fearful code of silence that had kept me capped all those years in my career. I am free. Afraid but free.

The story of Blake vs. the City of Los Angeles *went on for seven years. The U. S. Supreme Court returned the case to the Los Angeles Federal District Court for either trial or resolution by Consent Decree. On November 20, 1980, the City of Los Angeles agreed to implement a twenty percent quota of qualified women to the standing force; to promote by examination six women to Lieutenant rank; to pay each active duty woman officer monetary compensation for discrimination suffered while in the department; and to recognize minorities in the class action. The Blake case remains open until the LAPD successfully meets the quota imposed. Since the signing of the Consent Decree, over eighteen hundred women have been hired and, by the end of 1998, seventeen percent of the court order was met. Women have risen to the rank of Commander, now can compete for Deputy Chief, and are assigned everywhere at the LAPD. The Los Angeles City Council, noting the fine police work accomplished by the women, passed a resolution to elevate the Blake quota to forty-three percent of the standing force.*

Seven months after filing her lawsuit, Fanchon had a stress-related stroke at work. She retired from the force a few months later. Now seventy-seven, she has written her autobiography, The Silent Force, *with ghostwriter Ellie Bator. "To read Fanchon Blake's story," writes former Congresswoman Patricia Schroeder in the Introduction, "is to understand that the courage required to seek justice is not usually the kind that can be demonstrated in one fine, blazing moment of truth; rather, it must be summoned day by day, year after year, in the thousands of painful and humiliating incidents, both petty and large, that comprise prejudice in action. It is to understand that if a woman today finds her workplace free of discrimination or harassment, a host of other women have paid a heavy price to achieve that."*

Judy Chicago

"It was an important moment for me, choosing between what the world said and what I knew to be true."

Judy Chicago is an internationally known artist and author whose work, with its bold female evocations, stood the art world on its head. Her exhibit The Dinner Party *premiered at the San Francisco Museum of Modern Art in 1979, and since then, has been seen by more than a million people in sixteen exhibitions in the U.S., Canada, Scotland, England, Germany, and Australia.*

Over the years, numbers of people have told me that seeing my work changed their lives. For a long time, I didn't pay much attention to these comments, because most of the praise came from people who weren't in the art world. And the opinion of art critics was the only one on which I focused. But, when it became clear to me that the art world, or at least the New York art world, wasn't going to change its antagonistic stance toward me, I began to rethink why I worked and for whom. *The Dinner Party* had just exhibited in New York at the Brooklyn Museum. It was 1980 and I had been a professional artist for almost twenty years. I was well known and thousands of people were flocking to see the show, which the art system had tried to suppress. I was naïve enough to think that my success in the face of such resistance would bring me kudos from the sophisticated New York critics. But I was wrong. As a result, I began to pay attention to what people outside that small circle were saying, and to try to understand what it was about my work that caused people to say that it changed their lives.

For women in particular, seeing my work *The Dinner Party* or the *Birth Project* seems to trigger critical thinking about what it means to be female. A feminine perspective permeates the work, and I think the eager response to it is indicative of a widespread hunger for images of women that are empowering and affirming. With *The Dinner Party,* I wanted to educate a broad audience about the richness of women's heritage, and so I created a visual narrative of Western civilization as seen through women's achievements. Thirty-nine table settings, each honoring a woman or a goddess, feature place settings of painted ceramic plates and decorative needlework that display the combined image of a vulva and a butterfly — a visual symbol of liberation and the defining characteristic of woman in an almost metaphysical sense. These are set on an open, triangular table that rests on the Heritage Floor, a lustered porcelain surface upon which are inscribed the names of nine hundred and ninety-nine women who made a mark on history. Both the floor and the table are configured as an equilateral triangle, an ancient symbol of the Goddess and the feminine.

Standing in a room so imbued with feminine images, walking around the exhibit and seeing hundreds of names of women who accomplished so much and yet are not acknowledged in history, women responded on a deep level. I think it made them see themselves, as women, in a new light. It made them realize how many cultural assumptions about themselves they had accepted, but which weren't true. It presented a feminine image boldly, without apology, and it gave women a history.

Early in my career, when it became apparent to me that the art world was a man's world and that bringing all that is female — all that is woman — to my art would mean further exclusion, I struggled with whether or not to work from this perspective. For a brief time, I experienced a kind of terror about my creative urges, frightened by how strong they were. I struggled with the fact that, by expressing my full power, I thought I was doing something terribly wrong. I spoke with my friend Anaïs Nin about my feelings, and she reassured me that what I was experiencing was not some aberration of humanity, that she herself had felt such fears about the power of her creative drive. I really had nowhere to go but to follow that drive.

The images in *The Dinner Party* apparently rattled the art world, but the long lines at the exhibit and the enthusiastic response of the crowds made me believe that women's time had finally come. I was embraced publicly. I lectured constantly, gave innumerable interviews, signed many books about the exhibit. I forgot for a moment that women historically have been and still are excluded from defining art, or included only if they agree to work within the mainstream (clearly *not* the case with *The Dinner Party*). So, the fate of *The Dinner Party* — a hugely female experience — was sealed by an art world dominated by men.

Initially, positive reviews appeared in many publications, including *Ms.* and the *Village Voice*. *New York* magazine reported that, "*The Dinner Party* had caused more furor than any other contemporary sculpture." But later, when the show opened at the Brooklyn Museum, the *New York Times* ran an article by the most important art critic of the time. On the front page of the "Friday Arts and Leisure" section, he described *The Dinner Party* as "grotesque kitsch," little more than vaginas on plates. A few weeks later, a significant art writer for *Time* magazine, attacked the exhibit with a venom, making nasty references to pudenda (genitalia of a woman). A writer for the *New York Review of Books* called it entirely worthless.

The New York reviews really hurt. I didn't rebound quickly from them. I might have stopped making art altogether, but I was raised to believe in myself and to trust my own experience. Before leaving town at the end of the exhibition at the Brooklyn

Museum, I stood there one last time, watching hundreds of viewers silently walk around *The Dinner Party* — and it suddenly came to me: Who chooses? Who decides? A few critics in the art world or the viewers? Would I stand by my own experience of the piece, its beauty and its importance, or would I accept what was said by the critics? Like my cousin Howard says, "In the face of life's adversities, one either gives up or gets up, and in our family, we get up."

My father, Arthur Cohen, taught me this lesson. He also taught me critical thinking, which is essential to being able to stand up to the world. Without it, I don't think it's possible to have courage, because courage comes from believing in yourself, no matter what the world says. My father gave me this foundation, and what he taught me was tested when I was very young.

My father came from a long line of rabbis. His father was the twenty-third rabbi in an unbroken tradition. Given that most of our relatives lived in and around Chicago, the family gatherings were frequent and raucous. I was raised in a household where education was paramount, where the mind was celebrated, and where Jewish ethical values were instilled, especially the concept of *tikkun,* the healing or repairing of the world. I was taught that working to make the world a better place was what life was all about, and that material possessions were insignificant. My father would point to the many books and records in our house, which enriched the soul and mind, and say, "See these, these are the only riches that count."

He worked nights at the post office and was a union organizer. My mother worked days, so when I was little, he was always home when I woke up from my nap. He spent a lot of time with me and, through games, he trained me to think critically, logically. I guess, I came to assume that everybody thought this way.

My father was also a Marxist and a political activist during the height of McCarthyism. He was investigated for his political beliefs and eventually forced out of the post office job and the union work that he loved. His life was destroyed. He died of a stomach ailment when I was thirteen. I was dazed and stricken with grief beyond any imagining. My most beloved parent was gone. His death disrupted our entire family, and where it might have brought us closer, it alienated us from one another. My mother refused to talk about his death, and, as we sat over dinner night after night, with my father's absence an unbearable pain, the walls between us thickened.

Shortly after his death, the *Weekly Reader* at school began to run comic book pictures of bloated, swarthy men bayoneting beautiful, blond American boys. These swarthy men were the "communists," the "left wingers," the "Marxists." They were the bad guys. I remember going to school and seeing that *Weekly Reader* and thinking, "Is that ugly, bloated person who my father was?"

Peer pressure is intense in high school, and I struggled with those bloated commie comics. But I finally said to myself, "No, that's not who my father was, and I don't care what people say." It was an important moment for me, choosing between what the world said and what I knew to be true. My father was a wonderful human being, devoted to trying to make the world a better place, a brilliant man, generous, charming, and totally adoring and supportive of me. At that moment, I chose to believe my own experience in the face of the world's vastly different perspective.

This self-confidence continued to be a guiding principle in my life, through all those years when the art world trashed my work. I knew that people could be really, really mistaken. And people have been, about my father, about my work, about me. It's painful to be the subject of mistaken ideas, but what I care about is the impact of the work.

I was extremely fortunate that my father prepared me to trust my own experience and to think critically. "Know that what the world says is not always true," he would remind me. He left me with probably the single most important gift he could have given me — the ability to stand up to a world that demonizes female power, and that misrepresents many people all the time.

In a strange twist of fate, when *The Dinner Party* opened in Chicago in 1981, I was invited to appear on Irv Kupcinet's television show. A longtime Chicago celebrity, Kupcinet was beloved not unlike another famous Chicagoan, Studs Turkel. All Irv knew about me was that I was a hometown girl who had an art exhibit in town. Also appearing on the show the same night was Roy Cohn, the lawyer who had been in the spotlight during the worst days of Red-baiting because of his association with McCarthy. I didn't know Cohn was going to be on the show until I walked onto the set, live, on-air. He and Irv started talking to each other as if I wasn't there. I didn't exactly go for that. And, I sure didn't go for it when Cohn started talking about the Rosenbergs and what bad people they were. I interrupted their discussion, which startled them. I don't remember exactly what I said, but in no time, I was in a shrieking fight with Roy Cohn. All these years after my father's death, I was finally able to stand up for him and what he believed. My whole family was watching the show on television as I vindicated my father.

I make the decision over and over again, every day, to stand up for what I know to be true. Every time I read hostile or uncomprehending reviews of my work, I am forced to choose between what I believe about the importance of my art and what the so-called experts proclaim. Even after all these years of negative criticism, it still hurts — whether it be the drubbing I took after the premiere of the *Holocaust Project* (which I consider to be my finest body of work) or the asinine *Los Angeles Times* article — "Sexual Politics: Judy Chicago's *Dinner Party* in Feminist Art History" — that reappraised *The Dinner Party*. If I accepted these people's version of reality, I would spend the rest of my days in a mental ward. So, it is a good thing that I learned the lesson from my father that people can be very, very mistaken in their judgments, because it helps me in small ways to take a stand for myself, and, slowly, the small ways accrue until they become a lifetime habit. If I only had to take that stand once, on some big issue, it might be easy. Doing it every day is what's hard. And it takes more courage as you go along. But, what is the point of living carefully? So that the next time around you can pick and choose the risks you want to take? In my view, we have only one turn in the barrel and in spite of how hard it can be to stand up, one discovers that it doesn't kill you and, in fact, can be incredibly exciting.

Known as the founder of the feminist art movement, Judy's other works include the Birth Project, *the* Holocaust Project, *and her current* Resolutions. *Anaïs Nin called her autobiography,* Through the Flower, *"invaluable for all women." Judy's later book,* Beyond the Flower, *continues her commitment to the power of art as a vehicle for intellectual transformation and social change and to women's right to engage in it at the highest level.*

Riane Eisler

"So many of the models of courage we've had, ones that are still taught to boys and girls, are about going out to slay the dragon, to kill. It's a courage that's born out of fear, anger, and hate. But there's this other kind of courage, the courage to risk your life, not in war, not in battle, not out of fear . . . but out of love and a sense of injustice that has to be challenged. It takes far more courage to challenge unjust authority without violence than it takes to kill all the monsters in all the stories told to children about the meaning of bravery."

Riane Eisler gained international recognition with the 1987 publication of her book The Chalice and the Blade, *which was deemed by the anthropologist Ashley Montagu to be the most important work since Darwin's* Origin of Species. The Chalice and the Blade *stood history on its head, spoke of the Goddess and the Feminine as a force in history, and gave us Eisler's prominent theory of the dominator and partnership models of culture. For more than a hundred years, evolutionary theory has been one of the most prestigious of scientific fields and the most rigidly exclusive of men's clubs. Eisler is arguably the only woman to have shattered the glass boundaries of that circle.*

I was born in Vienna. When I was six, the Nazis took over. It wasn't just that the Germans marched in, there was a very strong anti-Semitic strain in Austrian culture. On Crystal Night, all the glass and windows in the synagogues and the homes of Jews were smashed. It was an official *pogrom,* the first mass roundup of Jews in Germany and Austria.

I will never forget the day they came to our home to drag away my father. A Gestapo Nazi official came with some Austrians, a looting party. They pushed my father down the stairs and were about to take him away when my mother recognized one of the young men. He had worked for the family business. My mother shouted at him, "How dare you! This man has been so good to you, and now you come to take him away. You push him down the stairs and humiliate him. You steal from him! I want you to give him back!" It was an extraordinary thing to do. She could have been killed. But she was driven by her love for my father. She had what, in my book *Sacred Pleasure,* I call spiritual courage: the courage to stand up and challenge something that was very wrong.

And something remarkable happened. The Gestapo officer said to her, "Okay, you bring such and such an amount of money to Gestapo headquarters and we will give him back to you." She did and they released him, but that wasn't all. She asked for safe passage out of Austria, because she knew the Gestapo would be back. If she hadn't taken that stand, we would all be dead.

We went first to Rome. One of my uncles was a physician there and he wanted us to stay. "The Italians aren't anti-Semites," he said. "I've lived here all these years, and they're not going to harm us." My parents almost stayed because it was so difficult to believe what was happening. In the end, my uncle was taken to a concentration camp.

After what had happened to us in Vienna, my parents decided to leave Europe altogether. They had to bribe officials to get visas for us. We fled to Havana, sailing on one of the last ships of refugees to leave Europe for Cuba.

One day, a short time after arriving in Havana, I was standing on a long avenue by the sea, looking out at a ship anchored offshore. Nearly a thousand Jewish refugees were on board, and the Cuban government wouldn't let them come ashore. The refugees had all purchased their "landing permits," but the Cuban government upped the price and demanded authentic visas. They named an exorbitant sum, which the Jewish Joint Committee couldn't raise quickly enough. It was, of course, all orchestrated by the Nazis. They were testing to see if the world would raise a finger about their Final Solution, and the world didn't. That ship was refused by every Latin American country. Not even the United States would take it. Finally it was sent back to Europe. Many of the refugees died in Nazi concentration camps.

I remember standing there, looking out at that ship, listening to my parents talk about it and not being able to understand. How could it be that the ship would be turned away? How? Why? What was wrong? These are questions I always ask now in my work. Questions that come from a very deep emotional place in me. Why is our world so full of inhumanity? How can we be so brutal to our own kind? What is it that tilts us toward cruelty rather than kindness, toward war rather than peace, toward destruction rather than actualization? Every one of us has asked these questions at some point, especially as children. When we see something unjust, we can't stop asking, "Why?"

Living through these times, I kept wondering why I had been spared. I began to feel that I was going to do something important in my life because I had been spared. That sense of mission disappeared in my teenage years when I became a properly socialized female — I had no role models for anything else. My main interest was in being attractive and having boys like me, which is very natural. But the luggage that went with it — that in order for boys to like me I had to abandon myself — *that is* very unnatural.

I had no clue what I was going to do with my life as an adult — except get married eventually. We had moved to the United States by the time I went to college. I studied sociology and anthropology and got my degree from UCLA. Then, because it was the shortest route to an advanced degree, I went to law school — and marked time. As soon as I got married, I quit.

In those first years after I had become a housewife, I read everything I could get my hands on about ancient mystery cults. In the beginning, I simply stumbled onto this material. I was always curious, and I was a voracious reader. I ended up giving myself an intensive education in material that would be extremely useful later. I began to trace the Mother/Goddess, reading myths about her and, not only her sons, but also her daughters like the Greek Goddess Demeter and her daughter, Persephone, or Kore.

I lived a very conventional life during this time. I did some work as a social scientist, but primarily I was a wife and the mother to two beautiful daughters. I tried hard to fit the conventional role of the woman behind the successful man. But, it was like living a dream dreamt by somebody else. I lost my true identity. Finally I got divorced — and this was at a time when people didn't divorce.

I went back to law school and got my degree, fascinated now by law as a scholarly approach to the study of society. I plunged into the human potential movement. I cofounded one of the first women's centers in the country and started a program called the Los Angeles Women's Center Legal Program, another first. It was like waking up from a long trance. I wrote many articles and two books, *Dissolution: No-Fault Divorce, Marriage, and the Future of Women* and *The Equal Rights Handbook.*

But, I needed to go deeper, to understand how we got to this place, to a world where the female half of humanity — and anything associated with women or the stereotypically feminine — is devalued, ignored. So I began my research, and it gave rise to the new method of multidisciplinary study I call relational dynamics, probing the two basic alternatives for structuring human relations, which I identify as the dominator and partnership models. Tracing periods orienting primarily to one or the other model, from prehistory to the present, I developed my cultural transformation theory and wrote my books *The Chalice and the Blade: Our History, Our Future* and *Sacred Pleasure: Sex, Myth, and the Politics of the Body, New Paths to Power and Love.*

There were times when doing this pioneering work was very uncomfortable and, in retrospect, I see that it took a great deal of courage. Women were not supposed to have intellectual authority, just as we were not supposed to have moral authority, the authority to say this is right and this is wrong. Why? Well, if you exclude woman from the priesthood, for example, what are you really excluding her from? You're depriving her, and her entire half of humanity, of moral authority, of the authority to say what is right and what is wrong, including what was and is done to us. And, if you exclude woman from intellectual authority, you are depriving her of defining not only what is, but what can be.

In my generation, we did not have role models of women in positions of either moral or intellectual authority and we had such a need for them. The courage I had was the courage to challenge all this. My work shows that we have alternatives: that male dominance, warfare, exploitation, conquest are not innate but socially constructed.

The task was very difficult because women are not supposed to say, "I am going to challenge a whole line of authority. I am going to formulate my counter theory — and I'm going to do all this without the beard of the wise man. I, a woman, am going to throw my hat into the arena of intellectual history."

At times, challenging an intellectual establishment that presented history in a certain way despite all the evidence to the contrary, I had a feeling of hubris, of *How dare I.* Hubris means quite literally challenging the gods. And ironically, of course, I ended up doing just that, by saying, "Look, there's enormous evidence from archaeology of a time before the dominator cultures, which viewed the power to destroy, to dominate, as the supreme power, when the powers that governed the universe were armed male deities, like Jehovah with the thunderbolt or Zeus with the sword." I found myself developing an analysis based on massive evidence from archaeology, from folklore, from the history of myth, and art history of a long span of time in an earlier era when the powers that governed the universe were primarily seen as the powers that give life, that nurture and, yes, that take back life. It was a time when a Great Goddess was worshipped and the sacred union of a female and male deity was a central religious mystery.

Those images of deity were nowhere in the conventional texts. So, I ended up challenging the gods, writing in *The Chalice and the Blade,* and later *Sacred Pleasure,* about female images of deity — the kind of images that gradually disappeared from Western culture — and about what I call a partnership rather than dominator way of organizing society, the kind of society we are today trying to recreate: a more peaceful, more just society, where stereotypically feminine values such as nonviolence and nurturance can in reality, not just in rhetoric, attain social governance. And I say stereotypically because, again, these traits are not something innate; clearly men can also embrace these values, and clearly not all women do.

Overall, my work has had a very positive response. My books are assigned in university and high school classes. They are discussed in conferences, in workshops, even in church groups. But there are also those who are trying to make my work disappear — the way other women have disappeared from intellectual history — or to marginalize it, the way anything associated with women has been marginalized by the dominator worldview. My work makes some men (and women) in the male intellectual establishment very uncomfortable.

Let's take the difference in the way I see female figures from the Stone Age.

If you're looking at them from a perspective in which the early history of humanity is the story of man the hunter and man the warrior, then you've got a particular paradigm or screen, if you will. And, consequently, when you find these figures, what do you do with them? You have to fit them onto that screen. So, they become Venus figures, strange pornography, a rather bizarre counterpart to *Playboy* centerfolds. But the point is, that's not what they were. They were representations of the life-giving and the life-sustaining powers in the universe. They have to be seen from a different paradigm altogether.

That was one reason why, in *The Chalice and the Blade,* I wrote that this book opens a door to new paradigms, to seeing new patterns. I'm not the only one who has said, "Wait a minute, we've been denied by history." There have been others. But, I think my main contribution was to provide the conceptual framework, to not only deconstruct, but reconstruct our past — and with this, the possibilities for our future.

This reconstruction, as I said, has required seeing patterns differently. Even in the nineteenth century, when archaeology was still in its infancy, some began to talk about societies where a great Goddess was worshipped and there were priestesses. But, what did they do? They called it matriarchy. Why? Because that fits into the dominator paradigm: if men don't dominate women, then women must have dominated men. And it must have been a primitive stage of evolution, which of course presumes evolution to be linear. Part of what I have contributed is a nonlinear approach to history, utilizing some of the same principles in my cultural transformation theory as chaos theory, as nonlinear dynamics. Basically, we know that change is not a linear process, that there are oscillations. In light of the barbarity all around us, to say that civilization is a linear process from savagery and barbarism to civilization is obviously absurd, isn't it. But, if you're within that old paradigm, you're stuck. So, I'm challenging those assumptions within a new theoretical framework. And because I'm a systems person, I don't fit into a cubbyhole, but draw from many different fields. Otherwise you don't see the patterns, you don't see that societies where a Great Goddess was worshipped were partnership models, some of them very sophisticated.

This work, by showing it can be done, is very useful to those who understand that to change our lives for the better, we have to change society. The father of social psychology, Kurt Luwen, spoke of action research. That's what I do. I have an enormous curiosity that drives me. I feel like an intellectual Sherlock Holmes at work, putting pieces together like a detective, seeing when something is actually a forced fit, then putting things together differently so that they suddenly make sense. That's really what my work is about — challenging the prevailing models of human nature, then changing the system to achieve a better, more natural fit that nurtures our greatest potential as a whole.

Riane's curiosity is insatiable. It's like an electric field around her. She thrives on questions, which, along with her long-standing love for her partner, scholar David Loye, and her rapture in the beauty of her natural enviornment, keeps her young and vibrant at age sixty-seven.

Marianne Williamson

"Maybe now I'll find out about courage."

Widely acclaimed author and lecturer, Marianne Williamson has touched millions with her books, A Woman's Worth, A Return to Love, *and* Illuminata: Prayers for Everyday Life, *as well as her most recent* The Healing of America, *all of which deal with universal spiritual themes. Over the years, she emerged as a leader in what one writer calls "the spiritual underground," time and again returning us to the power of love and forgiveness to heal ourselves and our world at large.*

I don't know if I know anything about courage, because I don't know if I have any. Others have called me courageous at times, but always in relation to situations where the more appropriate description for whatever they referred to was either naïveté or foolhardiness. So maybe that's what courage is, in some way: to act on the way you think things should be, rather than how they are, and to not spend a whole lot of time considering the consequences.

I didn't *know* how many people would not appreciate a Jewish woman talking about Jesus; I didn't *know* how much institutional resistance there is to thinking outside the boxes; I didn't *know* that there are so many unspoken rules against women truly owning their voices and how severely punished we can be for trying. Once I found out, I can't describe my reactions as courageous. Heartbroken is a better word. But maybe now I'll find out about courage. It isn't courageous to go forth when you don't know the dangers. But it's very courageous to go forth when you do.

Marianne recently founded the American Renaissance Alliance to "reawaken more Americans to the principles of nonviolence and the need to infuse spiritual values into our political system." Through Citizens' Circles, people work to become more politically aware and to take action to effect a more compassionate society. "The Twenty-first Century will see the world transformed by the genius of the human heart," she says. "It is not our technology, but our consciousness, which carries the power to create a sustainable, peaceful world."

Brooke Medicine Eagle

"I came to the defiant conclusion that I, a woman and not an elder, could attain spiritual knowledge on my own, going directly to Mother Earth and Father Spirit and sitting at their feet."

Born on the Crow Indian Reservation in Montana, Brooke Medicine Eagle is one of the most highly respected Native American teachers of our time. She is a healer, Earthkeeper and ceremonial leader, songwriter, sacred ecologist, and author of Buffalo Woman Comes Singing, *an autobiographical book of spiritual teachings.*

We were alone on our ranch on the Crow reservation in Montana, miles from anything, and he was beating her face bloody again. He was just as drunk and insane as he had been before when I had seen five husky men try to pull him off her as he struck again and again with all the power and fury he possessed. This time I could see his big shoulder muscles, hard from doing the heavy work of the ranch, and I could hear his fists connect with the flesh of her face as each blow landed. My older brother and I huddled together, shaking, so scared that our teeth chattered like dry bones on a desert.

Just then, my mom's nose gushed a red blossom of blood as he hit it directly. I couldn't wait any longer. I pulled away from my big brother's protecting arms. "Stay here, baby," he whispered desperately, "stay here!" But I was gone, running toward my mother.

At four years old, I could only get between their knees, but get between them I did.

"Stop hurting her!" I screamed. "Leave her alone!"

"Get away and sit down!"

"Stop it! Stop hitting my mom!"

I cried and I screamed, hitting and kicking his legs, climbing up on him to intercept the blows.

Mom tried to grab me and get me out of the way, but I held on with the strength of a young tiger. I had to. If my dad killed my mom and ended up in prison, what would happen to us kids? We had nowhere to go, no one who would take care of us. We would be lost, the whole family, if he killed her. He had shot at her before, in this crazed state, as she ran, ducking up the hill away from the ranch house. He was a dead shot, because he hunted for our only meat: hitting his target was almost instinct. I knew he missed because he had wanted to, but he told her if she ever ran off again, he would kill her. She was sure he meant it. Hiding the guns each time he went on a running drunk stopped the shooting; it didn't stop the beating.

I had to hold on. I had to make him stop. And finally, he did stop, for his tiny daughter was the only one he would listen to. He sat down and cried. And my terror began to subside, or rather, it submerged temporarily, because I knew this would happen again. Maybe three or four or six months down the line, but it would happen again. And again, on courage born of terror, I would sail into the fray to save my family.

Such experiences in my childhood enabled me as an adult to stand up against men who were "in charge" when I thought they were wrong. Nothing could be as bad as what I endured as a child. Nothing could be worse than the breaking point when I was eight: the year of the fire. To "make it go better," a neighbor boy poured gasoline on the fire my brother and I had built to make clay pots, and as the whole five-gallon can exploded, the blaze came right at me.

Death came close. I could see the flames around my face, knew my eyelashes were gone, smelled my hair melting. I screamed and ran. All the adults had just gotten in our old noisy jeep to drive up the hill. Dad later told me that his hand was on the ignition key when they heard me scream. Close, very close, death came, blowing its fiery breath up my nostrils.

They heard my screams and came running. Mom put the fire out with her hands. Then, we drove forty-five miles over backcountry roads to a doctor. I was out of it for most of the ride, but I clearly remember my dad carrying me in his arms, running into the hospital, crying out for help.

While I was in the hospital, my mom got to be away from the ranch for two months. It was probably the first "free time" she had ever had. She had grown up poor, slaving for her family until she met my dad. Then she slaved for us, carrying water to cook and wash, cutting wood for the cook stove and the potbelly heater, breaking horses and herding cows, stacking hay my dad tossed up with the old beaver slide.

During those precious weeks on her own, she got to meet people, to see the world outside the prison of our little ranch. As she watched the flesh rot and fall from my leg, and watched it try to grow back again, I'll bet she did some deep thinking, because within a year or so, she had found a way to get my brother and me off the ranch to a school away from the reservation. We all spent nine months away, coming home on weekends. Then summer at the ranch. After another school year had passed, she found friends and courage enough to hand my father divorce papers. My terror began to truly subside, to drain away, as I saw that we were free. He wasn't going to hurt my mom any more. At least this part of my family — I, my brother, and mom — were safe.

Thirty years later, listening to comedian Richard Pryor rap about being on fire, I understood for the first time that as a child I had made a choice from the deepest part of myself, too deep to recognize then, too painful. When I heard Pryor say, "I used to be an angry man, but the fire burned all that up," I felt like someone had knocked me over and I tumbled back in time to that day on the ranch, by the fire, when I was eight years old and the night had exploded. And something deep inside me knew that I had made that choice, I had taken on that fire, to burn up the anger. I burned up the anger, not only my dad's cruel anger and my mother's bitter anger, but mine: my anger that I had to save my family again and again; my anger that I didn't get to be a little girl safe in her parents' arms; my anger that no one was there to intercede, to help me. On some deep level, I had made a choice, to burn up the anger and change things, to wake up my parents or to leave life. Nothing else, not anything, not anywhere could be so bad as this. Something had to change.

Yes, being on fire changed things for me. There were heavy losses — the ranch with its green valleys, aspen trees, mountain springs, and my pony to ride wild over the hills. Yes, there were losses that haunted me for a long time. But the terror had gone up in smoke. What could anyone scare me with anymore?

It was facing the demons, facing death, that gave me the strength I would need in my spiritual quest as an adult. I graduated from the University of Denver majoring in counseling psychology and mathematics and was elected to Phi Beta Kappa. I had gone on to teach and was instructing in Minnesota when I realized that my academic career wasn't giving me the opportunity to do the kind of healing work that I wanted to do. The rigid rules and rote forms seemed to deaden learning rather than to create a living education. So, I decided to go back to get my Ph.D. in humanistic psychology with an orientation toward a more holistic body therapy, thinking this would enliven my work. I left my secure job, a circle of friends, a warm home, and sold most of my things, put the rest in a car, and headed out to San Francisco. On the way, I was given a vision. It came without my conscious summons and it called me back to my roots. It was a spiritual calling that led me back to my own Native spiritual ways.

My first and primary teacher was a wise old woman. When she went to the beyond country after I had known her only a few years, I sought other teachers. Most of the Native American elders I found to learn from were men, and most of them held out their spiritual knowledge for a trade. Directly or indirectly, they eventually would make it known that their teaching would continue only if I would have sex with them. It would have been different if I had fallen in love with one of them, but all I wanted was to learn and grow. I was a willing student and gave back good energy and support for what I was given, but that giveaway did not include my body. When the sexual pressure began, my opinion of them as wise men sank significantly.

I had to take a stand. I had to throw myself into the metaphoric fray, even if it seemed to go counter to the accepted way of Native spiritual learning, which included honoring one's elders and following their good direction. I became a mouthy woman in the good-old-boy system. Mouthy because I spoke the truth and exposed the sexual bribery. Mouthy in the most powerful, risky, and honorable sense of the word.

In the end, I turned away from human teachers and turned, instead, to the Earth and Spirit for guidance, taking quiet time on my own on the land. I started doing more and more vision quests, going out onto the land, into the sacred places, fasting and praying and asking for vision and numinous dreams. A vision quest is a retreat to a quiet place, sometimes a place that's traditionally sacred to Native people, letting go of food and normal life, sitting in the silence and praying to receive vision about what you're supposed to be doing in your life.

By now, I had left my doctoral program to travel around the country and teach courses in body therapy and sacred ecology. I'd go on vision quests into the Badlands of South Dakota or the Redrock Canyons in Arizona, or up to Mt. Shasta and Mt. Lassen in northern California, and any place where I felt a special power. Sometimes, I'd just put on my moccasins and run, and I'd find myself at a beautiful waterfall up a canyon somewhere, and I'd lie down and rest and be given visions and dreams. It was, in a sense, a kind of spiritual roaming. I was always on the lookout for someone who could be my teacher when I spent time on various reservations, contacted Native elders, and taught at the gatherings where other half-breed and full-blood teachers came. Yet, I never again found anyone who carried into everyday life and personal relationships the holiness I sought. Among my people, holiness is paying attention to the whole, not focusing on a God or a spiritual figure, but, rather, enlarging one's awareness to consciously include and respectfully consider All That Is, All Our Relations, all beings, energies, and things in the larger Circle of Life.

I came to the defiant conclusion that I, a woman and not an elder, could attain spiritual knowledge on my own, going directly to Mother Earth and Father Spirit and sitting at their feet. Following my new belief wasn't easy. It was bold beyond anything I had done. I stood alone, interpreting what was offered. No elder did the translating for me. I recognized that I possessed a kind of clarity, innocence, and integrity necessary to be present in this quest.

What I dared to do, at first, seemed to be a harsh break from the traditional Native way. People would accuse me of going against tradition, and that censure was challenging for me to face. But I came to realize that my quest was more deeply traditional than anything I'd done. The original Northern Plains spirituality was a mystical spirituality, in which the Great Spirit was honored as living in everything. In the truly traditional way, one recognized that the Great Spirit dwelt within oneself. One could ask for and receive messages from the Great Spirit — from within oneself or from a tree or from a crow or a deer or a vision or a dream. The great knowledge and wisdom was available in all of life, not simply in one book or from one person. One might ask an elder to help with a vision quest or with interpreting knowledge.

The wisdom of an older person who has been down the path for a long time can be invaluable. But the Truth itself comes from the Great Spirit. And it is more traditional in my mind to go directly to the Source for information than to what I call a priestly line, in which wisdom is considered to be the sole possession of one person who says, *I will put my hand on your head and pass wisdom to you, and I will tell you exactly what's right and what's wrong, and you will follow the rules of our order.*

The word "traditional" has come to mean that which people have been doing for the last hundred years, which doesn't have anything to do with what's truly traditional. Traditional is what happened before the white man came, before the Native way was stamped out. When Native people were restricted to certain areas, when they were forbidden to travel a distance away from trading posts, they stopped vision questing. And the mystical tradition became more of a priestly one, because people sought answers from elders who had lived in a time when they could still follow the traditional way. So, I realized that I wasn't breaking with tradition, I was breaking with a habit formed by oppression.

As my spiritual life burgeoned, I made contact with White Buffalo Calf Pipe Woman, who came to me in meditation and visions. In legend, she is a mystical being who came walking across the prairie and appeared mysteriously to the Lakota, worked with them, and gave them sacred rites. She brought with her the catlinite pipe to be used in sacred ceremony to bring about a reunion with all things in the Circle of Life — a remembering of ourselves as one with All Our Relations, the two-legged, the four-legged, the winged, and all that grows from Mother Earth. When she left, as she was walking away across the prairie, she turned into a white buffalo calf and disappeared in the distance. When she appeared to me, she told me that it was time for the awakening of the feminine, for women to stand up and lead. A balance was necessary: the positive feminine values of nurturing and renewing life had to become stronger than the degrading masculine ways of destruction and domination. This idea is obvious to me now, but twenty years ago, it was a life-altering revelation.

So, I have taken my stand with White Buffalo Calf Pipe Woman. I bring her message into the workshops I lead, the retreats I hold, and the lectures I give. Walking my daily walk, I try to bring her to mind as often as I can, to honor her message of unity and wholeness with all things in the Circle of Life. From the way I garden to the way I cut wood, I try to express holiness and oneness with All Our Relations. This spirituality is not about what I do on a Sunday or on any particular holy day, but what I do on all days, how I make my decisions and impact others, not only within the circle of life around me now, but for the seven generations of children to come.

Brooke has studied with medicine people and shamans in the U.S., Canada, and Peru, as well as with masters like Moshé Feldenkrais, the world-famous Israeli healer, with whom she apprenticed for three years. She has also studied body therapies and psychology at the Humanistic Psychology Institute in San Francisco and is a certified Neurolinguistic Programmer.

Now at home in the beautiful Flathead Valley of Montana, she conducts ceremonies, retreats, and vision quests there during the summer months and, in the winter, at Lake Buchanan near Austin, Texas. In addition to EagleSong, *her spiritually oriented wilderness camps, she teaches Earth Wisdom internationally and will soon offer a new training,* Wakantia, *focused on an emerging way of living powerfully and peacefully. Philosopher Jean Houston calls her "a new embodiment of White Buffalo Woman."*

The Courage to BE VULNERABLE

Salle Merrill Redfield

"Where I once found it safer to stay in the background . . . I've stepped from the shadows into the spotlight."

Salle Redfield is the author of The Joy of Meditating: A Beginner's Guide to the Art of Meditation *and* Creating a Life of Joy, *due out in the fall of 1999. She travels and lectures internationally with her husband, James Redfield, author of* The Celestine Prophecy, *which became the number one international bestseller of 1996 and was on the* New York Times *bestseller list for three years.*

When James wrote *The Celestine Prophecy* and we self-published it in 1993, we hadn't been together all that long. We had been married not quite a year when Warner Books bought the book rights and began spreading *The Celestine Prophecy* around the world. The book began to rocket up the bestseller lists when we were still in a honeymoon phase. It was a long honeymoon as it turned out — we spent the next three years traveling around the United States and parts of Europe lecturing and attending book signings. Although it was a wonderful experience that I wouldn't trade for anything, it was a challenge for me to go from being a massage therapist in a small southern town to touring all over the world with James. I had always been a private person and, suddenly, people were wanting to know everything about me. It was an exciting time and very different from the way we had been living.

After three years on the road with the book, we came home. And I came back to — me. Before the book's huge and unexpected success, I had been going through a deep soul-searching, facing my relentless desire to be the one taken care of, to be the rescued Cinderella. When our honeymoon was over and the uproar about the book died down, that desire was still there to a degree, because during those years traveling, lecturing, helping James present the message of his book and recording *Celestine* meditation tapes, I had been so busy that I had set aside personal work on my Cinderella complex. Simply being on tour with James and the book had changed me and given me confidence and, coming home, I didn't want to fall back into the unconscious trap of avoiding responsibility and giving away my personal power. When I began to feel the Cinderella complex creeping back into my daily life, it became important to me to take another look at my behavior and shift it. My desire for personal empowerment outweighed my need to be a victim.

I had been raised into a Cinderella complex: "Don't you worry your pretty little head" was the unspoken message of my childhood. Overcoming the desire to be rescued and taken care of has been challenging work. It was painful to admit to myself how I played the clinging vine, how I made others responsible for me, how I blamed others. Unconsciously, subtly, I loved the victim role. But, it was very empowering to recognize what I was doing and to stand up for myself. I began to say, *Wait a minute, I chose this.* I may not have realized in the moment that I was choosing it, but I did. And since I chose it, I can choose something else. Or I can embrace it and get on with life. It was refreshing not only for me, but also for those around me. As I grew to care more for myself, I was able to be more caring toward others.

I first learned about caring for myself in 1989 when my marriage with my first husband ended and I began taking steps toward being self-sustaining and depending upon my higher source, my inner source, my self. It was anything but natural in the beginning for me to say, "This is my place in the world, not my husband's, not my father's, not anybody else's." It went against everything I had grown up with, everything I saw around me. I had married an engineer who did very well financially, which meant I was free to work or not to work. After a few years, a friend and I had started a small catering business. It was a start toward greater independence, but it was a "proper" start, the kind of thing a good married woman would do as a hobby. I certainly wasn't driven by passion.

After seven years of marriage, the universe seemed to say, *Well, Missy, it's about time to wake up,* and just threw me out into the world at large. I was twenty-nine and truly on my own.

I was scared and unsure of myself when I got divorced. I was so fragile. Things that are inconsequential to me now were monumental back then. For instance, one time I went to a fast food place and the guy behind the counter asked, "Do you want fries with that?" and I panicked at my uncertainty. *Did* I want fries with that?

I was like a delicate southern magnolia blossom. In retrospect, the fast food incident is funny but only because I've grown to be so different than that frail flower. I think to move through that intense a fragility, you have to get in touch with the energy of Kali, the Hindu goddess known for her powers of destruction. That strong, aggressive energy is what I needed to destroy my self-doubt and to be able to stand up and say, "Yes, I have a place in this world, I have something to say."

In the years when I was married and not motivated by a career or a life purpose, I was afraid of the whole world. It was scary not having the confidence to go out and say what I believed, always hiding behind, "Well, my husband thinks . . . " And then, all of a sudden, I was divorced and had no husband. How was I going to take care of myself? Where was I going to go? What was I going to do? Financially, I couldn't afford to keep the house. Anyone who has ever lost a home understands how hard that was for me. But somehow, I was able to move forward and, in the year that followed, I began to mature and enjoy my new freedom. I realized that I didn't really *want* a husband — at least not until I understood myself better. I didn't date or go out much. I knew I had to take time to just be me.

With my new life came new friends. Synchronistically, many of these friends were massage therapists who were passionate about their work. Meeting them inspired me to make the decision to go to massage therapy school and become a massage therapist myself. I strongly believed in the mind-body connection and I knew that if people became more aware of their bodies, they would also become more aware of other aspects of themselves.

Because I couldn't afford to go to massage school without financial support, I approached family members about loaning me the money for tuition. I composed a very methodical letter that included a budget and all kinds of backup data, hoping it would appeal to their business side. I'll never forget the letters I got back: "No, I won't help you, and I won't loan you any money, because I don't see how you're going to be able to pay it back."

That's when I thought, *Wow, I am about to turn thirty and I am really on my own.* What a tough realization that was. I took a deep breath and reached down inside myself and said, "Okay, I'm going to do this anyway. I just have to get the money another way. I don't know how I'm going to pay it back, but I will." I got angry and determined and, for the first time, took responsibility for my destiny. It was a turning point in my life.

Feeling strong about myself and my course, I decided to ask my ex-husband for the money. This was no Cinderella looking for her prince's help, but a confident woman with a plan. Because he believed in me and wanted me to succeed, he loaned me the money. I think God had a hand in that decision. It was a gift on many levels, an opportunity for us to see how much we had grown when it came to communicating with each other and a chance to learn how to support each other without all the dependency of the past.

I graduated from massage therapy school, and built a practice with people who cared about me and about whom I cared. And eventually, I paid back the loan from my ex-husband, which was a moment of great pride for me. I will never forget writing that check.

Lately, when I contemplate that turning point and all the opportunities it opened up for me, I think about my grandmothers and wish they had had the opportunities and support that I was given. It was unthinkable for them to break out of the mold of the perfect wife and woman. In the South in the fifties and sixties, women weren't encouraged to find exciting personal projects or work. There weren't as many female role models for them as there are now. The media didn't support the idea of women having a strong place in society, outside of a traditional role. Society itself didn't support the idea. Both of my grandmothers ended up dependent upon alcohol and depressed. They died within a month of each other, both of them in their early sixties. They might have lived longer, definitely richer lives had they been encouraged to develop a strong, meaningful purpose beyond caring for those around them. They had no future once those who relied on them moved away. And neither of them had the support of a circle of other women. They grew lonely, with nowhere to go, nothing to do, with no joy, no hope.

Today, we have more options because of the courageous women who helped pave the way for us. And because of them, most younger women won't fall victim to the Cinderella myth. In my own struggle to overcome that myth, I have spent the last few years making my mark in the world and expressing who I am through the book I wrote, *The Joy of Meditating: A Beginner's Guide to the Art of Meditation,* and the meditation tape that accompanies it. The positive international support that I receive for my work has given me the strength and motivation to be more conscious when I find myself being too dependent upon James. If I detect too much dependency, I say to myself, "Now, wait a minute, what is this all about?" I'm learning to create a balance between my independence and my interdependence with him. I keep exploring who I am, my needs and opinions, my thoughts and feelings, so that I don't lean upon his approval or devotion. It makes our relationship better. It makes me more. I'm holding myself responsible for my own emotions and my own future.

It's new territory for me to really live my life the way I want to live it. Each small success I have builds upon the last one and gives me the courage I need to step even further out into the world. Any time I find myself wondering if I'm ready to move into a new phase of my life, I reach for what worked in the past. When I'm sure it's time to move into that new phase, I take the first step, and trust. It can feel for a while as if I'm between worlds, the known behind me and the unknown ahead. Eventually, I push myself to take the second and third steps and it feels really good. The whole process can be scary and exciting.

Publishing my books and tapes has given me a great opportunity to step outside my normal comfort zone. I've been popularizing the idea of meditation, which is a challenge in a mainstream population too busy to slow down. It's been an interesting adventure to introduce meditation, to talk about it, to be a part of a new wave of individuals and mainstream organizations like the National Institute of Health interested in this ancient technique.

It's taken courage and perseverance to move from behind the scenes, from being the support person behind my husband's book, into a person enjoying the success of her own books and projects. Where I once found it safer to stay in the background and push the energy of *The Celestine Prophecy* forward, almost helping birth it, I've stepped from the shadows into the spotlight. And I have grown to like my new role more and more each day.

Special women along the way helped me step out and be heard. Because of their encouragement, I have come to see that as women we need to help each other find our voices in society and to support each other in our passions and missions. We also need to listen to each other's stories, especially when someone says, "This is who I am, this is my path, this is where I failed and this is where I succeeded, and this is where I just wanted to die it was so hard." It's exciting to be a part of that honesty and strength. When you listen to someone say, "When I was twenty-one, I had a nervous breakdown, but I came through it and this is how I did it," you hear the real essence of a person. Being soulful, when it feels safe, can lead to enriching connections and deep respect among us.

As I look back on the twists and turns that my life has taken since 1989, I see that I was propelled into an archetypal journey of the self. Because of that journey, I have learned to honor the sacredness of my process and to listen to my inner voice. I have begun to reach out to other women and honor the paths they have traveled. And, I have deepened my own sense of what my role is in making the world a better place. Even though I am going where my grandmothers could not go, I am standing on their shoulders and on the shoulders of all the courageous women who play a part in furthering the evolution of what it means to be a woman.

In addition to her books, Salle has recorded an audiocassette version of The Joy of Meditating *and created meditations to accompany James' books, which are recorded on the audiocassettes* The Celestine Meditations *and* Meditations for the Tenth Insight.

Sabrina Ward Harrison

"I will dare to do just what I do. Be just who I am. And dance whenever I want to."

Twenty-three-year-old Sabrina Ward Harrison opens her recent book, Spilling Open, *with a quote from the poet Walt Whitman about "washing the gum from our eyes and dressing ourselves for the dazzle of the light." Witness to the struggles of women and men, Whitman threw them a challenge: "Long have you timidly waded holding a plank by the shore, now I will you to be a bold swimmer, to jump off into the midst of the sea, rise again, nod to me, shout! and laughingly dash with your hair." With this, her first book, Sabrina let go of the plank and dove deep, opening herself for all the world to see.*

I was living in Berkeley, a student at the California College of Arts and Crafts, when the chain of events occurred that would lead me to write *Spilling Open.* Not in my wildest dreams could I have imagined I'd be so vulnerable, that I would lay myself bare for all the world to see.

I hadn't planned to go to art school right out of my senior year at La Cañada

High School near Pasadena, California. I didn't know *what* I was going to do. All my friends were making college plans and talking about joining sororities. I was barely passing algebra and grateful to get accepted at my least favorite college. Then one day, my art teacher, Karen Mealiffe, who apparently saw a flicker of something in me, took me aside and said, "Get your head out of that dark hole." I went through horrible stages growing up when I doubted and doubted and doubted myself, when I hated myself. "Get out of southern California," Karen urged, "and go to art school."

"But I don't even have a portfolio," I protested. I was no child prodigy but a late bloomer, not discovering art until my sophomore year of high school. Who was I to think that I would be accepted by an art school?

To which, she replied, "I believe in you. You have something, you have an eye. I know, trust me on this."

At the California College of Arts and Crafts, I was studying with mostly second degree students who had already graduated from college. I, on the other hand, was eighteen and this was my college equivalent. The environment was very intense and competitive.

In the beginning, I was drawn to graphic design, the kinds of things you see in great ad campaigns. The power of words and images fascinated me. I loved the Nike campaign about women being women, unfettered. It ran powerful quotes about not being boxed in — "You do not have to be your mother unless she is who you want to be ... the only person you are destined to become is the person you decide to be." — over strong photographic images of women. I was captivated by the message. It was potent. It was honest.

When I signed up for a class called "Life Stories" taught by the poet, Opal Palmer Adisa, I had no idea where it would take me. The very first day of class, she did an exercise with us during which we closed our eyes while she led us through a guided visualization about trust, taking us on an inner journey to find ourselves, to trust ourselves. It reminded me of a time when I was rock climbing with my dad. I was ten years old and, at one point, the mountain got so steep that I froze with fear and started to cry. I couldn't go any farther. We were with a group of people, all harnessed in and, had I not gone on, everyone would have had a risky descent back down the mountain. Very calmly, my dad said, "Brave on the rocks," to remind me of how I would always walk on rocks when I was little. His voice was soothing and patient, "Close your eyes Sabrina, I want you to close your eyes and imagine your next step ... and then the one after that ... and then the one after that. Once you can see it, you can be there, the power is in seeing, being open to where you can go." It was a definitive moment in my life. I got to the top of that mountain and it gave me a powerful sense of what was possible in life.

And now, Opal Palmer Adisa was taking us on a trip of inner seeing to find our own true voices, to trust in what we heard. When we opened our eyes, she told us to take out a piece of paper and write, "I need to write because," and fill in whatever came to mind, uncensored. We were to get journals — "big and blank" — and write in them, "I have to write because," and "This is what I need to say," or "This is what I have to say." And so, I began my journals, getting what was inside of me out and slowly finding my voice.

During this period in my life, I was very uncomfortable, insecure, and struggling with my image. I had terrible acne and the medicine I was taking for it was so strong that it could only be purchased in conjunction with birth control pills because it caused birth defects. I was excruciatingly embarrassed by my face. I didn't want to be looked at, I didn't want to be noticed. So the idea of having a strong voice was confronting and, in the beginning, I could only explore it through other people, using them to reflect what I felt. I began photographing women my age and talking with them about their lives.

Gradually, I noticed that my journals were becoming a journey, not a simple destination. They were real life, happening in the moment. I'd complete a journal every two months. They were thick and full and ripe with feelings and thoughts and drawings and photographs. People would read them and say, "Oh, I totally feel this way" or "I relate to that so much." It led me to do a project called *A Descent into Limbo.*

At a lecture, I had heard Maurice Sendak, the children's book author and illustrator, speak about creativity as a "descent into limbo." It described perfectly how I felt as I turned nineteen. People would say to me, "Nineteen is so easy," or "You're so lucky to be nineteen," or "That was the time of my life." But I didn't feel that way. And neither did the people around me: My best friend was anorexic, another friend had been raped, another had just had an abortion. The people I loved, whom I was inspired by, had overcome incredible things by the age of nineteen.

Realizing the potency of the photographs I'd been taking of women my age, I put together a school show of large photographic panels with essays written by the women themselves about what was honestly happening in their lives and what they believed. I was fascinated with peoples' truths, how they were perceived by others and how that didn't necessarily jibe with what they felt. People would say to me, "You seem so together" when I felt so apart. And I knew I wasn't alone. We all have edges and the challenge is to not hide them.

I made a pact with myself to be as honest as I could and admit as much as I could and to share it all.

And then, just as I was finally clicking in, making friends, becoming part of the college community, I got mononucleosis.

My newly-spun world dropped out from under me and I suddenly found myself back home sitting in the kitchen in my mom's pajamas, disheveled and pale. I had to quit school. I thought I'd never get my life back.

Feeling funky in La Cañada, I read my favorite author, SARK, whose books — like *Inspiration Sandwich: Stories to Inspire Our Creative Freedom* — are wildly and wonderfully illustrated and written to encourage living life to the fullest. Her company, Camp SARK in San Francisco, has an inspiration telephone line that you can call and leave or hear an uplifting message. For some irrational reason, I decided to call and leave a message. "Hi, this is Sabrina, I just need to call and tell someone that I feel really disheveled. I know you want something inspiring on your machine, but I basically don't have anything happening and I just feel rumpled."

A week later, the phone rang. "Sabrina, this is SARK."

Ohmygod. I could barely speak. I'd been reading her since I was fifteen. My dad was in the background saying, "Write down everything she says, you'll never talk to her again, this is a moment in your life."

"Thank you for talking about being disheveled," SARK said. "Thank you for speaking about your real feelings."

We launched into a long conversation. She talked about her own insecurities, and it was a wonderfully ageless, timeless connection. Here was a woman I had admired for years calling me not because I was an artist — she didn't even know I was an artist — not because of my journals, which she also didn't know a thing about, but because I had told the truth.

Two months after leaving Berkeley with mono, I finally returned. Instead of going back to art school, I went to work at a clothing store so I could pay off my bills, which I had run up toward $900 before getting sick. When I wasn't working, I was home watching *Oprah* and trying to heal and regain strength.

And then, SARK called again. "I feel that I'm supposed to know you. I don't know why. But I feel it. And I was wondering if you'd come and hang out or intern at Camp SARK — you can lie down on the floor whenever you need to."

How could I pass up this great opportunity? "I have a job at a clothing store and I really need to buckle down and work," I said. "I've got all these bills to pay."

"Sabrina, I spent my whole life listening to my dad tell me to buckle down. I worked 250 jobs before I finally realized that life is about *unbuckling.*"

On November 4, 1996, SARK and I met at her house in San Francisco. As usual, I carried a journal with me. She took one look at it and asked to read it. "There's a book in this," she said after one page.

"Excuse me."

"There's a book in this."

I almost hated her for saying that. "You can say that because you're SARK, but I'm only nineteen." I didn't even want to think about being published. It was too much.

Over the weeks that followed, SARK read all my journals. Periodically, she would call and say, "Sabrina, would you please write a book."

"I can't . . . I don't know how . . . I don't know." I was still working at the store to pay off my $900 of debt. It was pretty bleak, but it was necessary.

"Okay, then what is it that you would really love to do?"

I told her I'd think about that and hung up.

I thought and thought about that question and finally realized that, if I could do what I really wanted to do, I would work with twelve- and thirteen-year-old girls, because that was the age when things were so awful for me. As it turns out, during a period when she didn't have any money, SARK had put together adventures for young artists. I liked that and set out to create a four-week, summer art course that would center on the emotional side of being twelve and thirteen years old. I'd have the kids keep sketchbook journals as a way of expressing how they were feeling, *spilling open.* Our focus would be growing pains, aliveness, being yourself. It was the course that I'd wished I'd been able to take when I was that age.

Nobody signed up.

It threw me into a tailspin. I had believed so strongly in the class that it hadn't even occurred to me that people would be anything but thrilled to enroll. I swirled ungracefully into self-doubt. It wasn't pretty.

"You could still think about doing that book," SARK encouraged.

"But, what would I do?"

"Create a few sample pages of your book, how you see it."

"But, I have no idea what that would be."

"Can't it be like your journals?"

"That would be really expensive, it clearly couldn't be in color ... no way."

"There's a lot of power in those journals, there's nothing else like it. Wouldn't you have liked to have them as a book when you were younger?"

I had to nod.

"Think about it as a big letter to the world."

I was terrified. Surely, people would say:

"How dare you."

"Who do you think you are?!"

"What are you talking about?"

"Who are you to think that, at nineteen, you're ready to write a book? You write a book once you've really lived your life and can look back on it all and reflect with the wisdom of experience. Who do you think you are to write it now?"

To which, SARK replied, "That's precisely *why* you have to write it now, because you're in the *middle* of it, it's visceral." She was right, of course. Many people have written about being young from a vantage point of looking back in time, but there's something about being *in* it and saying, "You know what, these are my questions, this is really where I'm at, and I'm going to speak about it now because that's all I can do."

I started going to bookstores with SARK, looking for local publishers, checking out the kinds of books they published. I made appointments with a couple of them and had pretty mediocre meetings, because I was looking for someone to tell me how to do the book. I hadn't made sample pages. I was going in with my journals, wanting someone to say, "We'll do it," and then give me the vision of what "it" was, to tell me how the book should look, and then I'd go off and simply do it.

My final call was to a publishing house run by a man who had written a book about visionary business. I met with him on the Fourth of July. I took my journals but, by now, I knew that no one was going to create the book for me, that I would have to step up to it myself. A very insightful and open man, the publisher told me about how he, himself, had had a dream to start a publishing company. At first, he didn't believe he could do it. But he worked on envisioning it, seeing it, believing it and once he could visualize it, it happened. I could almost hear my dad saying, *Brave on the rocks, Sabrina.*

I told him about the art class I wanted to do with teenagers, how I had this passion to help young people be themselves without the adolescent junk that makes kids feel awful about themselves.

"Well Sabrina," he concluded, "I think you should root the book in that art course and make up some sample pages."

"What should they be, can they have color?"

He didn't say, "Make them and give them to me and I'll think about publishing them." He said, "How do you see them?" In other words, make them for yourself and then you'll know what to do with them. He sent me off saying, "If I can do it, you can do it. If SARK can do it, you can do it."

I spent the next two weeks making eight pages of a book I was dreaming. During those two weeks, I was tortured and excited and euphoric all at the same time. When I was done, I felt oddly confident about what I'd created. I put the pages in brown paper and wrapped lavender and twine around them and drove back over to the publisher's office. I walked in, went upstairs, and passed by a glass boardroom where the staff were all sitting around a table looking sophisticated. I kind of waved and blushed and didn't say anything, because they were in the middle of a meeting. I leaned the package against the publisher's door and walked away.

Sabrina, you're such a dork, they're probably wondering, "What is that little girl doing out there?" I felt so crazy. But, at the same time, a thrill rushed through my body. I was *living, really living, risking, taking a chance.* I called my parents from the pay phone down the street and yelled, "I did it!"

A few days later, I left for Toronto, where my family lived before the move to California, which, by the way, was the call of a dream that my dad had answered, knowing that Hollywood was the mecca of film and that he, a filmmaker, would always wonder what might have happened if he'd gone there and tried to make movies that mattered. We still continued to summer on Lake Simcoe in Ontario like the three generations before us. It was there that I went into detail about leaving the package at the publisher's door and slinking away, which prompted my dad's speech about the importance of rejection, a subject with which he is very familiar, the film business being all about rejection and requiring great commitment in order not to compromise one's vision. "It's important that you did this," he said. "It doesn't matter what happens. You did it, that's the important thing."

Time passed and I didn't hear from the publisher or any of his people. Obviously, they hated my work. My friends asked how the project was going and I said that I was trying to get the artwork back. My dad told me to send a self-addressed envelope and ask them to mail it back. I couldn't face driving over there and asking for it.

And then, I got a call from the editorial director. "I opened up this package," she said. "It was sitting against the door for days and I couldn't stand it, I had to know what was inside. So, I opened it and I've been walking around the office with these art boards thinking how much I'd love to have my daughter read this. I'd like to meet you."

That was the beginning.

You know that feeling when you see a dream starting to happen? I was euphoric and terrified all over again. Because now, I had to go ahead and write the book and create the art. Could I really do it? Would they like it? Had I been deluding myself? Would I be able to do the other nearly two hundred pages as well as I did the first eight? For a year, I lived on edge, thinking that, at any moment, the dream could burst, the publisher could reconsider. I emotionally yo-yoed around until I finally accepted that, if the book was supposed to be in the world, it would be in the world — whether it was now or ten years from now or forty years from now.

I quit working at the clothing store and paid off some of my debt with money a friend lent me. While I wrote and worked on the book, I took independent classes through the California College of Arts and Crafts, working with Opal Palmer Adisa and photographer Chris Johnson, who was mentored by Imogen Cunningham and Ansel Adams and now was mentoring me. And, I began teaching that art course for kids, rooting the book deeper and deeper in what I was learning from them. At times, it was very challenging, because some of the kids had a lot of pain. And I might show up for class feeling completely insecure and pathetic and awful myself. I'd say, "Well, I'm feeling insecure and pathetic today, can we just lie on the tables for a little while?" I tried to be honest about myself instead of pretending. I was simply Sabrina, with her highs and lows. And I was astonished by how vulnerable the kids became, even the boys.

When I was in junior high school, guys made fun of me. It hurt — a lot. So, I was made whole in a way by seeing that the badass boys in my art class were, themselves, wounded. They felt things deeply. Being a badass came out of conditioning, out of pain. It wasn't personal. A ten-year-old boy wrote, "People crave to be loved, to be liked by one another. Sometimes people go to the borders of life, everybody will do what it takes to be normal." These children made me cry. A beautiful, blond girl — the kind of girl I was terrified of at that age — said, "I've created my own prison and now I have to exist in it."

What we don't let out traps us. We think, *No one else feels this way, I must be crazy.* So we don't say anything. And we become enveloped by a deep loneliness, not knowing where our feelings come from or what to do with them. *Why do I feel this way? Last week, I was on top of the world and now my feelings don't make sense.* Voicing it, getting it out and letting other people hear it, helps to dissipate it. The fears and self-criticisms begin to leak. And we begin to heal. In the same way, if we feel deeply about something and voice it, then we're made whole by standing up for ourselves and what we believe.

Over and over, I hear people say how grateful they are that I speak about these kinds of things, because they feel the same way. When I wonder why on earth I wrote *Spilling Open,* I think of them. And I think of my favorite writers, people who have let me in on their own personal processes, women like May Sarton and Anaïs Nin. What if they hadn't written their books? What if I hadn't had them to turn to when I felt so alone? Maybe someone will pick up *Spilling Open* when they're feeling lonely or confused. Maybe it will help them to feel a part of what we all feel. I don't claim to know the answers to life, but I claim to feel it.

Spilling Open was my catharsis and it continues to be a work-in-progress for me. Being human. Being real. Letting other people be real, be vulnerable. I often felt naked writing it in the moment rather waiting and gaining perspective, reflecting and designing my experience to look the way I want it to look. Even in the process of creating the art and rewriting the material, I noticed things that I'd worked through since I first wrote about them. Parts of the book I still can't believe I put in there. Some of the more vulnerable things, insecurities, are hard for me to read now. My critical voices scold, *Sabrina, that's not important to talk about, no one else feels that, take it out!*, even though I know it's something I wish someone had talked about when I was that age. It's real.

May Sarton said, "The deeper you go, the more universal you become." It's a reminder to me that those things I try to convince myself I don't need to admit are usually the things I need the most to say. Speaking the truth, in its most poignant details, is liberating and gives those around us the freedom to be real. SARK reminds me that the ultimate goal is radical self-acceptance. Get into who you are. In my book, I write about a photographer named Elizabeth Sunday, who said, "I believe in myself. I believe in my vision, my life, my talent, my art more than anyone. No one can take that away from me."

We can choose to be affected by the world or we can choose to affect the world. I never passed algebra, I'm not good at games involving balls being thrown or kicked towards me. For years, I struggled with all that I wasn't. But, seeing and believing in who I truly am has given me an unstoppable faith and conviction in what I can do with my life.

In *Spilling Open* I write, "I think when I can get to that place of self-acceptance and a sense of calm assurance in who I genuinely am, if I can believe in who I am, what I need, what I deserve, and what I must express, then I can let go of the struggle of self-acceptance based on 'their' approval of my beauty, boobs, thighs, or sketchbooks. I will dare to do just what I do. Be just who I am. And dance whenever I want to."

Sabrina is leading The Art of Becoming Yourself *seminars at places such as the University of Southern California,* Jump *magazine, and high schools, as well as privately with groups of parents and children. She is also painting and writing and dreaming of a year abroad, living in a writer's colony in Italy.*

Katt Shea

"At times, I felt like a lunatic on my private journey. I was so afraid to let go of everything I knew, in favor of something I didn't, even if it was better and larger. But, I didn't back away from the fear."

Katt Shea is a feature film director and writer, whose work has been honored in retrospectives at the Museum of Modern Art in New York and the British Film Institute. Her films include Poison Ivy, Last Exit to Earth, Stripped to Kill, *and* The Rage: Carrie II.

I have always been alone — but never independent. Finding my independence has been my most courageous experience.

For the last twelve years, I've been working as a filmmaker — a writer and director — supposedly the most daunting of career professions for a woman outside the presidency or priesthood. I made it happen by sheer will and by badgering Roger Corman (the "B" Movie King) for more than a year for the chance to direct my first movie.

I'd acted in a movie for Corman. I had been his second choice for the part of an Amazon princess in one of his many sword-and-sandal adventures. When his first choice got a television pilot (a much better career break), I was sent off to a Third World country where I fashioned my very serious part into the comic relief of the movie.

When it was over, I went back to writing screenplays with my then-husband. I lost a bet with him and was forced to go to see (horror of horrors) a strip show. At first, I was pretty abashed watching these poor women expose themselves in such a humiliating way. But as I watched, I saw something deeper and unexpected: the performers were using this venue to express themselves artistically. My husand and I came up with an idea for a movie to take place in this underworld, which at the time, 1988, no one had examined yet cinematically.

In the meantime, I heard that Mr. Corman was very happy with my Amazon princess performance, and so, in an effort to make the most of an opportunity, one afternoon I waited for him (practically lurking in the bushes) to come out of his office and walk up the street for lunch. I ran around the building, "accidentally" bumped into him, reintroduced myself — and hit him with my concept for the movie, which, at my husband's earlier prodding, I suggested we would write and I would direct. Incredibly, Corman was open to the idea and asked me to come in on Monday morning and pitch it.

The movie I pitched was *Stripped to Kill,* which has since spawned scores of imitations — actually it's been credited with an entire subgenre, "the stripper thriller." The story hinged on a female impersonator posing as a stripper. The audience would have to accept a guy dressed as a girl being sexually attractive in very little clothing. This was many years before *The Crying Game,* and Corman wasn't convinced it could be done believably — after all, the guy would have to wear a G-string! After weeks of trying to convince him it could be done — sending him pictures of transvestites and actual strippers, and writing on the bottom "Which is the real girl?" —

I made a surprise visit to his office with a female impersonator in tow. I'd found this performer, a somewhat effeminate guy named Bill, at a club called La Cage au Folle and asked him to come with me to do a quick favor: There in Corman's office, I quickly introduced him to Roger and said, "Listen to this!" with a nod toward Bill. Nervous about the task at hand, Bill sat down and described in great gory detail how he hid his genitalia while wearing skimpy outfits. Once he'd started, there was no stopping him, as he described the process, something about pulling the organ and stretching it up to fit into the crevice of his buttocks, I think — I don't know for sure, because I blanked out during the explanation, while Mr. Corman, my prospective producer, a very dignified, gray-haired, sixty-five-year-old, turned purple with embarrassment and tried to stop Bill from going on. But, as I said, Bill was on a mission and kept explaining until I snapped to and stopped him.

From the outside looking in, this entire escapade was a bold move. Equally bold was standing in front of an entire film crew as a first-time director, scared to death, and doing my first shot of that first movie. I've since made four more movies for Corman's Concorde Pictures: *Stripped to Kill 2, Dance of the Damned, Streets,* and *Last Exit to Earth.* My more well-known films, *Poison Ivy* and *The Rage,* were for bigger outfits: New Line Cinema and United Artists respectively. Each of the Corman movies was done on an impossible schedule with "student" crews (actually many of these kids weren't even quite students yet). I started out at Concorde a novice and ended there a pro, and, for this, I am deeply thankful to a man with whom I continue to have a love/hate relationship. It's all been an adventure, yet simply the stuff of which Hollywood is made.

People seem to think that respected directors are the strongest sort of people, impervious, mavericks, self-reliant individualists who hold themselves above criticism. I admit I thought that was the role I had to play, and I played it very convincingly. For the crew, my presence inspired fear (some would describe it as respect). I was never wrong.

Here I was, living a dream, writing and directing films for theatrical release. I was taken very seriously and often even critically praised. I was singled out in the press as a remarkable creative force behind the movies I'd made. The Museum of Modern Art and the British Film Institute both held retrospectives of my work, and I wasn't even dead yet — well, not on the outside anyway.

My writing partner-husband became my producer. Our lives centered on filmmaking. Nothing else mattered. All of my value in my eyes became dependent on being "Ms. Director." I was tense, stressed, and on the verge of an anxiety attack a good part of the time. My husband was hyperactive and driven; he didn't notice that anything was wrong. Success was so close he could touch it, taste it, feel it. He lived to prove himself worthy to his outrageously successful TV producer father.

The budgets for our movies were minuscule, our schedules preposterous, and I was bent on making art. I'd barely have enough time to shoot important emotional scenes and I'd get a demand from The Kremlin (Corman's office) to film additional nude scenes by the end of the day. If Mr. Corman wasn't throwing a wrench into things, then the city would be shutting us down for incomplete permits, or perhaps some Teamsters would show up to delay filming while they tried to get the crew to walk off the nonunion production. Or maybe my producer (that guy I was married to) would be throwing a fit because I'd filmed something in a different manner from what he'd expected or deleted something he'd written, which was now unnecessary and time consuming. I knew things had to change. My life was out of control. I was exhausted all the time, sick with some kind of flu every few months, and my shoulder muscles were chronically aching. Sometimes, while shooting, I would turn to the wall and cry when no one was looking — just for a moment.

When my writing partner-husband-producer announced one day that he was a drug addict, it didn't throw me much because so much else in my life was manic. Filmmaking is a world of ongoing crises, and I figured we'd get through this one just like we had gotten through every other impossible situation. When he "temporarily" moved out of the house and into his own apartment in order to "find himself" and sort things out, I kind of understood. When on Valentine's Day, we went on a date to dinner and he confessed that, for the last few years, he'd been having an affair with a porno actress, things became a little clearer. I had spent the last several years of my life metaphorically dead. My reflexes still worked, but I was emotionally and psychologically numb. I hadn't the foggiest idea what was going on in my life. This was a major revelation. It would have been easy to blame my freaky husband for what had happened, but I knew that would be cheating. I had to be as responsible for this nightmare as he was. Only by answering for the mess I was up to my neck in could I turn things around. This was some kind of wake-up call.

Breaking up with and divorcing my husband was especially scary because not only had he been my spouse, he had been my career partner. I relied on him enormously. I didn't know if I could get along in life, much less in my career, alone. In fact, I thought my career might be over. He was a great writer; his dialogue was always unique and unconventional, often even poetic. As a producer, he was always there, and I'd grown accustomed to his looking over my shoulder while I was filming to make sure things were right; his ideas would enhance my own. And maybe I even needed him to keep me from going over the edge in the midst of all the production chaos, to pour me my double (triple maybe?) shot of bourbon at night, the only thing that would help me to sleep. But I wasn't going to give him another chance at being a good husband, which he seemed to suddenly want, out of some last minute fear or desperation. I wasn't going to be a better wife — everything had gone too far, for too long. I was just going to have to take the risk of exploding into life, on my own.

First, though, I had to implode. I began by spending time with myself — I was so used to hearing his voice in my ears that I wasn't even clear who was thinking my thoughts for me. I was an act, a facsimile of what a powerful female director is supposed to be. I looked great, and everybody scrambled to do my bidding. When I ordered something, it was there half an hour later. I asked for something, and five people jumped to make it happen. But, real power comes from self-possession, knowing who you are, being an individual and trusting in the worthiness of that individual. I was just a shell of a person who relied on my husband to judge whether or not I was okay. The last time I could remember feeling like a pure, unadulterated "me" was when I was three years old.

I made a commitment to stop pretending, stop behaving the way I thought people expected me to act, to uncomplicate things by telling the truth all (well okay, 99 percent) of the time, and to be vulnerable. This meant I would talk about what I really felt, and what I really thought. If I was sent a script that was crap, I would politely and diplomatically say so, even if the studio thought it was terrific (translation: commercial). I would freely give of my ideas to improve it, ideas from the soul, not simply ideas that I thought a studio would be "open" to hearing. I couldn't be thin-skinned either; yes, I would give of myself entirely, be creatively naked, make suggestions that revealed tons about me, shamelessly, and if my thoughts and ideas were rejected or the studio people looked at me like I was crazy, I would just go right on about my business. I stopped second guessing others, stopped worrying about whether they'd respect me in the morning. It felt so good that I decided to accept the consequences even if it ended my damn career — the only thing that, at the time, defined me. The few friends I had thought I should see a psychiatrist.

I had been searching for a spiritual center for many years, and in the midst of the drama of making five movies in the same number of years, I'd lost track of it. I had to find that missing piece of myself.

One afternoon, a neighbor came by for coffee and inadvertently put me on track. Like a female, gentile Woody Allen, I was narcissistically describing the big empty hole I felt in my soul, the loneliness and desperation this swirling black abyss seemed to contain. She said that we women usually fill that void with men, but it never works. I asked her what we were supposed to fill it with and she shrugged like she was guessing, " . . . God." In the past, I would have just stared blankly at her, but I knew something deep and important was missing from my life. There was a hole. I was incomplete, empty. My career didn't fill it, men didn't fill it (for longer than a couple of months anyway), getting a new car, losing weight, even eating one of those ice cream cakes from Baskin Robbins didn't fill it. Something was missing, and if my neighbor wanted to call it God, well, okay.

I was willing to risk everything — even my sanity — to find the thing that would really make me whole. I say that because, for a pragmatic sort like me, looking for "God" seemed pretty loony. I'd wander around the city just thinking about completeness, whatever that meant. It turned out to mean trust and faith, two things I'd never had. I had always expected the worst. I liked to do that — so I'd be prepared. That way, I would never be disappointed. "Hope" was a ridiculous word to me. It seemed to connote a powerlessness on my part. I didn't "hope" for things, I went out and made them happen. That's right, I'd expect the worst, then go out and make something better happen (50 percent of the time). I had come to believe that I was in control of my destiny: If I worked hard enough, sacrificed enough, and tried with all my might, I could attain, accomplish, achieve. And I did. I attained a miserable life.

During the period of time I was searching to fill that empty place in my soul, people kept popping up to tell me I could do my work on my own, without my writing partner-husband-producer who was now becoming simply my ex. "You know Katt, you don't need anyone else, you can do this." That sort of thing. Even people who worked for me would say it and they'd say it with feeling, as if they knew it was what I needed to hear. I thought they were crazy — or, rather, uninformed. I figured they had no idea what a great contribution my partner had made to "my" work.

I threw caution to the wind and started writing. Put it out there for the world to judge — the most personal biographical stuff: a book, a screenplay, another screenplay. I supervised and contributed to other writers' visions, and started to teach acting. I've been praised and criticized and I take it in and let it all roll off. My job is not to judge, but to go deeper, be more honest. And more humble.

Little by little, I've found faith in the world, and ultimately in myself. I've learned to trust the mechanism of life, but it was hard and took tremendous discipline. I worked at it daily, thinking about what the concept of faith meant to me, defining my integrity and being true to it, keeping my word, being open enough to risk loving, expressing my feelings (positive and negative) to those around me. This is how I found out how I felt about things. And knowing how I felt made "me" exist. I no longer existed to impress others. I existed to live a life and make a difference. I respected myself now. I trusted myself. How could I trust a Higher Power if I couldn't even trust myself? Even about something as simple as how I felt. I went to a few meetings of Al-Anon — a support group for the friends and family of alcoholics and drug addicts — and found the Twelve Steps enormously inspiring. But, ultimately, the key was facing myself.

We all have our own ways of discovering what life is about, what faith means. I can "hope" now, because I don't try to control my destiny as I once did. I care more about people than business. I never purposefully try to impress anyone and honestly would consider it a waste of time. The world is a whole lot bigger than me, and it feels good to be a little insignificant. I feel freer now and think the quality of my work has improved. I'm not afraid of getting older and not attaining enough. And, I see how I was held back by the partnership that I thought was the sole reason for my success. I see that I held my former husband back as well.

At times, I felt like a lunatic on my private journey. I was so afraid to let go of everything I knew, in favor of something I didn't, even if it was better and larger. But, I didn't back away from the fear. And I didn't give up. And, in the end, I found the courage to give in to real faith. I didn't go insane (I'm fairly sure), and the abyss was filled with trust and hope. I think those things provide the space to love.

Now, I'm not alone, but I still wouldn't describe myself as independent. In fact,

I feel supported by many more people than ever before. Everything isn't perfect. My once chronic and unrelenting shoulder spasms still hurt like hell if I spend too much time hunched in front of the computer, and I'm still trying to get my rampant PMS under control. But I'm a person. My own person. My own woman. That gives me the courage to experience my life fully. To go out on a limb. To trust. To weather criticism. And to change and grow.

Katt lives outside Los Angeles with her husband, Danny, a musician; her dogs Buster and Minnow; and two horses, Guy and Henry.

Barbara DeAngelis

"It takes a lot of courage to be the same person on the outside that you are on the inside."

Barbara DeAngelis has been on the bestselling circuit ever since she wrote How to Make Love All the Time. *Her book* Secrets about Men Every Woman Should Know *kept her there; so did* Are You the One for Me? *and* Real Moments, *which Deepak Chopra called "a brilliant, groundbreaking book that will fill your heart and nourish your spirit." She is known to some as the Love Queen. She has only recently come home to herself.*

What makes me feel that I'm finally doing a great job with my life has nothing to do with what's happening on the outside. Yesterday was a very high-powered day for me — a lot of business deals were coming to fruition — but what made me feel I was doing a good job with my life was going outdoors at about five o'clock with my dogs and my cat and sitting on the lawn for an hour, doing absolutely nothing. It was kind of foggy, and I was having what I call a real moment. I took an hour doing what I used to think was nothing, and it was the most meaningful part of my day. Not my infomercial. Not book sales. Not seminars. Not business deals. After all my success, I'm just beginning to feel like I'm doing a good job with my life because I'm finally, day-to-day, creating happiness in the moment, irrespective of the other stuff, which comes and goes like the wind. Getting here has taken courage.

One of the most courageous things we do is change. If everyone says you're wonderful every time you wear a red dress, and you change to yellow, that takes courage. Writing *Real Moments* was like that for me. I had written one successful book after another on relationships, and my publisher thought my next book would be similar. But I knew I needed to write *Real Moments* for myself. I desperately needed to write it. It's a book about the search for meaning and purpose in life, about how to have more real moments with yourself and your loved ones, and about the process of living, finding ways to make every day sacred. My publisher didn't know what to make of it. I said, "Trust me, by the time it comes out, books about life are going to be very popular." She trusted me and I'll never forget the day *Real Moments* appeared on the *New York Times* bestseller list. I was so gratified.

I have never turned away from change. I've called on it, embraced it. I believe that we're all given access to certain doorways at certain times in our lives and that most people don't recognize them, let alone walk through them when they appear. I'm on the lookout for them.

In my second year of college I made a very important decision to drop out, become a teacher of meditation, and study with a guru, much to the chagrin of everybody I knew, including my family. I moved to Europe and lived in an ashram. I turned my back on the course my life was supposed to take: get your B.A., then your Masters degree, then write your book. I got off the ladder.

And I keep getting off the ladder, listening to my inner voice and filtering everybody else's. It takes courage for a woman to find her voice and use it. I still struggle with it every day in my relationship, every day in my work, every day dealing with high-powered people. I have to remind myself constantly of my right to my opinion and of my ability to voice that opinion. I have to remind myself constantly that it's okay if I make other people uncomfortable. To some extent, my instinct is still to diminish myself, to apologize. Sometimes I feel that little girl in me, whining, "Don't ruffle feathers," and I have to say to her, "Get back in your room, because it's not 1952, I'm running the show and I didn't get here by listening to you. I understand you're afraid that we're going to alienate everybody, but that's not how we do things."

I didn't have any female role models growing up. I had none when I began my adult life. It was quite difficult to try to define power and courage and still keep my sense of femaleness, because all my mentors were men. Women today are still fighting an uphill battle — we live in a misogynist world, in a sexist world, in a world that's just creeping out of a patriarchal society — and continuing that fight takes a tremendous amount of consciousness.

Meditation is one way I stay conscious and aware. I've been meditating since I was eighteen. It's the center of my life. My quiet time tunes me into myself. If there's something "off" and I don't know what it is, I close my eyes and it's instantly brought to my attention. Rather than thinking I'm just not having a good week, and then realizing months later that I'm upset about something, I try to clear out stuff every single day. It takes a lot of work, but I've experienced the price of not doing it: It takes a tremendous toll on my emotional health and my success.

I didn't really start becoming successful until I completed a lot of this personal work. I think what holds many women back is knowing intuitively that, if they don't have confidence, they're going to have a hard time performing the daily tasks that come with being empowered in their career. To get whatever they're striving for, they know they're going to have to make conscious decisions every minute — important decisions that involve saying no to people, that involve giving people feedback, perhaps displeasing people. And sometimes they know they don't have the guts for it, so they sabotage themselves and then salve over disappointment with excuses like, "It's just not happening this year." What they are really saying is, "I don't feel prepared, I don't feel strong enough for the battle I know I'm going to have to enter." And it is a battle. I readily admit that I've had to work at least four times as hard to get where I am because I'm a woman. No question. I truly think that will be the case for women, at least in my lifetime, because society doesn't just turn around when we start wearing pants and using birth control.

Probably one of the most difficult times in my life was when my husband Jeffrey and I were just getting together. I was in a very bad marriage, not my first. I was already well-known. I'd written a book — about love of all things. I'd been on television, so I had a certain public image. And yet, I was in a terrible marriage, one I should never have even entered, because I was trying to rescue someone who didn't want to be rescued. And then Jeffrey and I met. We were friends for a year and a half before we realized we were falling in love. My husband left when he saw what was happening. And I thought, I can't believe this is happening to me again, I can't believe I'm getting divorced again, I can't believe I made a bad choice again. Why was I so blind? How did I do this? What is everybody going to think? The weekend after my husband left, I was to give a "Making Love Work" seminar. People were coming from all over the country to hear the Love Queen. I had two choices: Get up in front of all those people and say nothing about what was happening or speak the truth regardless of what they might think of me.

That Friday night when I walked into the seminar room I was a wreck. I gathered my twenty-five-person staff who were going to be teaching the seminar with me and told them everything. I said, "If any of you want to leave, you can leave. I'm going to use the weekend to get through this, because I believe in the seminar so strongly." I was going to be a student in my own "Making Love Work" seminar. I was going to do a lot of healing just like everyone else.

Two hundred people were waiting for me to start my seminar. I got up on the stage in front of them — all these people who had seen me on television, who held me in a certain light and thought of me as a very together person — and I started to cry. I told them what was happening and asked for their support. I gave them all the option to leave. No one did.

That whole weekend, I shared about myself, I did every exercise, I went through the seminar as a participant, like everyone else. This flew smack in the face of the image of a good seminar leader: You have to look good; you have to be perfect; no one is going to respect you if you're not. I'll never forget, on Saturday night, a man stood up and offered, "Are you ready for another breakthrough?" I thought, *Oh man, what else can I do?* And he said, "Close your eyes." So, standing there on the stage, I closed my eyes and heard the song "Wind Beneath My Wings" begin to play. Two hundred people holding candles sang "Wind Beneath My Wings" to me. I couldn't stop weeping. They all came up on stage and enveloped me in a huge embrace. It was one of the most healing moments of my life. I knew they were telling me, "We love you for who you are, and, in fact, you're giving us permission to love ourselves for who we are." It was remarkable. I didn't realize how remarkable until, over the next few months, my entire way of teaching changed.

Emotional courage is what we're all striving for in the end. The courage to tell the truth is something people need to be proud of, as is the courage to be yourself, to trust love and the healing process.

Robert Frost wrote, "The only way out is through." Turning into the wind, the struggle, the challenge, is the only way to get through difficult times. It is what's *supposed* to happen. The challenge exists for a reason. I don't think anything is an accident. If you try to sidestep something, it's just going to get you ten miles down the road. There comes a point when a situation is scary, but the alternative is even more frightening, maybe not on the surface but in terms of your soul, in terms of the health of your being. Sometimes the fear of staying where you are gets worse than the fear of taking the leap.

Sometimes, that leap is a free fall into the unknown. I call it living in the in-between — that invisible world that's so powerful in women — and it takes tremendous courage to be there because we identify ourselves so strongly with the physical world. To not know, to lack certainty, to lack structure, is scary, but, it's essential at times. There has to be breakdown before there is breakthrough. There has to be a death before a rebirth. Many of us don't have the courage needed, so we don't grow. We hang on to stagnant, toxic relationships, with family, with friends, with our lovers, because it's something solid. We're afraid to trust that invisible world. We're so at home with it, yet we turn our back on it and let the other world speak for us.

Often, when I'm working only with women, I'll ask my audience, "How many of you have been divorced or in a bad . . . ?" and they don't even wait for me to finish. They all raise their hands. And I'll ask, "How many of you knew in the beginning." And they all raise their hands again. We talk ourselves into ignoring our inner voice because it's not honored by the male world. It takes a lot of courage to listen to that voice. It takes a lot of courage to make other people hear it.

If more women let themselves be on the outside what they are on the inside, they would experience the wholeness they're seeking. I think our deep, inherent fear of abandonment has made us entirely too dependent, holding onto things we really need to let go of. It pains me to see a woman afraid to be alone or afraid to leave a relationship because she'll lose the abusive person she's been with. This is how we tarnish our beauty and hide our power. We forget who we are and masquerade as impotent creatures who are content to accept a little scrap from somebody and pretend it's a great piece of cake. I've done it. I did it for years. So I'm not saying these things in judgment, I'm saying them in compassion. I know what it's like to sit curled up, crying hysterically while your husband is in the next room with the door locked, and not say to him, "If you don't come out and talk to me, get out of the house." I know what it's like to plead, "Honey, could you talk to me?" I've done it in my past relationships.

We have to stick together. I wish women would empower each other and be loyal to each other. I wish more women on every level would be courageous: women in the public eye, women not in the public eye. I wish more celebrities would use the responsibility that comes with being well-known — I call it a spiritual responsibility. I wish more women would be honest about their process so that other women could see how much is attainable. The big myth about powerful people is that they're so together, so confident. The closet secret is that inside every woman is a scared little girl, and it's just a question of who's running the show — the scared child or the clear, centered, stable adult. So many women don't have confidence, or at least they *think* they don't have confidence. But, confidence isn't the absence of fear, it's how you act in spite of fear. Confidence isn't waiting until you feel totally ready to do something. If you're waiting for that feeling, you'll never do anything.

Life is always uncertain. Nature is constantly in flux. If we're not living on the edge, to the fullest degree, it's usually because we're trying to control something that's really not controllable. We sleep on the same side of the bed. We park in the same space. We put lots of controls on our lives to keep things stable. But, the truth is, anything could happen at any minute. When we stop pretending that's not so and trust change, invite it in instead of hoping it'll go past our door today, when we let go and surrender — then life becomes magical.

Barbara's latest books are Ask Barbara: The 100 Most-Asked Questions about Love, Sex, and Relationships; The Real Rules; *and* Passion.

Rita Dove

"Courage has nothing to do with your determination to be great. It has to do with what you decide in that moment when you are called upon. No matter how small the moment, or how personal, it is a moment when your life takes a turn and the lives of those around you take a turn because of you."

In 1993, at age forty-one, Rita Dove became the first black U.S. Poet Laureate, and the youngest.

All of my life, I was very shy. I still am really, but no one believes it anymore. When I began writing poetry, what I wanted was a quiet life for the mind. I would write my poems and, hopefully, they would get published and I could keep writing. This was my ideal life. I never imagined I would be in the public eye and have to speak to people.

I was in a hotel room in Chicago in May of 1993, having given a poetry reading sponsored by Columbia College the night before. I was getting ready to come home to Charlottesville, finish grading papers for my university class, and return to writing, when I got a phone call from Prosser Gifford, Director of Scholarly Programs at the Library of Congress. I had been chosen Poet Laureate — which would mean serving as consultant to the Library of Congress in matters of literature and poetry for one, perhaps, two years; I would be expected to organize a reading series at the Library, as well as promote poetry in any way I saw fit. The Laureateship meant, simply, to serve as the spokesperson for poetry in this country.

The appointment, for me, came totally out of the blue. I was young. Any hope I might have had of being Poet Laureate was twenty years into the future. And not only would I be the youngest Poet Laureate, but the first black. One of the initial things that went through my head was, *How the hell did I get here?* And then I felt frightened: If they were choosing someone this young, if they were choosing the first black Poet Laureate, they didn't want me to sit back and do nothing. This was not simply an honor to accept, but a challenge.

The idea of mixing a kind of public activism — that is, a commitment to reaching out to the public in actual deed as well as in word — with a discipline as private and esoteric as poetry put me right on the edge, treading territory that hadn't been trod. The challenge to me was to bring poetry to the public. What was being asked of me, or at least what I was asking of myself, was to believe in poetry enough to forget my shyness, to go out there and talk about it, and to believe that it could affect people. That was the challenge and one I accepted because I knew I had to — I just had to do this.

In my career as a poet, I have come across countless people, myself included, who were apologetic about being poets or about liking poetry, thinking it's not for everyone, we're such a small group. I had retreated into the rarefied air of academia and universities, reading for intellectuals. I was, in fact, rather afraid of reading to "normal" people, ordinary folks, for fear that they would say "Who the heck are you?"

I sat down at one point and thought about who the heck I am. What had brought me to this place? And, I realized, in a certain way, that it had been coming all along, my whole life had been leading up to this. I had believed, all of my life, in the value of the individual and the value of reaching out no matter what you might get on the other end. And this is where those beliefs had met me.

I had won the Pulitzer Prize in 1987 for *Thomas and Beulah.* When I began writing that book of poems, I was scared because it was very different, a story told in poem form at a time when narrative poetry was not popular in this country among poets. Everyone seemed to be a lyric poet, writing about the moment and beautiful feelings. I had to leap over that shadow — my own apprehensions about returning to an "old-fashioned" poetic form — in order to write *Thomas and Beulah,* a story about my grandparents, two very ordinary people, to whom nothing extraordinary had happened. I not only had to write it as poetry, but I had to believe that their lives, and every person's life, was intrinsically interesting and essential. That gave me the kind of strength to finish the book.

And now, if I still truly believed in the essential mystery and majesty of every person, then being Poet Laureate would mean waking up in other people a recognition of their essential mystery and majesty. The first thing to do was not to apologize for poetry, but to actually speak about poetry as I felt it, as something wonderful that opens up your life if you just relax and let it open you. That took a little leaping over my own shadow — my own apprehensions — again. As a shy person, I have never been one to say, "Hey, you guys, this is great stuff! You ought to try it."

I gave a press conference three days after becoming Poet Laureate and every time a reporter would ask me, "Well, isn't poetry difficult to understand?" I would simply aim for the positive and say, "No, but it has been made to seem that way in this country." Rather than being defensive and apologetic, I went on the offensive. "Try to remember what it was like when you were first introduced to poetry. You were probably intimidated or afraid because you didn't understand it. Fear is the thing that shuts down all human responses and as long as someone is afraid of literature, of reading poetry, you don't have much hope of really getting into it and understanding it."

At first, the media didn't grasp what I was saying, but since I didn't give them anything else, they couldn't report anything else. At this time I was also learning how to talk to the media and I came to realize that you have to say something over and over and over again for it to finally make an impression, not just on the journalist but also on the public. I would answer questions like, "Well, what do we need poetry for?" by talking about the poet's original role as bard of the community, one who was present at all important functions — births, marriages, deaths — in order to speak for the community. That should tell people how important poetry is. Then someone would counter with, "Well, how many books do poets sell?" Rather than talk about print runs, I'd talk about why our society is hooked on fast consumption and quick bursts of success. I'd talk about poetry as something steady that goes on for a long time, that doesn't fit into that fast and quick scheme. In the end, I think the media and the public understood.

As I matured into the position of Poet Laureate — say, by the spring of 1994, two-thirds of the way through my first year — some of the most moving support I received came from "ordinary people" who wrote me letters and stories:

"I remember my first experience with poetry."

"I wish I wasn't afraid of poetry."

"I remember when I wasn't."

These people included massage therapists, teenage girls and entire classes of second graders, retired Marine officers, lawyers and housewives, soldiers stationed overseas, even a puppeteer. Their letters supported my belief that poetry doesn't have to be an elitist art form, that the power of poetry to move us transcends racial, social, and economic boundaries.

I began to realize that there is an incredible hunger in people to communicate. If I hadn't opened myself up in those initial television and radio and magazine interviews, I am convinced I would never have gotten such letters. Simply daring not to be esoteric, but to open up, was essential to communicating with the public, and to eliciting a deep and honest feeling from people about poetry.

One of the difficult things about being the youngest Poet Laureate was the pressure I felt from my literary community to prove myself. "Let's see what she will do. Can she really speak about poetry?" It was hard not to respond to that pressure by pontificating, but in fact to keep opening up — not to talk down, but to be real.

The little things that I did during those two years as Poet Laureate took a great personal effort, though I tried not to show it. For example, going to MTV and talking with their executives about programming for poetry and reading poems to them, which seems like a small thing. But I was determined not to cater to a bebop television audience. I wanted to show them, instead, where we connected. And I went to the U.S. Naval Academy to read and talk about poetry. My friends gasped. My own initial reaction to the invitation was, I don't want go anywhere near that place, especially after the Tailhook scandal exposing sexual harassment in the Navy. Then I thought, *Wait a minute, why do I react that way?* Isn't the Naval Academy exactly where I should go if I have such a violent reaction? Am I going to brush them off, or am I going to go and see for myself, maybe change somebody?

At the Library of Congress, one of the jobs of the Poet Laureate is to plan a literary season that is open and free to the public. Usually, poets from all over the world come to read. But I wanted to expand the idea of what a poet is, what makes poetry, and to include the D.C. community more, especially the community near the Library. Washington is an incredible place, the Library is at the center of it — and it is surrounded by slums. The Library is a foreign country to the people in those slums, who feel they cannot enter. I asked myself, *How can I open the doors to them?*

I organized an evening for D.C. school children to read their poetry in the Library. I got them on buses, gave them maps, and their teachers came along with a whole bunch of other people, and the children read. It was wonderful to see these kids, from fourth grade students to high school seniors, all dressed up because this was important to them. They realized the Library was a place for them, too, where their voices could be heard.

I also invited a group of Crow Indian children, mostly of junior high and high school age, to come from Montana to read in the Library, because their voices hadn't been heard in the nation's capital. Before they came, they wanted to know if they could go over to Congress and read there, too. I said I'd see what I could do. We all went over to Congress, and they met their Senators and their Congressional representatives and read poetry and talked to them about the need for having more literature and more literacy in the schools. The politicians hemmed and hawed and didn't know how to respond, and I saw them realize that poetry wasn't something that would bite them.

Soon after that, I gave a speech to the National Press Club, which was really scary, because I was speaking to a room full of journalists who are very good at high rhetoric, a rhetoric that distances you from your feelings. I titled my talk "Who's Afraid of Poetry" and I began at the nursery school level: I talked about basic fears, everyone's fear of the first poem that they didn't understand, and what we do when we don't understand things. I talked about "Jabberwocky" by Lewis Carroll and how, as a child, you don't understand every word of it, but you're told it's fun, it's fantastic, and so you open up and you get it.

I think that there are two kinds of fear around poetry. Most people are afraid of not understanding and that stops them before they reach the second fear, which is the fear of being vulnerable. Kids have no problem being vulnerable and, very often, a person will grow up liking poetry, even loving it. A poem will mean a lot to them. Then suddenly around junior high school, a teacher tells them they have the wrong idea, they didn't get it, which the student internalizes as, *What I'm feeling is wrong, I am stupid.* What a big blow to a young person, because it produces feelings of rejection, like opening up and saying to someone "I love you" and having them tell you to go jump in a lake. The fear of not being understood is a fear of being alone, and is associated with poetry.

Our fear can be the strongest factor working against us. We are absolutely terrified of feelings, and absolutely terrified of our bodies. I wrote a poem inspired by my daughter Aviva, who, as we were reading one night when she was three, suddenly wanted to inspect each other's vagina. It's a pretty frank poem. Even I thought, *Whoa,* after I'd written it. I made up my mind that I would read it at public events because standing there in the flesh, reading about that kind of a moment, scared me so much. The first few times I read it, I was absolutely wild with fear. But afterward women, particularly mothers, would say, "Thank you for reading that, thank you for talking about it. We have been so ashamed of our bodies for so long."

That kind of response made me realize how important it was to read this poem, which is what led me to read it in the most unlikely place. I had been asked, as Poet Laureate, to be part of an evening of laureate readings, along with four of the Nobel Laureate poets. It was to be held in New York at the Cathedral of St. John the Divine, a huge, amazing Gothic cathedral. It was a very rainy Sunday evening, and the place was packed with about three thousand people.

I had made up my mind to read this poem because I was the only woman on the program and I had seen the impact of it earlier, that it was important especially to women. The poets had been told that we would be reading from the pulpit. When I arrived and saw that the pulpit was a big looming rostrum that spiraled up, encrusted with gargoyles, I thought, *I don't know if I can do this.* My grandmother always said that once you decide to do something, do it, don't let your last minute doubts get in the way because they're usually wrong. I got up there and read, "After Reading *Mickey in the Night Kitchen* for the Third Time Before Bed":

My daughter spreads her legs
to find her vagina:

hairless, this mistaken
bit of nomenclature
is what a stranger cannot touch
without her yelling. She demands
to see mine and momentarily
we're a lopsided star
among the spilled toys,
my prodigious scallops
exposed to her neat cameo.

And yet the same glazed
tunnel, layered sequences.
She is three; that makes this
innocent. We're pink!
she shrieks, and bounds off.

Every month she wants
to know where it hurts
and what the wrinkled string means
between my legs. This is good blood
I say, but that's wrong, too.
How to tell her that it's what makes us —
black mother, cream child.
That we're in the pink
and the pink's in us.

No one tarred and feathered me. Later, I received letters from people who said that when they heard me announce I was going to read that poem, they thought:

Something has changed in American poetry. If she dares to talk about that at a Laureate evening at St. John the Divine, something has changed.

Courage has nothing to do with your determination to be great. It has to do with what you decide in that moment when you are called upon. No matter how small that moment, or how personal, it is a moment when your life takes a turn and the lives of those around you take a turn because of you.

Rita Dove is married to German writer Fred Viebahn. She holds the chair of Commonwealth Professor of English at the University of Virginia and has received numerous honors, among them sixteen honorary doctorates, and most recently, the Heinz Award, the National Medal in the Humanities, the Sara Lee Frontrunner Award, and the Barnes & Noble Writers for Writers Award. Her play The Darker Face of the Earth *was originally produced by the Oregon Shakespeare Festival in 1996 and had subsequent runs at the Kennedy Center in Washington, D.C., and other theaters.* Her *song cycle* Seven for Luck, *set to music by John Williams, was premiered by the Boston Symphony Orchestra at Tanglewood in 1998, and her latest book of poems is* On the Bus with Rosa Parks.

Maxi Cohen

"A few months after we began filming, less than a year after my mother had died, my father found out that he had cancer. I was just beginning to get close to him and suddenly, I could lose him. It seemed more important than ever to keep filming. I couldn't stop. I felt like I was making this movie for all daughters, for all children."

In 1973, filmmaker Maxi Cohen set out to make a feature documentary about her father. Joe and Maxi *became an intensely personal and intimate portrait of a father-daughter relationship.*

I grew up in a junkyard filled with pre–World War II tankers, gas station pumps, tires, old school buses, and taxicabs. This was my father's domain, his palette, my playground. Though my father started as a truck driver, he built a trucking company in the midst of the stuff he collected, traded, and sold. And though I never saw his heart directly, I knew how big it was, because he let a homeless man live in a school bus, he lent money when he had little, and he let people trade the most useless things for the money they owed him, like row boats and water skis that fit no one we knew. My father loved transportation. He bought a plane that he flew (without a license) to check up on his trucks and then later on his boats, when he expanded his business to catching fish and clams. My father had that American pioneering spirit and felt he could do anything. To me, he was larger than life, charismatic, some kind of Jewish John Wayne, a man who only did what he wanted, never caring about pleasing others or keeping up an image. I always wanted to be like my father. Actually, I wanted to be him.

I have a snapshot of him posing with me next to his truck when I was three, but it seems like fiction. I don't remember him much in those first eleven or twelve years. He was busy and preoccupied with his growing business and rarely paid attention to my two younger brothers or me. I am sure he didn't know what grade I was in or what interested me; and because he never asked me anything, I was certain he didn't care if I even existed. I grew up hungry for his attention.

When I was twenty-three, my mother died of cancer. And though I was very close to her, so close that at times I felt I could not breathe without her, I was also about to experience being with my father for the first time. Sitting in a car with him on the way back from visiting my mother in the hospital, I felt overwhelmed with exhilaration: I had never done anything alone with him, not even a car ride.

My only ambition when I went to New York University Film School at age seventeen had been to make a movie about my father, because I felt he was "a great character." But, as the idea of the film stirred in me, I knew it would be my way of getting to know him, to understand him. It was that day in the car six years later, when he was talking to me for the first time in my life without my mother as a buffer, that I knew I had to start filming right away. And I knew the film would be not only about him, but about us, or the becoming of us, a daughter-father relationship that I was just beginning to have.

Even before finishing film school, I had begun applying for grants to make the movie with my father. The applications changed as my understanding of what I wanted to do evolved, especially after my mother died. I was fortunate to get a grant that same year, which I spent in one weekend of film shooting. My collaborator and cinematographer, Joel Gold, and I followed my father around while he worked on the fishing docks and later at home over dinner. Capturing my father on camera was a way to literally hold on to him. In this way, I got him to stop long enough to talk to me, and so a relationship began. That first weekend something happened (exactly what I no longer remember) that sent me screaming and crying to my room. My father came in, sat on the bed next to me and put his hand on my back. It was the first time that I remember my father ever touching me. And each time he did, I cried more and louder, until the touch stopped feeling like the solace of a compassionate father and more like a sexual caress. I quickly regained my composure. My father had such a hard time knowing how to be a father, or even how to conceive of himself as one. I was surprised over and over again that he could not understand what it meant for me to be his daughter. Once he said, when I suggested we go out for dinner, "I can't go out to dinner with you; you're my daughter."

For the next year, I followed my father around and filmed him, cinema verité style. At the time, this was a radical departure in form from the documentary films that were being made, which had narrators and "objectivity." My quest to be as honest as I could at twenty-four frames a second was deeply personal — it was raw and exposing. (Once, after a screening in Los Angeles, a man asked who played my father. The film was so real that this man had been completely transported and thought he had been watching fiction.) In the middle of that first weekend of shooting, Joel pointed out that it would be impossible to make the film without me in it. And so I became part of the story in front of the camera, not because I wanted to but because I realized that, to tell the story about our relationship, it was essential to the integrity of the movie that I be in it.

A few months after we began filming, close to a year after my mother had died, my father found out that he had cancer. I was just beginning to get close to him and suddenly, I could lose him. It seemed more important than ever to keep filming. I couldn't stop. I felt like I was making this movie for all daughters, for all children.

The process became much more difficult for me, because my roles as filmmaker and daughter were often in conflict with one another. Sometimes, things I wanted to know, or felt were needed for the film, the daughter in me didn't want to ask. Being compassionate and caring and, at the same time, thinking about story continuity was paradoxical at best. I filmed at times that I'm sure were not only uncomfortable for my father and my brothers, but made no sense to them and seemed like an unnecessary imposition. Only later, seeing the finished film, did my brothers understand and appreciate why I had brought the camera into the dining room or the living room at night to capture a rare moment simply "hanging out" with my father.

Some friends said spending so much time and money making a film about someone nobody had ever heard of was stupid; others said filming my father, especially now, was courageous. Stupid or courageous, making the movie was a necessary act of passion. I needed to make the film in a way I had never needed to do anything else in my life. I was getting to know my father as a real person. The film was becoming a story about expressing and withholding love.

I knew that the camera was a seducer, a way of keeping him in conversation with me, a way of creating intimacy. I think my father enjoyed the attention. He didn't change his behavior for the camera at all, probably because he didn't take me seriously and thus didn't take my filming seriously. He just allowed it, until what would become the very end, one dramatic moment on the fishing docks when he told me to stop shooting. "This is not a documentary," he said frustrated. "I am not a document. I'm a person." Sensing this was the climax of the movie, it was the last time I chose to film him. The next day, he wanted to know where the camera was, and, I think, he missed my not hanging on his every move.

The film took me six years to make: one year of shooting, four of editing, five concurrent years of fund-raising. Telling the truth during the filming wasn't nearly as hard as exposing myself and my relationship with my father to the public. Being raw and vulnerable in front of a camera was one thing, but to have that rawness and vulnerability aired in front of thousands of people was a far different thing. The fact that someone would see it, me — my face, larger than life on screen, unable to deal with my father and far from perfect — was painful. It wasn't the pimples or baby fat, it was the exposure of myself with my father, of things I couldn't even articulate. In the making of the movie, I had been fearless. Now I had to sit back and give myself up to public scrutiny. I would be judged, not just as a filmmaker, but as a daughter and human being.

I was riding the New York subway one day, and I started to wish the whole film would just burn in the vault. I had fantasies of it all going up in smoke so I wouldn't have to go through with releasing it. I was terrified of the film's potency, and proud of it at the same time. Irrationally, I felt like I'd get killed if I exposed myself, and I would die if I didn't. Either way, I felt doomed. So I chose to open the film with posters all over town, going all the way.

One of the great rewards of making *Joe and Maxi* was seeing how it opened up people, to themselves, to their parents. The film was a catalyst for people's emotions. And whether twenty years old or seventy, the viewer always saw the film through the child's eye, through the eyes of the child in them. "I saw your film and called my parents for the first time in fifteen years." "I never knew anyone else had a relationship like that with their father." How could I want anything more than to create work that provoked people to reconsider their lives in the most essential ways?

Despite receiving kudos upon its release in the U.S. and Europe, the film garnered a terrible review from the *New York Times* film critic. He was apparently so disturbed by the film that, despite his review on Wednesday, he brought it up again in the

Sunday "Arts and Leisure" section, and even used it later in a year-end quiz. Had I been more mature, I would have taken the fact that the film had such an intense impact on him as a compliment. Instead, he symbolized all the rejection I feared for thinking I could make a movie about my father as a way to know him and hold him. (This was before the age of home video cameras, before intimate documentaries became commonplace, and I had no role models.) It didn't matter how many good reviews I got, the authority of the *New York Times* devastated me. It eroded my fearlessness.

To pick myself up and take a risk again, to make another film that would go where no one else had gone, that would expose truth and reveal things that were uncomfortable, was hard after being raked over the coals for doing just that. It took me some time to work up the courage. But I have leapt into the fire time and time again. Once I had given voice to something I thought was important, I couldn't seem to stop.

Maxi went on to make many films, which have been shown on television and in movie theaters and museums. Her most recent documentary feature film, South Central LA: Inside Voices, *was made after the Los Angeles riots. By giving video cameras to African Americans, Koreans, and Latinos who lived and worked in some of the hardest hit areas, she found a way for their voices to be heard. Their video diaries tell stories from deep inside their neighborhoods, a raw and in-your-face portrait of prejudice and racism. The film premiered on the Showtime channel on the fifth anniversary of the riots. Maxi is now working on a fiction feature film about sex, power, anger, and the ethics of documentary filmmaking, as well as photographing and directing a series of short videos entitled* Ladies Rooms around the World as Far as I Have Gone, *and writing a novel on the side.*

Gail Shibley

"When we persevere and act from our convictions and from our integrity, we change the world in a way that we may never fully comprehend."

In 1991, Gail Shibley became one of only five openly lesbian women in U.S. history to become a State Representative.

My appointment to the Oregon legislature was a momentous, newsworthy event — in fact, the only thing that took my story off the front page of every daily and weekly in the state was the Gulf War, which we entered into on that same day. In 1991, Oregon had never had an openly gay legislator. (I was chosen to fill a seat made vacant when Secretary of State Barbara Roberts was elected Governor and appointed State Representative Phil Keisling to complete her term, leaving a vacant seat in the House.)

I had experience in Oregon public life, having worked for Congressman Jim Weaver for six years and at the City of Portland's Office of Transportation. I also had private-sector experience, having worked for a Portland advertising firm. Serving in the Oregon Legislature allowed me the unique opportunity to take what I'd learned from both worlds and shape public policy that made sense for Oregonians.

To move into the thick of political life was invigorating, as I had grown up with the highest regard for public service. Being a public official, as opposed to working in a support position behind the scenes or in a private business, meant that I was expected to stand up and speak out for what I believed. It was a job description that fit me to a tee.

The year 1991 was an especially important time in Oregon's political life, following the 1988 and 1990 anti-abortion and anti-gay ballot measure campaigns of the Oregon Citizen's Alliance (OCA). As a lesbian, I felt it was particularly important for my brothers and sisters in Oregon's gay and lesbian community to know we had arrived — publicly and proudly — in state government, and I said so in a news conference held just hours after my swearing in.

I also knew all Oregonians would be watching me closely, which is why I made a conscious effort to form legislative partnerships with both likely and unlikely allies. For example, I worked closely with conservative Democrats from rural Oregon on a variety of transportation issues ranging from trucks to bikes. My legislative priorities of promoting alternative transportation, protecting our natural resources, fighting for education, and championing civil rights provided unique opportunities to also forge alliances with conservative Republicans from rural Oregon — something unusual for a liberal Democrat from Portland. I came to appreciate that my personal connections with colleagues were as important as my legislative successes. Without that human element, it would have been a very different experience.

In 1992, I ran to keep my seat. It was a volatile time. Public sentiment was working itself into yet another anti-gay ballot measure (Oregon's infamous Measure 9) drummed up by the OCA. When the group's director was asked about me, he said he hoped the public would vote me down, send me back to where I came from, the belly of the beast in Portland. I was on the front page of the OCA newsletter, targeted for defeat.

Since I was running for the first time on a ballot that also contained Measure 9, I felt that to be fair to my constituents, I needed to make sure that they understood who I was, what I'd done, and what my legislative priorities were. I literally walked my district, "coming out" on every doorstep, which was daunting. It can be hard telling your best friend of your sexual orientation, but imagine telling complete strangers over and over and over and over again, regardless of who they are, regardless of their party affiliation or household structure. As challenging as it is to solicit votes face-to-face, going from door to door, it was particularly difficult to talk about gay rights, which was on the minds of many people at the time because of the OCA ballot measure. Supportive friends volunteered to walk with me as I canvassed, but I thought if I went alone I'd have a better chance of connecting with people.

Campaigning, for any candidate, is extremely stressful, but as tiring as the rest of my political campaign was, it didn't compare with the personal fatigue and, at times, fear of coming out person-to-person, face-to-face. People literally thumped me away from their doorsteps with Bibles. I was threatened and, at times, physically frightened.

These experiences made me even more determined to get out and meet as many voters as I could. Although all candidates use personal contact to build name recognition and get out their message, I knew it was especially important for me to do: it had the added dimension of educating the voters. Ignorance breeds fear, fear breeds resentment, resentment breeds hatred, and hatred breeds discrimination — and violence. I felt that personal contact — allowing people to see our commonalities rather than imagined differences — was the best way to counteract the ignorance, because it broke down the stereotypes that form the barriers of mistrust.

Consequently, canvassing neighborhoods had the potential both to energize me and deflate me. Whenever I met someone particularly virulent in their prejudice, I became all the more determined to garner support (and lawn sign locations) among their neighbors. By the end of the campaign, I'd canvassed almost every neighborhood in my legislative district.

I also appeared on television talk shows and at town hall meetings and other types of forums where I made clear who I was and for what I stood. Subsequently, I received death threats, harassing phone calls, and hate mail. My home was egged, my car vandalized, my things stolen. I was harassed beyond the bounds of the constitutional right of citizens to shout me down or vote against me or run against me.

In the end, all the canvassing, fund-raising, mailings, and hard work paid off. Facing a three-way contested Democratic primary, I was nominated with eighty-eight percent of the vote. My general election opponent was a pro-choice woman with a solid reputation in the district; as hard as she worked, I worked harder, and won 75 to 25 percent. Measure 9 was narrowly defeated.

Running for office is difficult as a woman, but even more so as a member of a group that traditionally has been shut out of positions of power. I seem like a "normal" human being. I can string two sentences together. I can fit in because of my white skin and the way I dress. I don't match certain lesbian stereotypes. But, during my campaign, I was stripped bare of all the other elements that make me who I am — I was identified solely on my sexual orientation. I faced an attitude that said I am allowed to walk my walk, talk my talk, make my money, spend my money, that I can be smart, I can be educated, I can give my best, but, by God, I'm just a dyke, and in the end, that ultimately defines, in a very derogatory way, all I'll ever be. It was a dangerous, frightening attitude that I didn't think about much during the race until later when I remembered that not everybody has to get an unlisted phone number, not everybody has to sleep with a crowbar under the bed.

Those of us deemed "minorities" — who, together, make up the majority in this country — continue to face prejudice, discrimination, and artificial barriers in all we try to do. Our leaders have traditionally been straight, white, middle-class males, and anyone not fitting that profile is, by definition, challenging tradition. I hope that, by facing the challenges I did, and triumphing, I have made the road a little less rocky, a little less intimidating for others — so each individual can realize the absolute fullness of their potential in whatever it is they choose to do. I think every person of every generation has an obligation to those who follow — we must keep in mind those who will travel the same road. It is my fundamental wish and design that people whose lives I touch will benefit from the sacrifices I make and the leadership I provide as a woman, as a human being, as a taxpayer, as a legislator, in whatever I do.

I'm in this political world — despite its moribund traditions — because I truly believe in our democratic process. And I refuse to be held back. My ideas may crash headlong onto the shores of public opinion sometimes, but I refuse to accept that I will be stopped by factors of culture or ethnicity or gender. I believe in the power of ideas to change lives, and I'm committed to using my skills to change things for the better. I believe our country's founding declaration that "all men are created equal" and that, to be true to our Constitution, there can be no higher calling than to strive to "form a more perfect Union." For a nation, a state, or a community to succeed, every citizen must have a legitimate place at the table of public discourse. As an American, as an Oregonian, I demand no more — and no less. I am committed to leaving my part of the world a better place for having been here.

I look forward to the day when "lesbian legislator" is as passé as the phrase "lady lawyer" is today. I look forward to the day when people are judged by their character and the competence with which they conduct their profession and not by extraneous factors that have no bearing on their worth.

My first week as a legislator had some rough edges, but I carry with me always a clear memory of stereotypes crumbling steadily. As a Representative in the House, one can enter the Member's Lounge in the Oregon Capitol. There, seated up to six to a table, legislators talk and laugh and break bread together, sharing a drink or a meal. During my first couple of weeks going to the lounge after a House floor session, people would glance surreptitiously at me and pretend that they weren't looking, and then they'd look again and whisper behind my back. Without overhearing anything, I knew precisely what they were saying: "Wow, she eats, she drinks, she laughs, she talks, she seems almost normal. If I didn't know better, I'd say she was a regular person." At the same time, I received many notes, cards, and comments from my new legislative colleagues, welcoming me and telling me, "I'm glad you're here." Soon, even the whispering stopped and I became quite popular, because of both my personal demeanor and the cracking of the stereotypes.

We may think we're just eating lunch but, in fact, we're breaking down stereotypes, we're changing people's attitudes, we're providing an example and shifting the paradigm for people, not just right then, not just right there, but in all their interactions in all their years to come. When we persevere and act from our convictions and from our integrity, we change the world in a way that we may never fully comprehend.

In the spring of 1998, Gail accepted an offer from the White House to become Director of Public Affairs within the Department of Transportation, and moved to Washington D.C.

The Courage to HEAL

Laura Evans

"I was in a hallway, walking slowly toward what I knew would be my death or my salvation and knowing that either way, what I was about to undergo would be horrible."

At age forty, former fashion designer Laura Evans was diagnosed with breast cancer and given a 15 percent chance of surviving three to five years. That was ten years ago. After fighting back, she founded Expedition Inspiration with the dual mission of taking other survivors of breast cancer with her to the mountains she loved to climb and of raising money for breast cancer research. In January of 1995, she co-led a team of forty-three people that included seventeen survivors — who ranged in age from twenty-two to sixty-two — up Aconcagua in the Argentine Andes, the highest mountain in the Western Hemisphere. Her experience is intimately captured in her book, The Climb of My Life, *which illustrates the parallels between surviving a life-threatening illness and climbing mountains. Her story is being developed as a television movie by Barbra Streisand's production company, Barwood Films.*

As a mountaineer, I'm often asked, "When were you the most afraid?" Those who have lived on the edge probably have a lot of answers to that question: times when their hearts beat faster, when they prayed hard to God, maybe even when they wished they could turn back time. For me, only one moment stands out, so completely etched in my mind that even now, many years later, I can still taste the fear, can feel its tendrils wrap around my very being, tightening its grasp.

I wasn't hanging off the side of a mountain. Instead, I was in a hallway, walking slowly toward what I knew would be my death or my salvation and knowing that either way, what I was about to undergo would be horrible.

Although I started climbing in 1983, it wasn't until 1989 that I thought of mountaineering as more than an occasional diversion. I recently had returned from Nepal and an arduous 250-mile trek as part of the support team of Lou Whittaker's successful American Expedition on Kangchenjunga. This was my first trip into the "big" mountains, to the base camp and on up to 18,000 feet, and I was hooked. But my climbing "career" suddenly ended before it really began.

Six months after my return from the Himalayas, I was diagnosed with an aggressive breast cancer that had metastasized to my lymph system. In a matter of months, I went from feeling stronger than I'd ever felt to being ravaged by a disease that could very quickly claim my life. I sought opinion after opinion and mountains of advice from doctors. The consensus was that I participate in a clinical trial. The treatment would include two surgeries, three months of outpatient chemotherapy, seven weeks of radiation, and a two-month stay in a bacteria-free isolation room where I would undergo intensive chemo followed by a bone marrow transplant. I would be one of the first people in the country to go through this particular medical protocol. There were no statistics on how many people might be cured by it, only the certainty that not everyone who entered the therapy would survive the massive doses of drugs.

I put away my hiking boots, backpack, tent, and dreams of climbing. A different challenge lay ahead, one that would require every ounce of physical and emotional strength that I possessed.

On March 28, 1990, I walked down the hallway that led to the bacteria-free room where I would reside, alone, until either I or the cancer won out. I walked more slowly than I ever had, measuring each step, savoring my last moments of freedom. What would it be like in there? Would I ever come out? And if I did, what would my life be like? The only thing I knew for certain was that I would miss the outdoors, desperately. I could barely remember a day that had passed without my being outside, if only briefly, to inhale the sweet aroma of fresh air.

I spent seven weeks, twenty-three and a half hours each day, in bed on my back. The other half hour of each day I spent throwing up or sitting on the port-a-potty emptying my aggravated bowels. I was kept alive, barely, by a catheter that protruded from my chest, through which drugs and food were dispensed into my system. I thought only of surviving. I'd stare for hours upon hours out my window at the lush green park across the way, bringing all my focus to the memory of wind through my hair, the warmth of sun on my body, the satisfaction of muscles and lungs that burned from good, honest physical exertion. And then I'd collapse back on my pillow and pray that if nothing more, I would walk again, out of this hospital, through that park.

On occasion, I would dream about climbing again and would fantasize scenarios where, after a tough but successful climb, I would stand on the top of one of the world's highest continental summits. In my dreams, I would climb them all. But, in reality, I was very sick.

One day, all incoming calls to my room were stopped. I was put on oxygen, morphine, and three types of antibiotics in an almost futile effort to combat the pneumonia that had invaded my lungs. The doctors came to my room more often. My husband prayed. And I stood at death's door, for the first time in my life unafraid of the deep, dark void that stretched out beyond it. But also certain, for no defined reason, that it wasn't yet my time.

Before long, I was out of danger. My immune system built back to the point where I was able to be moved out of the isolation room to a nonsterile room.

Shortly after, I was released. That very day, I walked through the park that I'd been staring at morning, noon, and night for seven weeks. With my husband, Roger, at my side, I walked four blocks, willing my atrophied muscles to take one more step, then another, into the warm embrace of that garden. At the top of the steps, I raised my fists into the air. Behind me, at the base of the hill, was Pacific Presbyterian Hospital and the closet of a room where I had endured for almost two months.

That was a summit I will never forget.

It was inevitable, as I built my body back up, that my mind would return to the unfinished business of climbing. After six months of light hiking, I pulled my backpack out of storage and thought seriously about the mountains. Two years after my painful yet exhilarating walk through that San Francisco park, I stood atop Africa's Mt. Kilimanjaro, running the last twenty feet to the crest. Statistically, I should have died or been severely debilitated by the harsh treatment and agonizing side effects of my cancer treatment. But, instead, there I was, standing at 19,000 feet with a renewed appreciation for the human spirit and the body's ability to heal itself.

It was shortly after my Kilimanjaro trek that I made a personal commitment to the millions of women suffering from breast cancer and to a Higher Power that spared my life. The result was Expedition Inspiration, a climb up Aconcagua in the Argentine Andes in 1995, the highest mountain outside of the Himalayas. Lou Whittaker's son, Peter, who owns Summits Adventure Travel in Eatonville, Washington, became my partner in Expedition Inspiration. With the help of Peter, who would lead the climb, I put together a team made up of seventeen breast cancer survivors. The goals of our climb were to raise awareness, much needed research funds, and hope. The average person, if asked to give a synonym for cancer, would without hesitation say "death." Cancer is one of the scariest things one can ever face. Another of the objectives of Expedition Inspiration is to demonstrate that not only is the disease survivable, but one can go on to achieve goals that are otherwise seen as unthinkable.

We spent twelve hard days of scrambling over rocks, scree, ice, and snow often in cruel weather, to reach the top. The most emotional part of the climb was shortly before the summit when we radioed down to the trek team at base camp 8,000 feet below us, telling them that we were going to make it. Hearing their elated screams of joy from so far below pushed us on toward the top. At the summit, we radioed down again. It was a wonderful moment knowing that all of the effort that had gone into the project, and all that we were trying to do for the cause, was going to be a success. I know it was equally emotional for everyone at base camp. Some of the women had not gone as high as they'd hoped, but we were no less a team — I and the two other women who stood on the top represented all that we were doing as a group. Whether on the summit team or the trek team, none of us lost sight of why we were there and the fact that we were climbing for so many other women.

Aconcagua is a big mountain, but I would climb it again any day, rather than walk down that hospital hallway again. With the support of my husband, Roger, and of Peter Whittaker and our team of breast cancer survivors, I stood at 23,000 feet, battered lungs and all, to honor the will and determination that exists in each of us and to pay homage to the thousands of individuals who have drawn on that strength in an effort to stay alive. It was one of the greatest moments of my life.

The Aconcagua climb was made into a PBS documentary, "Expedition Inspiration." Expedition Inspiration annually conducts numerous climbs and other outdoor adventures, including bicycle tours, treks, and climbs up Mt. Whitney, Mt. Rainier, and Mt. Kilimanjaro.

With the support of her board of directors, Laura also runs a program called Help Breast Cancer Take-a-Hike, which she started "to involve the many people who believe in our mission: to support, educate, and honor the thousands of women going through this illness, and to encourage people to take responsibility for their own health and welfare by getting outside and doing something good for themselves." Drawing 100 to 800 people, Take-a-Hikes are two-hour treks with just enough vertical ground to give people a feeling of what it would be like to go on a climb. Half of the pledge money raised is donated to a local hospital or breast cancer center. Take-a-Hikes have been held in Boise, Sun Valley, Tucson, Denver, Seattle and Los Angeles, where Cindy Crawford was Honorary Chair of the event.

Dana Reeve

"I'm a very pragmatic person. I don't normally operate on planes of the spiritual, but without even trying, without even knowing, our whole family shifted into this other realm. Anyone who has been through profound suffering or drastic change must experience this. I live life on a deeper level by necessity."

Dana Reeve is a singer, mother of six-year-old Will, and wife of Christopher Reeve, who came to movie fame as Superman and, in 1995, was left immobile from the shoulders down when he was thrown by a horse and broke his neck.

My life was so radically changed by Chris's accident. It was the most profound change I've ever experienced, that I ever hope to experience. I think anybody who goes through this kind of suffering or tragedy is acutely altered.

There were two moments after the accident that, for me, speak volumes about a transformation that happened, which I wasn't even aware of at the time. These are not the obvious moments, not the time when I was first told about Chris's accident, not when I heard the depth of his injury: that he was going to be paralyzed from the neck down and that he wasn't breathing on his own. That was a shock of a magnitude beyond all words. There were other defining, subtle moments that I look back on and see the internal shift that took place in my life. One occurred as I faced calling relatives and friends about the accident. The other I saw in my son Will, as he faced his fear of seeing his daddy for the first time after the accident.

One of the things that had always frightened me was how difficult it would be to make a phone call to a family member or to anyone I cared about with bad news. I had never had to do that, but the idea of breaking the news that someone had died, or had been in a terrible accident, terrified me. And, of course, that was exactly what I faced.

The person I called when I was first told about the accident was my father. He's a doctor, and I needed him to talk to the doctors at the hospital where Chris had been taken, to help with the translation about the injury. I knew how serious Chris's condition was, but it somehow helped me to hear it from my father. I'm very close to my parents; they've always been a tremendous support to me, and at times I've leaned on them heavily, as I did then.

Later, I phoned them back to let them know that Chris had been transferred safely to a hospital in Charlottesville and that he was stabilized, but that the news was still bad. I made that call with the intention of begging my mother to make some of the difficult phone calls for me, to Chris's mother, his stepmother and brother, because I couldn't bear describing again what had happened. I spoke with them briefly, and then my mother, on her own, offered to make calls. "Do you want me to call Chris's mom?" she asked. In that instant, I realized that it was my responsibility, it was my job to do this. Very peacefully and confidently it came to me, *This is the beginning. I've really got to stand on my own here.*

I got off the phone and began to make the calls. And, as I was making them, I was stunned at my ability to remain calm, courageous, peaceful, and supportive of the person to whom I was telling the news, knowing what they were going through. I was suddenly in the role of the supporter. It's remained thus ever since. I've thought about this often, because I've always been a supportive person; but this was the defining moment when my role radically changed and I became someone on whom people needed to depend, for news, for support, for comfort, for fulfilling needs.

Ever since then, I don't sweat the small stuff. There is so little that I find daunting, so little that is difficult for me, and in an odd sort of way that's been a gift. I feel that I've been able to overcome a lot of the everyday kind of fears, because the reality that we went through was so difficult. It was the worst of nightmares, and we lived through it and survived. To go through something like that, especially the initial shock and trauma, is to rise up into another realm, to enter into a different sphere of living. I know that sounds esoteric, but it's true. I'm a very pragmatic person. I don't normally operate on planes of the spiritual, but without even trying, without even knowing, our whole family shifted into this other realm. Anyone who has been through profound suffering or drastic change must experience this. I live life on a deeper level by necessity. It's not even by choice. It just is. And, making those first calls was the defining moment of this shift. It was the beginning.

I saw a similar thing happen to our son, Will. Both Chris and I felt a tremendous concern for the children at the beginning. The two older ones were able to process the news in a way that Will, who was not even three yet, couldn't, and we had to be very careful to be as honest as we could without scaring him.

For the first week after the accident, Will was terrified. He didn't want to go to see Chris. He didn't want to be near him. He was afraid to go into the Intensive Care Unit. And, he didn't want me to go. At home, he would act out the accident. He had a little horse in his playroom, and he would ride on it and fall off and moan, "My neck, my neck." It was very difficult to go through, but I think it was his way of processing it.

After a week, I slowly, slowly brought Will closer and closer to Chris. First, we went to the door of the ICU, then we went inside, and then we saw the nurses. Then finally, we went in and he saw Chris, and this was Will's defining moment. Chris was there, he was smiling, he was daddy, and he was alive. From that moment on, Will experienced a transformation of courage that was phenomenal. His bravery exponentially increased. I saw it in things like his behavior around swimming. He would jump off the side of the pool, swim underwater, things he had never done. He was suddenly embodied with this kind of courage that makes you feel you can overcome anything. He had overcome his worst fear, just like I had.

I was able to see in Will, in a much more primitive way, what was happening with me — this realization that, if I can get through this, I can get through anything. It was a quiet thing. It wasn't a revelation full of thunder, but a shift in perspective that was very profound. I will never be the same because of it. The way I approach my work, the way I approach my relationships with other people, has been deeply changed. It's a beautiful thing. In all of this suffering is a gift. There have been many gifts. And this is one of them. To be living life at its extreme.

The Chinese philosopher Lao-tse said, "Because of deep love, one is courageous." From the moment I heard the news, this is what drove me. I could not fall apart, because I had to take care of Will. I had to make sure he was emotionally okay. I had to pack. I had to get to Charlottesville, find the hospital, the emergency room. There was no way around it, no one to take care of me. It had to be me who took care of me. Something just clicked in, some strength I wasn't really aware of, and off we went. I was outside of myself, because I had to take care of someone I loved.

People ask me now, "How did you get through this? How did you cope? How can you even get through the day?" It was never a question, and still isn't. I do it because I love. Chris is a very independent person, but needs a tremendous amount of physical care now and much more emotional care than he ever did before. But, giving it has never been a decision. It's simply something I do because I love him. And what I get in return is tremendous.

It seems heroic to people, but it isn't. It's just a new definition of my life, new parameters. And there's an effortlessness to it, because of this heightened sense, this other realm. It's as if we borrowed another life and now we're living it. And one of the things about this life is that it is deeply lived and deeply felt.

It's hard to pinpoint, but I am aware now of a feeling of strength and abandon that I've never had before. I see it in my work. I'm a singer and at first, having been away from it for the year it took me to get our lives back together, I was awkward. A friend of mine is the artistic director of a Shakespeare festival, and she offered me a role in a musical version of *Two Gentlemen of Verona.* At the first rehearsal, I felt like I was all wrapped up in cotton. I wasn't present. I felt like a visitor from another planet. I kept thinking, *What am I doing here?* And yet, this was my work, the theater was my world. As the days went by, the cotton slowly started to pull away and I became immersed, and the singing filled me with such joy and was such incredible therapy that I relaxed. It fed me in a way that it had never fed me before. And that was a gift.

Before the accident, I never studied voice seriously. I simply had a good enough voice to sing professionally. I dabbled a bit with lessons, got coached off and on for auditions. But, after the accident, I started studying in earnest. And the change was remarkable. My fear was gone. I didn't worry about being judged. I felt that wonderful sense of abandon. It felt good, it felt therapeutic. I found places within my voice that were incredibly strong and incredibly effortless at the same time. I was committed in a completely new way. I was no longer satisfied with simply dabbling, which is metaphoric for my whole life now. I am no longer satisfied with simply dabbling. There is too much of life to be lived deeply.

Dana is in the early stages of preparing a CD of her singing and is working on a book due out in November 1999 titled Care Packages: Letters to Christopher Reeve from Strangers and Other Friends.

Sharon Gless

"My mother said, 'Sharon, I want you to pack your trunk and another smaller suitcase. You have two hours in which to do it. . . . ' She then sat down in the living room with a book, and in the two hours I was given to pack, she never turned the page."

Sharon Gless is a two-time Emmy award-winning actress, most noted for her role as Christine Cagney in the groundbreaking 1980s hit television series Cagney & Lacey.

This is a story about a woman in a bus station — a woman who risked everything she thought safe in her world in order to buy freedom for her daughter. It was a moment when she dared to cut her daughter free from her own family, fiercely presided over by a grande matriarch. The woman was my mother. The moment can only be fully understood by knowing what led to it.

My mother was the eldest of four children. Her father was a prominent entertainment lawyer in Los Angeles. He was sole counsel to Howard Hughes, Cecil B. DeMille, and Louis B. Mayer of MGM, to name a few. There's even a salad named after him at the Polo Lounge of the Beverly Hills Hotel.

Her mother was one of the last of the grande dames, the kind you used to see in the movies, only she was real. She was very elegant, very disciplined, very New England, and very controlling, specifically when it came to my mother and me. And my mother worshipped her.

Mom was raised in the enormous and rather opulent home her parents had built. She was an adult with her own family when her parents separated and each moved away, and my grandmother asked her if she would move back into the house and look after it. My mother said yes, and she and my father, my older brother Michael (age five), and I (age two) moved into the house where I spent all of my growing years. My younger brother, Aric, was born there. My mother spent her entire married life in the bedroom suite she had had as a child. My grandmother's quarters, which she kept even though not living there, were strictly off-limits.

I think I am accurate in saying that my mother's clearest dream all her life was to be blissfully married and have lots and lots of children. Part of the dream came true. She gave birth to five children. She lost two children after birth. The three of us that survived were a handful. The other part of her dream didn't work. She and my father separated after twenty years of marriage. And through the loss of her children, my grandmother was there. And through the end of her marriage, my grandmother was there.

After my parents' divorce, when I was fourteen, my grandparents became our sole means of support. I loved my father, but he wasn't a very good husband and he wasn't around to help raise my brothers and me. When Mom divorced him, he stopped supporting us financially, so my grandmother stepped in and all of our expenses were now paid by her. And the purse strings she held were very tight.

Eventually, my grandmother (Grimmy, we called her) moved to Carmel, California. She took my mother and younger brother with her. She even bought my mother a house of her own. By this time, I had been in boarding school for two years — financed by Grimmy. Everything was taken care of by Grimmy — Michael's college education at USC, my boarding school in Monterey, Aric's private school in Pebble Beach, my debuts (two of them), our clothes, food, allowances (even my mother was given an allowance). Grimmy literally had taken on another generation.

Since my mother had no money of her own, she was totally dependent on Grimmy. I don't know what kind of life that was for her emotionally, what she had to give up. My mother was a very proud woman, but she didn't have so much false pride that she wouldn't accept my grandmother's help. She had three children. And they had to be educated and clothed and fed.

Throughout, my mother adored Grimmy, loved living near her, and was completely devoted to her. For example, although my grandmother had hired help, she said no one made a bed like my mother did. So, happily, every day, Mom would go over to Grimmy's house and make her bed.

Now, the good news about this story is that none of us ever "went without." My grandmother made sure of that. But, with this generosity came a price. I would hear my mother say, "Oh, thank you, Mother!" at least ten times a day. "Oh, Mother, how perfect!" I said, "Thank you, Grimmy" constantly, for the smallest thing. Once, my mother made me write a thank-you note when Grimmy bought batteries for my little radio.

I sound ungrateful. I am not. But the pressure on me to perform became intense. Grimmy told me that she and my grandfather looked upon me as an investment. "We put money into you, and we expect dividends." I felt scrutinized and afraid of not "conducting myself properly." Even my tone of my voice was listened to carefully and corrected.

Of Grimmy's seventeen grandchildren, I looked the most like her and was told I was her favorite granddaughter. She said that, because she loved me more than the other girls, she expected "more" of me.

When I graduated from boarding school, I was drastically overweight. Grimmy was furious with my lack of control and was determined to take the weight off me before Christmas, as I was to make my debut in Los Angeles that December (all paid for by my grandparents). She said she'd be damned if I was going to "walk down that aisle looking like Moby Dick!" (The remark was in reference to the fact that we all wore white gowns.) So, I moved in with her.

I had just spent the last four years in a boarding school and had never lived with my mother in her new home in Carmel. All that time, we hadn't gotten along because I was angry at her about my parents' divorce and was too young to see what an impossible situation it had been for her. Nevertheless, Mom came to Grimmy's house and said that she wanted me to live with *her* — that I was *her* daughter. I don't remember a lot about this confrontation, except that I was frightened — for me, for my mom. I only remember that the conversation went on a long time and Mom begged Grimmy, "But Mother, I can get the weight off of Sharon. Please, she's my daughter!" And Grimmy answered back, "No, Marjorie, you're not strong enough. The child can too easily trick you." And then Mom whispered, "Oh, Mother ..." and ran out of the house, crying as if her heart would break. And I just sat there.

Neither my mother nor I ever contradicted Grimmy. To go against her wishes was not an option. I lived with Grimmy for several months. She took forty-five pounds off of me. Looking back, I don't remember my mom in those days.

After my debut, I returned to Carmel and promptly fell in love with an older man. He was twenty-four. When he came to the house to take me out, Grimmy would invite him in and talk with him about his ambitions in life. It was always a short conversation, because he didn't have many. That, taken together with our late night necking in her living room, made Grimmy nervous, so she sent me back to live with my mother.

I was unhappy in Carmel. Except for my twenty-four-year-old, I couldn't see a future. I was lost. I wanted to be back in Los Angeles. I wanted to go home. Instead, I was sent to Gonzaga University in Spokane, Washington. Having gotten over my twenty-four-year-old-with-no-ambition, I soon was making friends and having a wonderful time, which lasted well into my sophomore year. Then, with only two weeks to go before finals, I got involved in some mischief — innocent stuff — but I was stupid enough to get caught. And suspended. They said I could come back the following September and take my finals then.

I was petrified. I started laughing. I couldn't stop. I was laughing at how much trouble I was in. I laughed so hard I had to sit down on the floor. No one else saw the humor in my situation. It didn't matter. I knew I was dead.

During my travels back and forth between Washington and California, my grandmother always sent me by plane. But now, I returned to Carmel by Greyhound bus. It was a twenty-six-hour ride. When my mother met me at the station, she helped me into the car and then said, "I think you should call your grandmother and apologize to her." So I did. And Grimmy said, "Well, I might as well have flushed that money down the toilet." I said I was sorry. She said she wasn't going to send me to school any more.

I stayed at my mother's house. I was silent about my feelings for awhile. Then one day, I confided to my mother that I wanted to go away. She asked me where. I didn't know, back to Los Angeles maybe. She said no. She said my grandmother would have a heart attack if I left. And I, like my mother, never did anything without Grimmy's consent.

That summer, I sank into a deep depression. Honestly, there are whole sections I don't remember.

The most important thing that happened that summer was the wedding of my best friend, Susan. I was her maid of honor, and the wedding was held in Los Angeles at her house, which her parents had recently bought from Grimmy. It was the same house I mentioned earlier. I had grown up in this house. All through my childhood, Susan would come to play with me there. As we grew older, she would come over almost every weekend to spend the night. Now, I was returning to watch my friend be married in it. The reception was the same sort of formal one that my mother had

had when she married my father in that house so many years before.

I remember that night very clearly and still not without pain. I remember when Grimmy entered the house. I watched her and wondered what this must be like for her. There she stood, quite regal, in the house that she had designed and built, the house in which she had raised all her children, the house where her marriage had ended — the same house where my mother had raised all her children and where my mother's marriage had also ended. Three generations of us had lived in this house, and there the three of us stood. Grimmy, Mom, and me. None of us ever mentioned it.

I laughed a lot that night, and drank a lot — and cried. All I wanted was to go back to when everything was fine. When Susan would come over and spend the night.

After the reception, a bunch of us, in our formal gear, crashed another party. By the time I came home, it was very late and I was quite drunk. But I remember the conversation with my mother. Grimmy's apartment was dark, but I knew my way around. I went into my mother's room and even though there was no light, I knew by the absolute silence that she was wide awake. I could feel her. We couldn't really see one another. I sat on the floor in my formal gown and cried. I told her I was so unhappy and I needed to go away. We both were whispering even though we were the only ones in the apartment (Grimmy was staying with another one of her daughters). Mom again said that if I went, it would kill my grandmother. I had to return to Carmel and get a job. And I said something that I had never said to my mother. I don't know where it came from. It wasn't meant to be hurtful. Crying softly, I said, "But Mom, if I stay she'll ruin my life the way she has yours." I couldn't believe I had said that. I said it so quietly, I hoped she hadn't heard me. But I knew she had. The room went quiet again. She said nothing. Eventually she said I should get to bed.

My mother and I returned to Carmel. My grandmother remained in Los Angeles. I don't remember the days following. I must have continued doing what I was supposed to do. But my depression grew deeper. One night, I woke up with the most violent headache. In tears, I woke up my mother, thinking even as I touched her shoulder, that I was too old to wake my mother up just because I was sick. She called the doctor, and he told her it was nerves. He said to pack my neck with ice. She did, and as I went numb, I fell back to sleep.

I don't know what my mother was thinking and feeling over the weeks that followed, but it must have been building to the fateful day I am about to describe.

I had a houseguest from boarding school. Her name was Edie. One morning, very late, I awoke to a totally empty house. I couldn't find my mother or Edie. Maybe they had gone to church together. My mother went to mass daily. That would have been like Edie — always doing "good" things. Eventually, however, they returned. Edie looked concerned and had a rather strained smile. I asked, "Where were you?" My mother replied, "Sharon, I want you to pack your trunk and another smaller suitcase. You have two hours in which to do it. While you're packing, I want you to decide where you would like to go. Anywhere in the United States. When you get there, you can call me and tell me where to send your trunk. I only ask that you do not go to Los Angeles."

I was stunned. It was so abrupt. Some voice inside me whispered, "Sharon, this is what you said you wanted." She reiterated the part about wanting me to be ready in two hours. I asked what this was all about. I thought maybe she was angry at me for something. She said she and Edie had been to see Dr. Burleson. To this day, I don't know what she told him, but it's not important now. Burleson told her she had to cut the "apron strings" and let me go.

She continued: "I've been across the road to the Roots' house, and I've borrowed two hundred dollars from them." (My mother had no money of her own, only what my grandmother gave her to run the house and raise Aric. She had to save her receipts to show where the money went, and was never able to save.) She said, "I'm giving it to you. It's all I have, but it should be enough to hold you until you can get a job. You'll have to go by bus. I'll send your trunk when and where you tell me. You might want to stay in a YWCA until you can find an apartment." A part of me was so excited, and a part of me wanted to cry. I can't tell you how petrified I was. I began to cry. I started to say something and she stopped me. "Do what I say, Sharon." She said it so softly. She then sat down in the living room with a book, and in the two hours I was given to pack, she never turned the page. Not once.

My grandmother had been in Los Angeles all that summer, but was returning to Carmel by train the day that all this was going on. She'd be arriving in three hours, and the only way Mom could get me out was if Grimmy didn't know. This was her last chance to help me. It was not a coincidence that my mother had chosen this day. I just hadn't figured that out yet.

Within the two-hour period that I was given, I packed all my things. It was very quiet. None of us talked during this time. I think we were all numb, protecting ourselves from pain. I put my suitcase in the car, and my mother took me and Edie to the bus station. She made sure I got my ticket (I had picked Seattle, Washington), she kissed me good bye, and left me there with Edie. She was rushing, as she was supposed to pick up Grimmy in Salinas. Her train was coming in at 4:00 P.M. My bus was leaving at 4:15. She had it timed just right, so that when Grimmy found out, it was too late. The bus had already left, and Grimmy couldn't stop it. By 4:20, driving Grimmy to Carmel and knowing I was now gone, she told her what she had done. She then turned the car back toward the bus station and picked up Edie.

Me, I cried a little — not too much — a little, for so many reasons. It was a long bus ride to Washington, but the farther I got from Carmel, the more I knew this was the only way it could have happened. I prayed my mother would be all right. I knew I would be. I was young and filled with possibilities. All I wanted was to make my own money, because I knew that my own money would buy me independence.

I went to the YWCA, got a room, and bought a newspaper. My first day there, I saw an ad that said they would pay me a lot of money to sell aluminum siding for houses. (Johnny Carson loves this story.) I went out in my pink linen suit, high heels, and white gloves and tried to sell aluminum siding to someone who lived in a brick house. I lasted one day. Eventually, I found a job I liked, went to school at night, made good friends, and became "financially independent."

My grandmother did have a heart attack, about a month after I left, but it was not because of me. She had been ill. Happily, she recovered.

After a year, I returned to Los Angeles, and slowly Grimmy and I started to "circle" one another, cautiously establishing our territories. We grew very close and spent many times together, laughing and learning to respect one another's company. We never mentioned that day I left.

Many years later, I asked my mother what Grimmy had said when she told her what she had done. "Nothing," she replied. "What could she say?" She then said, "I had to let you go. You were dying."

This amazing woman, whom I have the good fortune to call my mother, risked everything she knew to get me on the bus that late summer day thirty-five years ago. If she hadn't, I doubt if I would have the life I am enjoying today. I am free. I don't depend on anyone for anything. My money is the money I earn. In the late 1980s, while shooting *Cagney and Lacey,* Tyne Daly and I became the highest paid women in the history of television. I'm sorry that Grimmy didn't live to see it.

I received a note from Edie a few years ago — thirty years after the event — apologizing for being in on the "exile." It wasn't necessary, but it let me know how powerful that day had been in *all* our lives.

My mother lived in the same house in Carmel until she died at eighty-four. I believe she would be very proud of me today. I believe she would be proud of all her children. And why not? She did a wonderful job. I love her so very much, and I kiss her feet for having the courage to set me free.

Sharon lives in Florida with her husband, Barney Rosenzweig.

Carole Isenberg

"Moey was gone, and he had died in my home, and in the end it was the most natural thing that could have happened."

Carole Isenberg was associate producer of the film The Color Purple, *executive producer of the television series* The Women of Brewster Place, *and executive producer of the feature film* This Is My Life. *She currently works with teenage girls and their families.*

~

"Stupid, you're an idiot!" hissed the frail man in the wheelchair at my side. The spittle had collected at the corner of his mouth, and his angry hazel eyes were magnified in the lens of his glasses. I should have expected it, but was still stunned that it took only from the time the plane touched down to our arrival at the luggage carousel for this outburst. My husband, Jerry, who was waiting for us, shook his head as he heard the familiar eruption. "Welcome to Los Angeles, Moey," he said as he bent down to kiss my father. I thought, *What have I done? This could be a big mistake.*

Twelve years later, I don't remember what caused Moey's outburst. It didn't take much to set him off. I had flown back to New York to accompany him on this trip, using my frequent flyer miles so he could sit in first class for the first time in his life. Moey had visited Los Angeles yearly for the nineteen or so years that I had lived here. His greatest joy in life was being with my teenage sons, Joshua and Zachary. But this was not one of those yearly trips — he was returning to my home because I wanted to care for him. Moey's supposedly curable prostate cancer had metastasized to his bones. His doctors in New York gave me a diagnosis of about three months for him to live.

My mother, Evie, had died of breast cancer six years before. Evie was the one who made the social plans, stayed in touch with the family, kept them connected to the world. My parents were a volcanic duo. When Evie and Moey weren't fighting, they spent months in icy silence. I estimate they probably didn't speak for about half of their forty years together. Yet, without her, Moey was bereft and became a hermit, sealing himself off in their apartment in Queens. Moey lived a marginal life. For meals he would prepare a stew that would last for a week, and he spent most of his time submerged in his vast collection of periodicals and months of saved sections of the *New York Times.*

When my mother was diagnosed with cancer, I had begun researching alternative methods of medicine and healing. Carl Simonton, a well-respected physician, was a leader in the field of guided visualization techniques, using the imagery of destroying the cancer cells and nullifying their power. His work was very successful for many patients. My mother had refused to speak about her illness, much less consider anything alternative. But I now thought my father, always more open, would try one of these possibilities. I even fantasized about taking him to the treatment centers in Mexico that specialized in coffee colonics and special herbs. I couldn't accept the fact that his illness was so far along.

"Carole, we had to put him in the hospital; he was shrieking from the pain." It was my Aunt Ethel, Dad's sister. "Dr. Rosenberg was wrong. The radioactive isotopes he planted in your father's prostate didn't nuke the cancer. It's in his bones." My heart sank. The swift progression of the bone cancer left Moey incapable of living alone without nursing help. And his volatile nature had become even more explosive with the pain. The turnover in practical nurses was constant: Latitia, Mary, Rhonda, Willie June, Sylvia, Doreen. Moey quickly developed a nursing alumni association.

During my last visit to his apartment, I walked in on Moey hobbling around and shouting, "Stupid! Can't you do anything right?" to his latest practical nurse, Geraldine. The place was a mess, and an unsavory odor wafted throughout. Geraldine was sassy, but there was a hard gleam in the woman's eye and not a hint of compassion. I was afraid she'd harm him. I'd just read an exposé about elderly patients being abused by their caregivers. My younger sister, who lived only a few blocks away, made it clear she wanted nothing to do with this problem.

Back in Los Angeles, after endless conversations with Jerry, he finally said, "It's okay to bring him here; you'll feel better." We had known for years that, in the end, we would take care of Moey, and the time had come. I hated seeing him so alone and so isolated. I felt he was my responsibility as his daughter, and I wanted him well cared for. I knew being in my home was where he was supposed to be. It was the right choice. My only choice.

"So, Jerala, shayner boychik (my handsome boy)," Moey began his good-natured needling of my husband as our car sped from the airport to home, "you're thrilled to have me?" Jerry was one of the few people that Moey respected. He never got out of line with Jerry. "Moey," Jerry responded, "I hear you're taking a sabbatical from the *New York Times.*" They kept up their usual banter, and I was very quiet. I knew what Life with Father was like, that he could be very loving but was often impossible and bullying, with an unpredictable proclivity for tantrums and outbursts. What I didn't know was how to be the caretaker of a terminally ill person. I think my ignorance gave me the courage to attempt something I probably wouldn't have attempted had I known more.

As we turned the corner to home, I noticed the gold-and-rust-colored amber trees were in full June bloom. We pulled into the driveway as my blue-eyed boys, lean Joshua and husky Zachary, rushed out the front door. They gently helped my father out of the car and assisted him in his arduous walk to his new bedroom. The room had belonged to my housekeeper, Letty. It was a small room tucked behind the kitchen, but it was the only bedroom on the ground-floor level of the house and would give him more mobility.

To prepare for Moey's entry into our lives, I had met with Sue, a compassionate, motherly woman who specialized in gerontology. The soothing, pale gray walls of her office were filled with black-and-white photographs that captured the beauty, dignity, and wisdom of aging. In her organized and peppy way, Sue navigated me through a labyrinthine to-do list for Moey's physical needs. Then she turned to the emotional impact of caring for my father. "There might be a point when you find it difficult to continue having him live in your home. I know some excellent nursing homes." I thought of the movie *Where's Poppa?* George Segal was being driven crazy by his loony old mother, played by Ruth Gordon, but couldn't even bring himself to say the words "nursing home." Could I, a nice Jewish girl, ever put my father in a nursing home? When Sue started to say, "If he should die in your house — ," I felt revolted and frightened, cutting her off with, "No! No! There's no way he can die in my home."

Moey's room was fairly consumed by the hospital bed. My boys had experimented with all the settings. A gleaming chrome wheelchair sat in the corner. The portable commode and shower bar for assistance were installed in the bathroom. I watched Moey sit on the side of the bed with difficulty and sigh while his few belongings were brought to him. My father, who had been six feet tall and always chunky, was now emaciated and shrunken. He smiled at me and I kissed his head. "Mamela (little one)," he said, "I can't even drive a car. How can I be living in Los Angeles?"

Once Moey arrived, his needs were my first consideration, and we quickly fell into a routine. I took care of him at night and in the early morning. He was always his sweetest in the morning. I would bring him a tall glass of orange juice about seven o'clock, and he would take his complement of potions in his shaking hands. "Caroluchala," he would say, "you're still my pussycat princess." Jerry usually peeked in on him before he took a jog.

The day nurse's shift was from ten until six. He disliked Lucille, the first day nurse, hating her perfume and convinced she was out to get him. Thank God, our angel Ralph appeared. He was a beautiful, gentle black man who could bathe and turn Moey easily, shave him with precision, and keep him in good humor. Ralph became friendly with my quick-witted housekeeper, Letty, so there was always laughter coming from my kitchen. Moey flirted with Letty, who was devoted to him. But no matter how immaculately she kept his room, a sweet fetid aroma would emanate from it — illness has a pungent scent. Because my office was only about fifteen minutes from my home, I could return easily for doctor's appointments, swing by for lunch, or just check in.

The only stylish piece of furniture in Moey's bedroom was a bamboo étagère whose glass shelves were filled with all the vials and containers for his assorted medicines, the most important being the morphine that he took every four hours for pain. Moey was in a continuous state of mild hallucination from this opiate. When the pain became intolerable, Jerry, who had been a medic in the Coast Guard, would take a syringe from its crisp paper jacket, fill it with Demerol, and shoot it into Moey's nearly nonexistent tush. As time went on, those crisp paper jackets were opened so frequently that Jerry was afraid he would overdose Moey.

I could never have cared for Moey without Jerry's support. He knew only too well how difficult a character my father was. But my extraordinary husband said, "Assisting you with Moey is my honor, because of my love for you. I love Moey for creating you." I can still see the two of them in the sun-dappled breakfast room sharing the *Los Angeles Times*. Jerry, who has a sharp, black sense of humor, would say, "Moey, I think there's less of you today than yesterday." Moey, who was pretty wry himself, would retort, "I'm glad my diet is working."

When the doctors had given me the three-month prognosis for Moey's life, I couldn't accept it as final. It seemed impossible that the doctors could put a date on my father's death. I felt I could inspire him to choose healing, to choose life, willing him to turn back the tide of this illness. I wanted to explore more alternative healing methods.

One afternoon after he had been settled in my house a short time, we took a ride into Santa Monica to visit the Wellness Community, and my special friend Gloria Carlin accompanied us. Within a small craftsman bungalow was a unique healing center dedicated to cancer patients. The entry table was filled with information on meditation and guided visualization, the technique of using mental imagery from the meditative state. That afternoon, we participated in a drop-in rap session, which was available three times a week to give patients and the people who love them a chance to talk with others in similar circumstances. Actress Gilda Radner was leaving as we entered, and she was radiant. I heard her say, "I finished a round of chemo. We're leaving for Paris tomorrow."

Twenty or so people filled the funky living room that afternoon. We — children, parents, husbands, wives, and lovers — looked pretty solemn. The facilitator, Julia, a pale, lovely, soft-spoken woman of about fifty, who was a two-time cancer survivor, began the session by talking about her own experience. Julia felt it was worth trying anything that gave you hope, medical as well as alternative methods. We then took turns telling our stories. When it was Moey's turn, my father, who always had loved being the center of attention, mumbled, "This healing stuff is for my daughter. She believes in it. She deserves it. Not me. I'm too far gone. It's no use for me." My heart tightened and tears rolled quietly down my cheeks. To humor me, Moey went back to the Wellness Community a few times to listen to meditation tapes.

Still, I couldn't give up trying to work with Moey, trying to assist his healing when there existed even a vague possibility that his quality of life could improve. So,

I turned to my vivacious friend Rahla Kahn, who created a unique workshop called Playshop, which grew out of her training as an actor and used improvisational techniques to encourage people to play with life. She worked with Moey individually. "She's adorable," was all he would say. He never refused to try any of the alternative programs I suggested. But my father, who was a Jew well educated in the teachings of the Torah and Talmud, was a confirmed atheist and had no spiritual life. Moey never believed there were other possibilities, and it saddened me that he felt so impotent and spiritually void.

At night, we kept the intercom open between our bedroom and Moey's room so we could monitor him. One night, when he had been with us for six weeks, the intercom was inadvertently shut off. In the morning, I was horrified to find my father on the floor, soaked in his own urine. He'd tried to get to the bathroom by himself and had fallen. There wasn't too much left to Moey, physically, but I didn't have the strength to lift him. We now needed round-the-clock assistance.

Sometimes, when I would go into his room in the afternoon, the shades would be half drawn, and my father would be sitting in his wheelchair reading a newspaper that was weeks old. "News isn't dead until I finish reading it," he'd always say. In areas like current events, he remained sharp, never relenting in his tirades about Ronald Reagan or George Bush. Sometimes, I would come in when he was propped up in bed, and I would sit next to him and hold his hand or put my head on his chest, remembering when he was Daddy, completely invincible. As a little girl, when I heard the click in the door at night, I would scream, "Daddy's home" and run to him, hurling myself into his arms. Moey would pick me up to kiss him, and I can still remember the intoxicating scent of "Daddy." I loved to feel the velvety texture of his ears, especially if it was winter and frosty outside. My memories of father were potent. I adored him. His being in my home was my way of honoring him.

Moey was grateful to be with me and often said, "It's so good to be here," but he was still Moey. It was impossible for him not to do what was essentially his nature.

Outbursts like the one at the airport continued until, one day, I'd just had enough. "Daddy," I said, "I'll take care of you, I'll do everything in my power to make you physically comfortable, but I won't allow you to be verbally abusive with me anymore." He looked at me sheepishly, like a little boy who had been chastised. "But I'm dying," he said. I thought, how very Moey. "No," I said, "dying isn't a good excuse."

The only relationships in Moey's life that were pure and clear were with my sons. They loved each other unconditionally. Moey's presence didn't alter their teenage lives very much. Moey loved to see his boys every day, and they would take him for a trip around the block in his wheelchair. It was a maturing experience for Josh and Zach to watch the death process from the front row. They were disturbed at the way their grandfather was wasting away, but they were always kind and loving and so gentle with him. To this day, they've kept his slippers and glasses.

By the time Moey had been with us for three months, I had to accept the fact that his death was near. His stay had forced me to take a really good look at myself. I wasn't always compassionate. At times, I felt more like Nurse Ratchett than the healing grace I had fancied myself. The word "healing" developed new meanings for me. I always thought it meant remission of disease. I began to see healing as a place of consciousness, heartfulness, and forgiveness. It felt right to have Moey at home with us, for him to be with those who loved him while he was dying. It was an awakening for me to experience the dying process when I was in the fullness of health. That death is the duality of life, the natural completion, and the absolutely inevitable conclusion were, until then, foreign concepts to me. Living with death diffused the fear. I only wanted one more thing for my father — some spiritual connection. He remained steadfast in his atheism to the end. I don't think he ever experienced completion or peace.

At our last visit to his oncologist, Moey was clearly failing. The doctor suggested checking Moey into the hospital for several days and explained, "He should be hooked up to an IV and given a transfusion, a major overhaul." Moey asked, "What if I don't go into the hospital?" The doctor said quietly, "You'll die shortly." Moey looked at me and nodded, "I don't want to do anything. This is no longer a life that I'm living. I'm ready to go." I had a lump in my throat. I was nauseous. I felt both sadness and relief. Daily life had become increasingly more difficult for him and more stressful on our family.

Moey was feverish that night. He was hallucinating intensely. Jerry went into his room about eight o'clock in the morning, and the night nurse Katherine smiled, "Your father had a difficult night, but he's sleeping comfortably." Jerry looked closely at Moey and saw he wasn't breathing. "This isn't sleep," he said. "Moey is dead." She had never been with a patient who had died during her service and she was extremely upset. Jerry met me in the hall and held me while he told me that Moey was gone.

Moey was gone, and he had died in my home, and in the end it was the most natural thing that could have happened. On some level, I think I knew all along, from the moment that he came to live with us that, for me, the experience would be about learning to accept death. And having him die at home made death real for me in a poignant and beautiful way. I went into his room to say good-bye, and he was still warm. I put my hands on his face and felt his ears. I pressed my cheek next to his and gave him a kiss. I held his hands in mine and whispered, "Good-bye, Daddy. Good-bye, Moey."

Carole is the founder and president of Just For Us Seminars, Inc. and works to strengthen families through programs designed to enhance communication and nurture the full potential of each individual. Workshops for mothers, preadolescent, and adolescent daughters enhance self-esteem and communication; father-daughter workshops focus on the pivotal role fathers play in their daugthers' lives.

Penelope Pietras

"I was angry at her, at everyone who believed that suffering was a ticket to heaven, and at doctors who poked and prodded at my baby's cells and then left me with a decision that no one should ever have to make."

Penelope Pietras is a freelance writer and editor living in Washington D.C. She teaches memoir-writing workshops and is at work on a novel.

My dear baby daughter,

I am so sorry that things turned out this way for us. There is so much I wanted to give you. A happy, secure home. A good education. Lots of experiences to help you grow and find out who you are — dance lessons, music, horses, soccer — whatever captured your imagination. But some awful twist of fate has deprived us of all this. In the smallest part of our world, in the very cells where your life began, something went wrong. And so, it turned out that I couldn't even give you a healthy body or a sound mind with which to start this journey. . . .

This is how I communicate with my unborn daughter. Letters in a blue floral journal tucked in a drawer with a dog-eared copy of *What to Expect When You're Expecting,* handmade cards from the couples in our prenatal loss support group, letters from friends, and the tiny, soft infant sleeper I bought back when I was full of certainty about life. It is all I have of her, and it looks like very little, these bittersweet mementos from a pregnancy. But wrapped around them are the cherished lessons she taught me.

Joyfully expecting for the second time, my husband and I decided not to have amniocentesis even though I was thirty-nine years old. Because I'd lost my first pregnancy at ten weeks, the tiny chance that the amnio procedure could cause a miscarriage was more real to us than any of the statistics about genetic disorders. "Besides," I argued to those who encouraged prenatal testing, "even if there is something wrong, I'd never have an abortion." But I was about to learn the most valuable lesson of my life: I don't know what I'll do in a given situation until I'm in that situation.

Sixteen weeks into my pregnancy, a blood test indicated that our baby might have Down's Syndrome, and I rushed to my doctor's office for amniocentesis. Three weeks later, our worst fears were confirmed with the lab report.

When amniocentesis reveals that a fetus has Down's syndrome, it tells you that and only that. The doctors can't give you any idea of how severely it will affect your child's mind or body. In the weeks that followed, two images played tug-of-war with my heart. One was of the young man with Down's who was the star of a popular television show about whom I'd read an inspiring article in a women's magazine. I'd also heard that such mild Down's cases were the exception rather than the rule. But, I kept wondering, *What if our baby is like him?* Surely we could handle that and raise a child who would be able to function in the world and experience some satisfaction with life.

The other image was more persistent, however. It plagued me, a vivid childhood memory of visits to a state hospital in Michigan where my mentally retarded uncle lived most of his life. He roomed in a dormitory with about a hundred other innocent, childlike men. Usually several of them gathered around us when we came to visit. With their needy stares and garbled words, they would try to tell us about Uncle's girlfriend in the women's dorm, about the Tiger baseball score, what was for lunch in the cafeteria. I was a little afraid of them and curious, but mostly sad. They seemed to want something from us so desperately, something more than our awkward smiles and fleeting attention. I didn't quite understand what it was they needed, but I knew clearly, even then, that I didn't have it to give.

I began to think about abortion, me who had so righteously proclaimed that I would never, ever.

"God never gives you anything you can't handle." The nuns in my parochial school had taught us that and it haunted me now. Maybe this was God's plan for me. Maybe I had no right to try to take control. I even wondered if our child's soul had chosen to take on such a limited physical body in order to work out some karma.

Every time I felt the faint stirring in my womb, I agonized about a decision I had to make. In the end, those long-held memories from the state hospital prevailed. And along with them, that early, painful awareness of my own limitations. I decided to have an abortion.

That week, I was anchored to the phone, confiding our heartbreaking news to family and friends. "It isn't fair!" cried my friend Lynda, a mother of seven. And yet, she quietly agreed, "You know what you have to do. It would be no kind of life for that child."

My sister Pam let out a long, uneven sigh. "Would you believe I was selling Right to Life Christmas cards in our church lobby three weeks ago? But, if I were you, I'd do the same thing."

A longtime friend called me every day with growing concern. She had enlisted her neighbors to pray that I would make the "right decision." Then one day, she bluntly asked me if I knew what I was doing. She had contacted the Down's Syndrome Society, and there were people who wanted to adopt my baby. "No!" I railed at her. "You don't get it! I don't want to bring a child into the world for that kind of life!"

Another acquaintance said, "God must love you very much to give you such a special gift." I was angry at her, at everyone who believed that suffering was a ticket to heaven, and at doctors who poked and prodded at my baby's cells and then left me with a decision that no one should ever have to make.

So what did God give me? Ovaries with haywire eggs? Or the wizardry of prenatal testing? The only answer seemed to be that God had given me a choice. I finally went to the clinic at peace with only this: I might never know if what I was doing was right or wrong, but it was the only thing I could do.

Because I was five months along, an abortion would not be quick or simple. It would take three days, and during that time, I would learn more lessons. Every door and window of the clinic was guarded with alarms and bulletproof glass. Along with instruction sheets on medication, my husband and I were given procedures for gaining access should the site be besieged by protesters. The need for these security measures — as if we were doing something covert, illegal — sparked a new fear in me. It was a humiliating, terrifying feeling to know that what I was doing was, in the name of God, condemned by some people.

On the first day, we sat in a waiting room with several other couples. Some of them, like us, were "fetal anomaly" cases. Others appeared to be more what I'd imagined: scared young girls with solemn boyfriends. People who, a year ago, a month ago, I might have criticized for not going through with their pregnancies. Now, looking at them, I knew they had not come here easily. On all our faces, pale with pain and fear, in all our eyes, swollen with tears, was the same sad surrender.

My sister came along to lend support, and the faces of the other patients weren't lost on her. "I can't go back to those Right to Life meetings anymore, not after this," she whispered to me. "If anybody is outside this place tomorrow, harassing us, I'll go right over and ask them to sign up to take care of your baby and pay for the millions in medical expenses." In that moment, I loved my sister more than ever before. The sharp tongue and temper that had wounded my thin skin a thousand times while we were growing up was now, instead, on guard to protect and defend me.

The first step at the clinic was another ultrasound. The pictures showed a fetus several weeks behind schedule in its development. The next day, we learned that there was hardly any fluid in the amniotic sac. The doctors suspected that our baby's kidneys were already failing. On the third day, I went into induced labor, and when it was over, the kind, motherly counselor who had comforted us through the whole ordeal told us about our child. "You had a little girl," she said, "and you didn't really have a choice." I listened to her gentle, heartbreaking description of the doctor's observations, and I was thankful that I'd trusted my intuition.

In the weeks that followed, I awoke most mornings crying, groping my way through a strange kind of grief. In my mind, I'd already developed a relationship with my daughter. I'd taken her on a hundred outings, from the neighborhood pool to the Grand Canyon. I'd taught her to tie her shoes and had sent her off to college. Yet now, I had nothing tangible to show that she was anything more than imagination.

So I began to write to her. I told her about her Dad's love and her Aunt Pam's fierce devotion. About the friends who had cried with me at her memorial service. About the strangers who had shared the stories of their own losses and had become our friends. About the new compassion I felt when I saw another person struggling to make a good decision in a bad situation. About healing.

Mothers often talk about how much they learn from their children. Although I don't have the day-to-day joys — or the trials — of raising a child, I always nod in quiet agreement when I find myself in one of these conversations. The pain of letting go, the power of an open heart. I've learned these, too, from my daughter.

Eventually made a grandmother by her stepdaughter, Penny finds great comfort and pleasure in doting on nieces and nephews and the children of several friends who call her "auntie" regardless of blood affiliation.

Patty Rosen

"I stared at her, unable to fathom what I was about to do, what I had to do."

With her children grown and on their own, Patty Rosen left her San Diego home and moved to Oregon, full of the anticipation that comes with change, with turning the page on life. A nurse by profession, she settled near Portland. When her daughter Jody called to say she was coming up, Patty realized how much she missed her. She didn't realize what a terrible road they were about to walk down together.

It had all started in July of 1985 when Jody, my third child, joined me to live in my home just outside of Portland, Oregon. I had moved to Oregon four years earlier, having raised my children in San Diego, California. But they were all grown, and I had decided it was time for me to live closer to nature and the mountains. We are a close family, and it had been painful leaving, but my sons Mark and Eric had come with me. My daughter Laurie was married and settled in San Diego. Jody was there studying to become a medical assistant. I missed them both terribly and was ecstatic when Jody finished school and called to say she was moving up.

Twenty-five years old and full of the spirit of life, she arrived complaining of a nagging backache. The pain had been so bad that she had gone to the emergency room of a San Diego hospital before starting her trip north. The doctor diagnosed a kidney infection. Medicated, she'd climbed into her VW van and headed toward Oregon. By San Francisco, she was in such pain that she went to another hospital emergency room. Three days later, she finally pulled into my driveway. Carefully, she slid out of the van and into my arms, sobbing uncontrollably. We held each other tightly, my heart soaring to have her in my arms but aching because of her distress. Soon the worst nightmare either of us could have imagined began. Within a ten-month period, her painful backache that defied diagnosis was finally identified as the end stages of bone cancer. She was immediately put to bed, given high doses of drugs, and underwent surgery to remove the thyroid where the cancer had started. Even at the time of diagnosis, however, there was no hope for recovery. By then, the cancer had invaded most of her bones, making them fragile and weak and eventually causing many to fracture. There is no cure for such an invasive condition. The onset of a fast, painful decline to death had begun.

The third of my four children, Jody had always been special. Her birth had been easy, but it was immediately apparent that she was "different" — she never cried and wouldn't wake to nurse. Even though I was young when I had her, only twenty, I knew something was wrong. "There's a chance she's cretin," I was told over the phone by a young, frustrated pediatrician. "What is cretin?" I asked. "She won't grow physically or mentally," he said. I was stunned. This precious, cuddly new baby was a cretin? I didn't know what to do. Helplessness overwhelmed me as it often would when it came to Jody. That diagnosis proved untrue and, although she never developed at the normal childhood rate, she survived as a sweet, endearing, charming baby and grew to be a seemingly normal, healthy young woman, vibrant and beautiful and gregarious. Both her father and I were enchanted by her and, throughout her short life, that never changed. I considered Jody an "old soul," always wise and compassionate beyond her years.

And now she was dying. And now, I would learn the rage of medical misdiagnosis. Jody had had Sipple syndrome at birth, a condition marked by abnormal cells in the thyroid, adrenals, and parathyroid. The thyroid goiter had first appeared when she was eighteen, but the doctors hadn't diagnosed it, hadn't removed it when it would have meant she would live on to enjoy a healthy life. How I hated this cancer! How I hated the doctors for their failure to diagnose it.

"We can't find anything wrong with her" was all the doctors in Oregon could say. Desperate, I finally took her back to San Diego, where I had had a long medical career and knew doctors I thought I could trust. The trip was excruciating. Jody was so fragile, so deathly looking, that I had to convince the flight attendants we could make it. Within twelve hours of our arrival, we had the fatal diagnosis and the shocking news that it could have been prevented with a simple blood test for the goiter and a simple operation to remove her thyroid earlier — much earlier. We're so very sorry, said the doctors I thought I could trust, the very same ones who had misdiagnosed her.

I was stunned when one of the residents at the hospital, standing by Jody's bed, said, "The cancer is going to win." I saw Jody's startled look and I wanted to shake him for the cruelty of his comment. Any hope, any will that she had to fight, dissolved. I saw her turn inward. She begged to go home.

Because I am a registered nurse and certified nurse practitioner, I possessed the skills that would now be necessary for her care. She didn't want to stay in the hospital and I took her home where Mark, her brother and soul mate, could also be in constant attendance. Together, with our hearts breaking, Mark and I kept her as comfortable as her condition would permit. I would find Mark, night after night, sitting on the floor beside her bed silently weeping, totally overwhelmed with the hopelessness of the situation.

During the time she was approaching death, we shied away from talking about it. But occasionally, when we could no longer ignore the obvious, she would ask me to tell her again what I thought dying was. Thank goodness it wasn't the first time for these conversations. I had always discussed death with my children and shared my spiritual beliefs, which had been passed down to me by my Irish grandmother. But now it was completely different because Jody was facing death, and I was frightened. I would find myself panic-stricken by the enormous responsibility of stating beliefs that were now so significant to both of us. Although I had always held them to be true, they had never been tested. Now my faith in those beliefs was undergoing the ultimate challenge. But, when she asked, I would hold her hands, look into her sad eyes, take a breath, and say, "Jody, I believe that death is not an ending but a passage. I have no doubt that we have known each other before and will see each other again." I silently prayed that these words were true.

From the time she was told "The cancer is going to win," I intuitively knew that Jody would ask me to assist her death. Her training and work as a certified medical assistant had put her face-to-face with dying patients, and she had always been outraged that their last request to die was ignored or contradicted. "Terminally ill patients should have the right to die when and how they want," she would say angrily. So, I knew and I waited. And then, the day came.

Two months after the diagnosis, she called me to her room and asked me to sit beside her. Taking my hand in hers, she looked straight into my eyes and began, "Mom, look at me, really look at me. I'm not going to get better. And, this isn't any fun. I can't move, and I can't eat. I sleep twenty-two out of twenty-four hours, and when I wake up, it's only to take drugs and go back to sleep. My bowels are gone, and I'm going blind." Sobs wracked her frail body. "Please, Mom, don't let me suffer any more, help me die now."

Nothing could have prepared me to hear those words. "Oh, Jody, my darling child . . . " Tears and grief overcame us, and we cried together in desperation. What could I do? I understood what she was saying too well to refuse. My daughter was trapped in her bed, with no sense of dignity left and nothing to look forward to but torturous pain. She wanted to end the suffering and to pass over to the other dimension. Was that so unreasonable? No. No, it wasn't. I fought back my tears and the moan of desperation that tried to escape from my quivering lips. She hated to see me cry. She would always say that it was bad enough to be dying, without having to watch me grieve, so I tried not to sob. As I had done so many times before, I excused myself and ran to the bathroom to stuff toilet paper in my mouth so she wouldn't hear the sounds of my sorrow.

When I was able to return to her bedside, I begged her for time to adjust to the idea, because my mind wouldn't allow me to think of letting her go. How could I do it? How could I kiss her good-bye forever? I had given her life and now she was begging me to end it.

In answer to her request to assist her death, my mind first said, "Okay," and then a warm cocoon of unreality enveloped me and I felt myself falling into an abyss. A transformation of my spirit was beginning, and I felt I was slowly losing my mind. Many times during this experience, I thought of all the brave women around the world, throughout history, who have faced what I was facing. How did they do it? And I thought of the women of the Holocaust who saw much worse than I. How did they stand it?

My first attempt to help her die was not really an attempt. I just wasn't ready. I had begun to administer the drugs when, like a bolt, my mind screamed, *No! There will be a miracle! Jody* will not *die! I will save her!* The next day, when she regained consciousness, I was so ashamed. I had let her down. Once again, she was facing this cruel existence. "I'm so sorry, Jody," I started, trying not to cry. "I'm just not ready. Don't you realize how difficult this is? When I kiss you good-bye, I'll be kissing you good-bye forever . . . forever . . . " By this time, I was sobbing, becoming hysterical. I couldn't even take her in my arms to comfort her, because I could easily fracture another of her fragile bones. So I sat beside her bed, with my head next to her as she stroked my hair and patted my shoulders. "It's okay, Mom, I understand." My dying daughter was comforting me. How absurd. It was all too much.

Finally, six months after her first request, I could no longer stand it. I had to help her. I'm not sure how someone in such bad condition could get worse without dying, but Jody had. Her strong heart and constitution had kept her going. Now she was a mere seventy-six pounds. On her five-foot-six-inch frame, seventy-six pounds was, literally, only skin and bones. All I could see was her shrunken, frail body with her huge blue eyes glazed over in pain. Tremors shook her. Pain, even treated with massive opiates, whether she was awake or in a drug-induced sleep, made her moan and writhe.

"Okay, Jody, I'm ready," I whispered. Tears covered her pale face. Sobs filled the room. "Oh, Mom, thank you. This is the happiest day of my life. I'll be free of this body. Oh, thank you."

It was the worst day of my life. I was frantic. I could no longer fool myself that Jody's cadaverlike state was temporary. The Angel of Death was no longer an imaginary hoax that I could push away from her. This was the end. I would no longer have Jody. No more phone calls, no more letters, no more talks over coffee, no more shared laughter about some silly, wonderful thing. I stared at her, unable to fathom what I was about to do, what I had to do.

I'm not sure if I can describe, so that anyone will understand, what happened to my mind at this point. During all of Jody's illness, I bounced from being clinically withdrawn from the situation — a skill I had practiced for fifteen years in medicine — to an abject state of disbelief and horror. But I was her mother, and I eventually saw the stark reality of the situation. In my commitment to do what must be done, I allowed my mind to fully slip away. It started with a ringing in my ears, then the feeling of a haze surrounding me. I found myself walking and talking, but as an outsider, disconnected. When I looked at anything, I stared, blankly, my mind fixated on what I was about to do. Was I in a trance state? A dream state?

It was like the time I was given a preoperative drug. I could hear what was going on around me, I could respond, but I was once removed.

I couldn't let anyone know what I was going to do. Even though Jody was in the end stages of life and begging for relief, assisting her death would be a felony offense. I desperately wanted to call a doctor friend for advice about the drugs I should use and what I might expect, but I couldn't do that for fear of making him an accomplice. I was going into uncharted waters and my daughter's safe, peaceful passage depended on me. I started to chant to myself, "You can do this, you can do this, it will be okay, she will be okay." I have never felt such isolation and desperation.

Tenderly, I tucked the bed covers in around her and kissed her, knowing it would be the last kiss, that I could not fail her. I was shaking from the very core of my body. It is nearly too painful to tell, the anguish too absolute. "Jody, honey, swallow these pills," I whispered. "Here, honey, can you take more?" It wasn't like what you see in the movies. It wasn't a matter of "she swallowed a massive dose of drugs and died." No, it took hours for the pills to take effect, long hours that allowed my mind to vacillate between "No! I have to stop this! This isn't real! She's going to be okay!" to the reality of her condition and "My God, Jody, please, please die!" I knew she might vomit the pills, and the horror of failing her swept through me like a hot wind. I had to turn her to give her a suppository to keep her from vomiting, and yet, simply turning her could fracture bones. I babbled uncontrollably, "Jody, my darling, I don't want to hurt you," as gently, gently, I turned her, willing my hands steady. By this time, Jody was in a deep coma, slowly making the transition into death while I was making my transition into oblivion.

Silence. She had finally stopped breathing. "No no no no no no!" I wailed and sobbed as I climbed into her bed and gathered her in my arms. I held her, stroked her hair, and kissed her gently. It was over. Jody was dead. I slipped further into my comforting cocoon. I felt safe and protected, swaddled in a fuzzy warmth.

In the weeks following her death, I watched life go on around me from my safe

Never-Never Land. I watched myself stumble through the days. I didn't fight it, I couldn't fight it. There was nothing I could do. I was totally without any sense of my being, in grief and shock. During my waking hours, in solitude and privacy, I grieved like the wailing women of tribes and religions that honor grief, the women who shroud themselves and beat their breasts and wail until they have no breath left. I allowed myself to be angry, sad, hysterical. I cried. I moaned. I rocked back and forth, wishing I could tear my aching heart out. I prayed that it wasn't real. I fantasized that somehow I must be caught in a nightmare. Jody wasn't dead. I had dreamed the whole thing. Of course! Any minute now, the phone would ring and I would hear her happy little voice say, "Hi, Mom, I love you!" I would sit by the phone for hours begging it to ring, praying for it to ring.

I became afraid to go to sleep, because my dreams recreated, in minute detail, the last very painful year of Jody's life, which wasn't really life but a slow death. I'd wake up screaming, flooded with an extraordinary helplessness and hopelessness. Over and over, a voice inside chided, *You were her mother and you couldn't save her!* Friends rallied around as best they could. They were also going through the pain of losing Jody and struggling with their own grief. My three grown children stayed in close contact as we all muddled toward an acceptance of some kind.

Madness is powerful. Grief is powerful. I knew if I wasn't careful, I would stay distant and removed. I also was constantly fighting the seductive urge to commit suicide. I desperately wanted to join Jody. However, my children were suffering enough and would never have understood or forgiven me if I'd died at by own hand. No, it wouldn't be fair. I had to find a way to go on. I knew, because of my strong spiritual beliefs, that I could learn from all of this if I could just hang on. I had to find the way. It was a strange dilemma. I couldn't commit suicide, and yet I felt hopeless to cope with my memories. *Hang on, hang on, hang on*: It became my mantra as I struggled toward sanity.

I hiked. I taught dance. I taught cross-country skiing. I taught high school equivalency courses to kids. I looked normal, but I was locked away in my own world. I kept myself busy to the point of exhaustion, but quickly found out that didn't work. If I became too tired, I would lose my limited self-control and would end up totally unhinged and grief stricken. It was a burden for my family and friends to watch me and know there was nothing they could do to help. I had to hang on. There would be an answer.

I joined Compassionate Friends, a group for family and friends who have lost a child. It was one of the best things I did. In the safety and care of this group, I learned that I wasn't going crazy. Everyone waited for the phone to ring. They all expected their child to walk through the door. These hopeful fantasies were common. We all wanted to believe that the death of our child hadn't happened. So our minds worked to bring us comfort, no matter how unrealistic. I learned that the hours I spent rocking and hugging myself were shared by many parents, as were the anger, agitation, and sleeplessness. It was extraordinarily comforting to listen to other bereaved parents tell their stories, share their grief, and to feel normal and supported. The only difference that was uniquely mine was that I had helped my child to die and that was a crime. It had to remain my most precious secret, and did, until 1993, when I put all my efforts into the Oregon ballot measure to legalize physician assistance in dying. My promise to Jody was then fulfilled: I told the world, so that "no other mom would have to go through this."

I never felt guilt or remorse for assisting Jody's passing. It was an act of love from a mother to her dying, suffering child, and I was only grateful that I had had the strength and the courage to carry through with it. No, the sorrow and grief that tears me apart isn't related to helping her pass but is much more fundamental: I grieve because she suffered so harshly for so long. I grieve that she died. I grieve because I have to go on without her. I grieve because I miss her.

Seven years after Jody's death, the ballot measure Death with Dignity, Physician Assistance with Dying for the Terminally Ill passed by a vote of 51 percent. In 1994, Oregon became the first state to legalize physician aid in dying. Jody's story, and her mother's role in it, was told nationally and internationally and was felt by many to have been the deciding factor in the passing of this historic legislation. Her story was also part of the state of Washington's legal brief presented to the U.S. Supreme Court in January 1997 in argument for the legalization of physician-assisted death.

EPILOGUE

"You have to risk stepping outside the circle that has been drawn around you."
— Lourdes Saab, former chief of protocol, mayor's office, Los Angeles

Every act of courage takes us outside the circle drawn around us into unfamiliar territory, to places we never thought we could go, where things are messy, not so comfortable, predictable, where we don't know what to expect.

At first, we're scared, excited, anxious, exhilarated. Most certainly stretched. We become more of who we truly are, who we can be. Time goes on. We get comfortable. The edges of the familiar fill in. Perhaps unnoticed, a circle draws around us again. Our next act of courage may be something we couldn't have faced from inside the first circle. But now, we're ready, more confident. And so we dare to step outside yet another circle — and on it goes, as we continue becoming more, tapping into reservoirs of power, realizing our talents, our gifts, our strengths.

That's what I wanted this book to be about, stepping over the edge. Scary. Chilling. Sobering. Thrilling. A moment when life suddenly becomes bigger, when we see more clearly into our soul's eyes. And what we see is surely worth the telling. Because as we tell our stories, more of us dare to be a little more courageous, to risk a little more, to reach deeper, to travel wider in our lives.

The daring, bold, mouthy women in this book give a precious gift to us, men and women alike. Their shared storytelling helps us value who we are, truly. Their accumulated experience is rich and deep. I hope you've found much here that you can identify with, that makes you ponder a moment of courage in your own life, that inspires you, encourages you to stand up, to say "Yes I can!"

ACKNOWLEDGMENTS

To each and every woman who so generously and vulnerably gave of her story for this book. I am honored and humbled. If I could have, I would have used them all.

To my incomparable husband, Franc Sloan, whose deep love and courage has and continues to change me and whose book this is as much as mine, having given hugely to it in ways that only I know. To my magnificent son, Ben, wise beyond his years and a constant inspiration, one of the finer human beings to grace the planet.

To my parents Virginia and Stuart Lane, who have always encouraged me to be more and gave me the precious gift of unwavering love and the strong foundation to do so. To my mother-in-law Joan Martin, for believing in me and for daring to live a life of great curiosity.

To my agent, Ken Sherman, gracious champion of my work and a man of uncommon honor, integrity, and tenacity.

To my editor Becky Benenate, whose passion for this work runs deep, whose talent and vision are great. To publisher Marc Allen, a blessing on the world of publishing and Arielle Ford, a blessing on the world of publicity. To Lisa Schneiderman, passionate advocate of the book, and Kathy Buttler, the first to champion it, patiently fleshing out the heart and soul of every story.

To my compassionate and insightful review board, who saw me through the early times with encouragement and support: Sunni Kerwin, Cynthia Price, Jane Lancellotti, Robin Damore, and Penny Winton. And to Julie La Fond, who became pivotal in *Women of Courage* finding a good home.

To Peny and Michaell and Jach, who are an ongoing source of courage and illumination, and to my dear dear friend Lazaris, whose guidance I cherish.

To Riane Eisler, whose great belief in and enthusiasm for the book were pivotal. To Karen Kinsey-House, coach extraordinaire.

To Poet Laureate Rita Dove, who so generously gave of her work. The epigraph is excerpted from her poem, "Ö," in *Selected Poems,* Vintage Books 1993, by permission of the author, copyright 1980 by Rita Dove. "After Reading *Mickey in the Night Kitchen* for the Third Time Before Bed" is from *Grace Notes,* W.W. Norton, New York, copyright 1989 by Rita Dove.

To A. T. Birmingham, who tirelessly connected me with daring women and gave me a tremendous appreciation for the work of the Giraffe Project in Langley, Washington, which honors people who stick out their necks for the common good. And similarly to Ken Sloate, a generous resource for winners of the prestigious Goldman Environmental Awards. To Irene Stuber for being bold without compromise and her Abigail's Rebels. And to Women of Vision and Action for inspiration.

And to the following people who helped in one way or another with individual stories: Rhonda Grider, manager of Ann Bancroft. Fanchon Blake's ghostwriter Ellie Bator. Heidi Heyman, public relations manager, Barbara Brennan School of Healing. Pat Page who worked for Judy Chicago's nonprofit corporation Through the Flower. Martha Cole, personal assistant to Barbara DeAngelis. Leslie Williams, formerly executive secretary to Rita Dove. Kory Johnson's mother Terry. Linda Schoeneck, executive assistant to Michele Lee. Annette Booth, executive assistant to Senator

Patty Murray and Press Secretary Rex Carney. May Kay Moment, managing associate for BrainReserve Inc. Michael Manganiello, executive assistant to Dana and Christopher Reeve. Debbie Taylor, researcher to Anita Roddick, and Laurie Wilson, who was in charge of special projects in the U.S. for The Body Shop. Lucy Lytwynsky from the Astronaut Office, Nassau Johnson Space Center, Houston, Texas. Cindy Chandler, office manager, Planet Hope. Gowri Priya Reddy, assistant to Barbara Trent at the Empowerment Project, and Pat Jackson, executive assistant to Lynne Twist. Courtney Carlson, assistant to Marianne Williamson, and Maggie Lang and Megan Taylor, who also worked with her. And, Vivian Lee Sampson, personal assistant to Susan Winston at Blanki and Bodi Productions.

And to the intelligent and tenacious Munro Magruder and Marjorie Conte and everyone at New World Library who in any way worked on this book and all the bright and talented people at Publishers Group West.

DIRECTORY

Ann Bancroft
Base Camp Promotions
Minneapolis, MN 55401-1790
Phone: (612) 333-4996
Fax: (612) 333-1325

Rebecca Black
Gladys McCoy Academy
3802 NE Martin Luther King Blvd.
Portland, OR 97212
Phone: (503) 281-9597
Fax: (503) 281-8817

Fanchon Blake
2226 Ridgeway Drive
Eugene, OR 97401
(541) 684-4561

Barbara Brennan
The Barbara Brennan School of Healing®
(BBSH™)
P.O. Box 2005
East Hampton, NY 11937
Phone: (516) 329-0951 or
(800) 924-2564 Fax: (516) 324-9745
E-mail: bbshoffice@barbarabrennan.com
Web site: http://www.barbarabrennan.com

Judy Chicago
P.O. Box 1327
Belen, NM 87002
Phone: (505) 864-4080
Fax: (505) 864-4088
E-mail: throughtheflower@compuserve.com
Web site: http://www.judychicago.com

Maxi Cohen
565 Sunset Avenue
Venice, CA 90291
Phone: (310) 392-1246
Fax: (310) 450-7385

Barbara DeAngelis, Ph.D.
12021 Wilshire Blvd.
Suite 607
Los Angeles, CA 90025
Phone: (310) 535-0988

Rita Dove
University of Virginia
Department of English
219 Bryan Hall
Charlottesville, VA 22903

Riane Eisler
Center for Partnership Studies
P.O. Box 51936
Pacific Grove, CA 93950
Phone: (831) 626-1004
Fax: (831) 626-3734
Web site: http://www.partnershipway.org

Laura Evans
President/CEO
Expedition Inspiration Fund
for Breast Cancer Research
P.O. Box 4289
Ketchum, ID 83340
Phone: (208) 726-6456
Fax: (208) 726-2040
Web site: http://www.expeditioninspiration.org

Janelle Goetcheus, M.D.
Christ House
1717 Columbia Road NW
Washington, DC 20009
Phone: (202) 328-1100
Fax: (202) 232-4972

Cheri Honkala
Kensington Welfare Rights Union
P.O. Box 50678
Philadelphia, PA 19132
Phone: (215) 203-1945
Fax: (215) 203-1950
E-mail: kwru@libertynet.org
Web site: http://www.libertynet.org/kwru

Carole Isenberg
11041 Santa Monica Blvd.
Suite 708
Los Angeles, CA 90025
Phone/Fax: (310) 473-8889
E-mail: justforus@earthlink.net

Jako
Phone: (503) 222-5349
E-mail: fixfs@earthlink.net

Cora Lee Johnson
Treutlen County Community Sewing Center
411 New Street
Soperton, GA 30457
Phone: (912) 529-6238

Michele Lee
c/o Joan Hyler
Hyler Management
25 Sea Colony Drive
Santa Monica, CA 90405
Phone: (310) 396-7811

Katherine Martin
P.O. Box 931
Lake Oswego, OR 97034
Phone: (503) 697-2947
Fax: (503) 697-2948
E-mail: PeopleDare@aol.com
Web site: http://www.peoplewhodare.com

Brooke Medicine Eagle
#1 Second Avenue, East – C401
Polson, MT 59860
Phone: (406) 883-4686
Fax: (406) 883-6629
E-mail: bmeagle@cyberport.net
Web site: http://www.medicine-eagle.com

Senator Patty Murray
111 Russell Senate Office Building
Washington, DC 20510
Phone: (202) 224-2621
Fax: (202) 224-0238
E-mail: senator_murray@murray.senate.gov

Elizabeth Pirruccello Newhall, M.D.
Downtown Women's Center
511 SW 10th Avenue
Suite 905
Portland, OR 97205

Heather O'Brien
E-mail: obrien2@un.org

Judith Orloff, M.D.
2080 Century Park East
Suite 1811
Los Angeles, CA 90067

Penelope Pietras
PennyPG@aol.com

Mary Pipher, Ph.D.
3201 S. 33rd Street, Suite B
Lincoln, NE 68506

Salle Merrill Redfield
Satori Publishing
P.O. Box 360988
Hoover, AL 35236
E-mail: salleredfield@celestinevision.com
Web site: http://www.celestinevision.com

Dana Reeve
c/o Dan Strone
The William Morris Agency
1325 Avenue of the Americas
New York, NY 10019

Anita Roddick
The Body Shop
Watersmead, Littlehampton, West Sussex
BN17 6LS, United Kingdom
Phone: 011 (44) 1903 731500
Fax: 011 (44) 1903 726250
E-mail: anita_roddick@bodyshop.co.uk
Web site: http://www.the-body-shop.com

Rhea Seddon, M.D.
3601 TVC
Vanderbilt University Medical Center
Nashville, TN 37232-5100

Katt Shea
c/o Director's Guild of America
Phone: (310) 289-2000

Gail Shibley
U.S. Department of Transportation
400 7th Street SW
Washington, DC 20590
Phone: (202) 366-0660
E-mail: gail.shibley@fhwa.dot.gov

Kelly Stone
Planet Hope
8205 Santa Monica Blvd., #1-441
Los Angeles, CA 90046
Phone: (310) 479-3434
(800) 314-4673
Web site: http://www.planethope.com

Barbara Trent
Empowerment Project
Phone: (919) 967-1963
E-mail: project2@mindspring.com
Web site: http://www.webcom.com/empower/

Lynne Twist
#3 Fifth Avenue
San Francisco, CA 94118
Contact person: Pat Jackson
Phone: (707) 963-1322

Sarah Weddington
The Weddington Center
Fax: (512) 478-7184
E-mail: sweddington@mail.utexas.edu

Marianne Williamson
Web site: http://www.marianne.com

Susan Winston
Blanki & Bodi Productions, Inc.
3599 Cahuenga Boulevard West
Suite 440
Los Angeles, CA 90068
Phone: (818) 753-7644
Fax: (818) 753-7652
E-mail: BandB03@aol.com

NEW WORLD LIBRARY
publishes books and cassettes that inspire and challenge
us to improve the quality of our lives and the world.

Our books and tapes are available
in bookstores everywhere.
For a free catalog of our complete library
of fine books and tapes, contact:

New World Library
14 Pamaron Way
Novato, CA 94949

Phone: (415) 884-2100
Fax: (415) 884-2199
Or call toll free: (800) 972-6657
Catalog request: Ext. 50
Ordering: Ext. 52

E-mail: escort@nwlib.com
Web site: http://www.nwlib.com